POSTCARD HISTORY SERIES

Westport and Weston IN VINTAGE POSTCARDS

POSTCARD HISTORY SERIES

Westport and Weston in Vintage Postcards

William L. Scheffler

ARCADIA PUBLISHING

ISBN 978-0-7385-9042-4

Published by Arcadia Publishing
Charleston, South Carolina

Printed in the United States of America

Library of Congress Catalog Card Number: 98-87781

For all general information contact Arcadia Publishing at:
Telephone 843-853-2070
Fax 843-853-0044
E-mail sales@arcadiapublishing.com
For customer service and orders:
Toll-Free 1-888-313-2665

Visit us on the Internet at www.arcadiapublishing.com

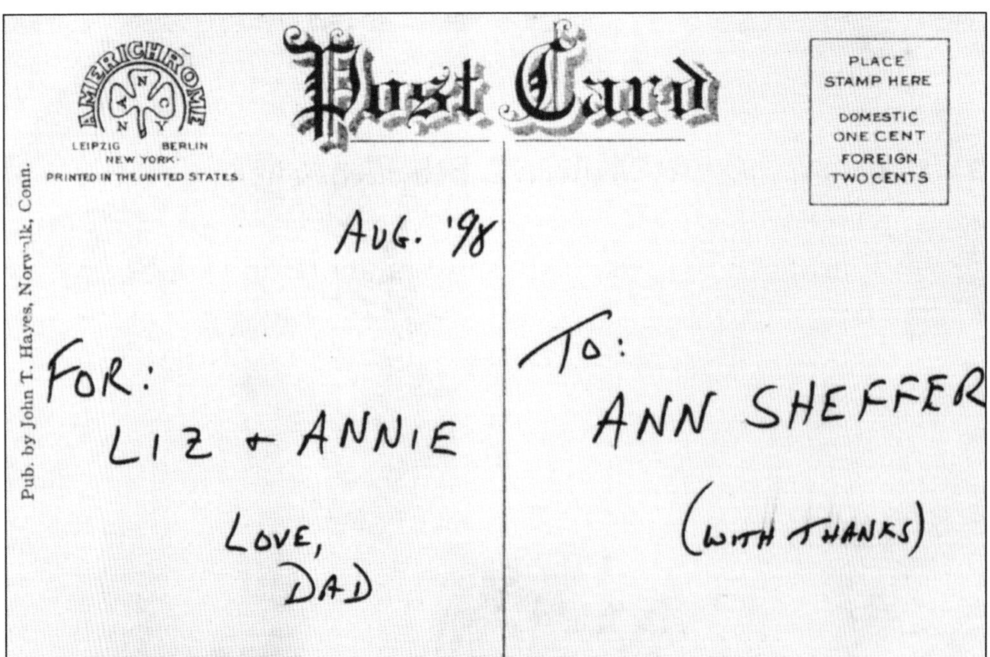

Contents

Introduction		7
1.	Downtown: Main Street and the Post Road	9
2.	Commercial Westport: Businesses and Factories	25
3.	Residential Westport: Houses and Street Scenes	35
4.	Institutional Westport: Churches and Schools	47
5.	Tourist Attractions: Hotels, Restaurants, and Clubs	61
6.	The Beach: Compo, Old Mill, and Sherwood Island	81
7.	Weston: Town and Country	107
8.	Odd Lots	117

INTRODUCTION

"*Am having just a grand time down at Compo.*" —A.L.B., August 1908

"*Are you living? If so let me hear from you.*" —Love, Eddice, March 1909

"*We are having some more of the old fashioned winters. Are just over the effects of one big storm that disabled trolley trains and telephones when lo, another arrived last evening.*" —Vera, December 1915

"*Some place and a fine trip and we are enjoying every minute of it. Salt water tastes good and makes fine bathing.*" —Everett, July 1917

"*Please come in Friday about 8:45 for this week's lesson.*" —Mrs. C. Brockett, May 1920

"*Remember the spot? Very hot here and full of New York people.*" —The author, 1950

The above are messages from Westport and Weston, delivered over the years, each providing a glimpse of our towns, a snapshot of familiar scenes. Postcards capture the essence of a place, to save or show a friend. And when mail delivery was more frequent, up to five times a day, postcards took the place of telephone calls for quick messages—for only a penny!

I've collected postcards of Westport (where I live) and Weston (where I grew up) for many years, finding them at tag sales and antique fairs where dealers sit with musty shoeboxes sorted by place. Then, in the spring of 1998, when I offered to mount an exhibit for the Westport Historical Society, I discovered that there were other serious postcard collectors in Westport, as well as many "old timers" who could tell me details of where long-gone buildings had stood or what was now on the same site.

The exhibit, entitled "Having Just A Grand Time Down At Compo: Postcards from Westport's Past" forms the basis for this book. I am grateful to Gordon Joseloff for adding his postcards to those of the Westport Historical Society for that exhibit; and to James H. Gray (formerly of Westport) and the Weston Historical Society for providing additional cards for this book. In addition, materials compiled by Allen and Barbara Raymond, Westport's town historians, and comments from Bill Gault, Harry Audley, Lou Santella, and Eve Potts were very helpful in providing background information about Westport's history. Susanna Flood helped organize the manuscript.

I've tried to convey, in the captions for these photos, a sense of Westport's unique character—in the choice of subjects for both sides of the card. For a fuller history of our town, we will

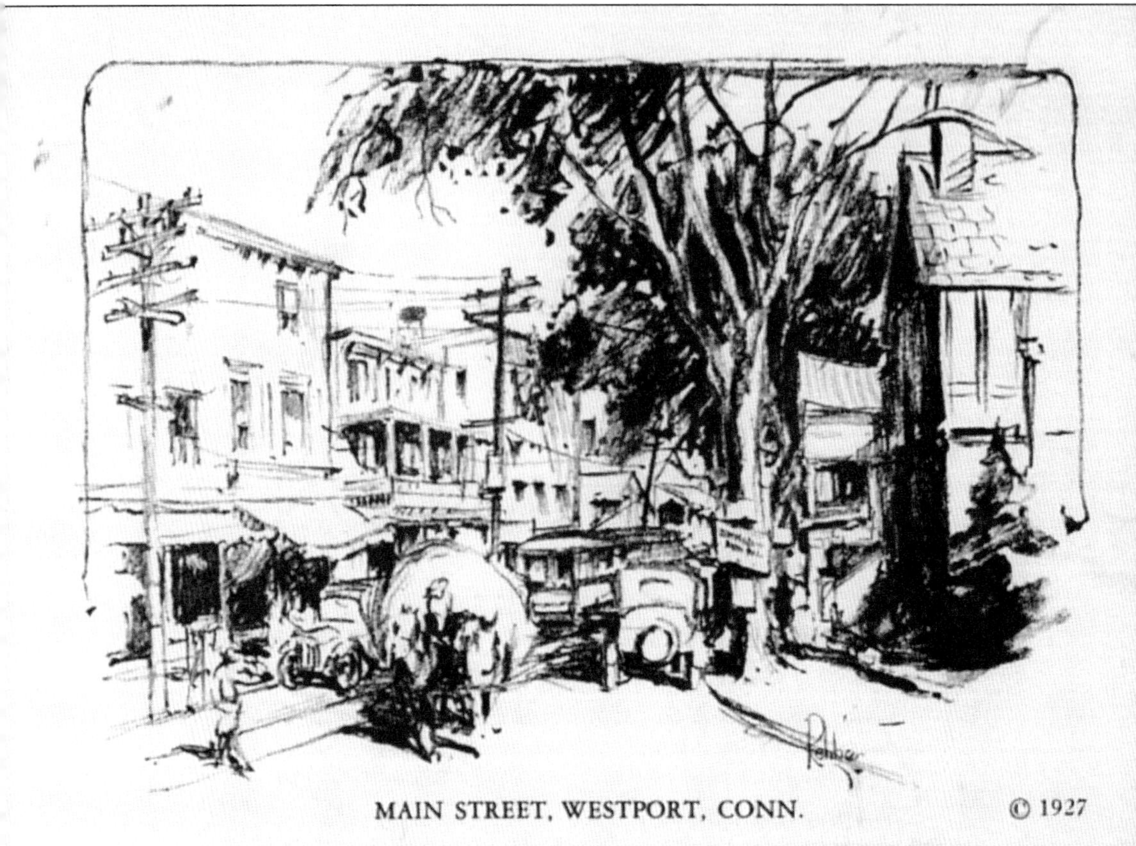

have to wait for the definitive book commissioned by the Westport Historical Society for the year 2000, currently being written by Woody Klein and designed by Miggs Burroughs. These postcard images are a look back, and a promise of more to come.

A note about postcards—before 1907, writing was not permitted on the address side of a postcard, so most publishers left a wide border on the side or bottom of the view side so a short message could be added. Beginning in 1907, postcards were made with a divided back—that is with a vertical line down the middle—so that the address could be written on the right side and messages on the left. Since many cards are saved without being sent or postmarked, these features are helpful in dating older cards.

One

Downtown:
Main Street and the Post Road

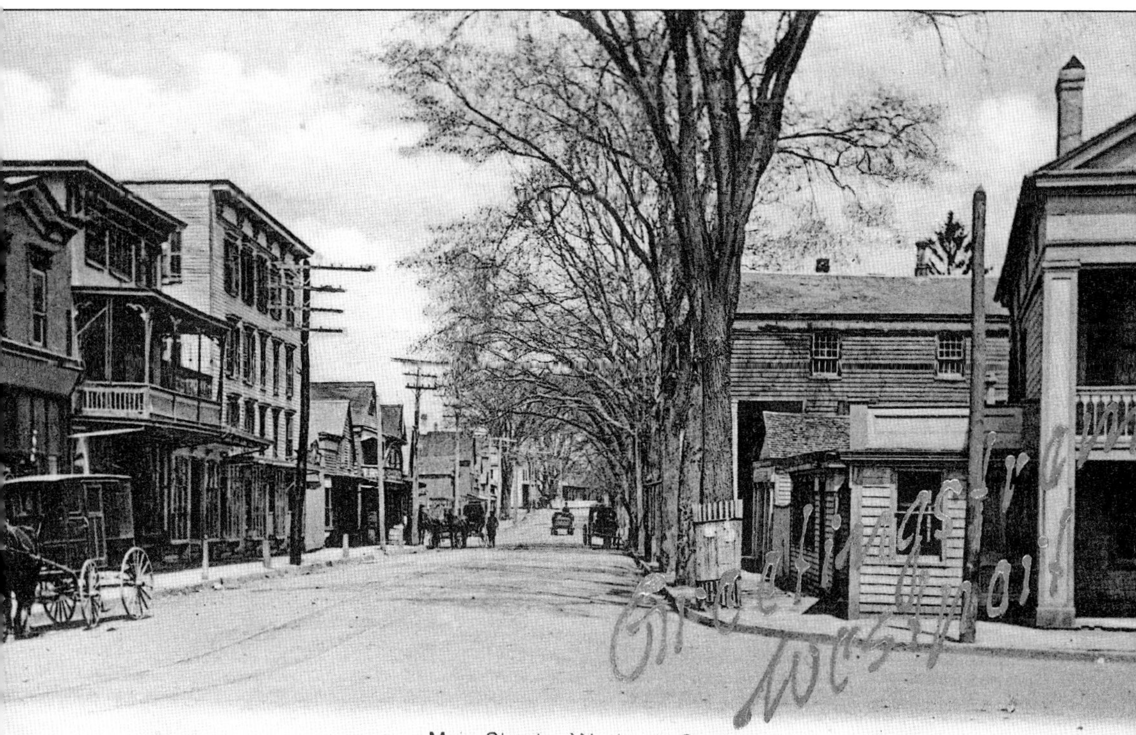

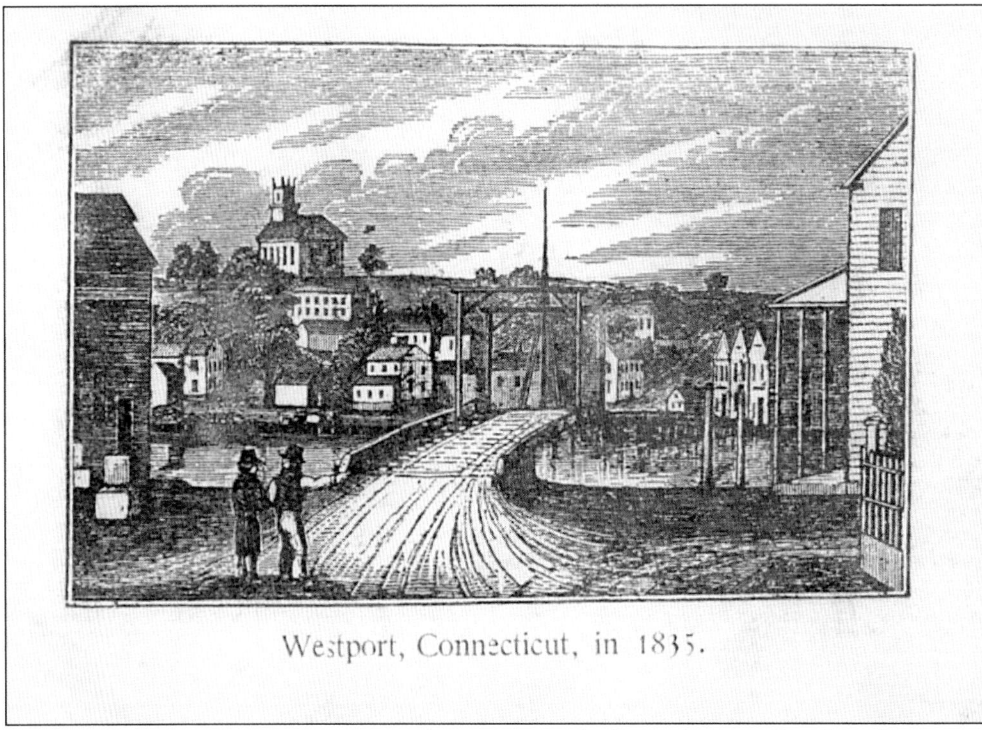

This early view of downtown, reprinted as a postcard, shows the Post Road in the year of Westport's incorporation, as seen from the east shore of the Saugatuck River.

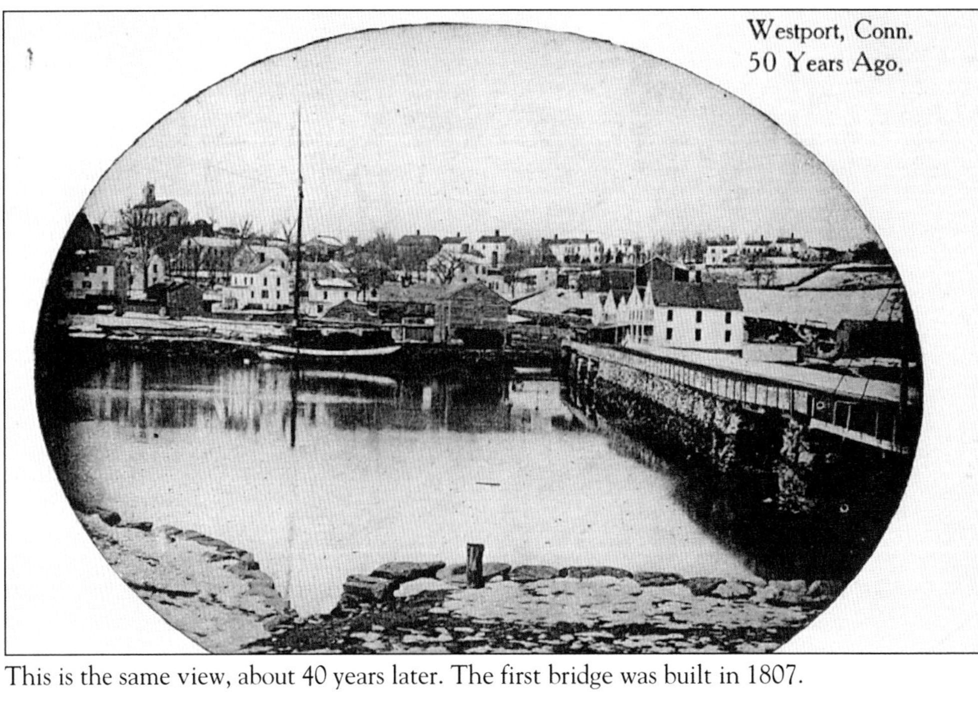

This is the same view, about 40 years later. The first bridge was built in 1807.

This card shows the Post Road, looking west, about 60 years after the town's incorporation.

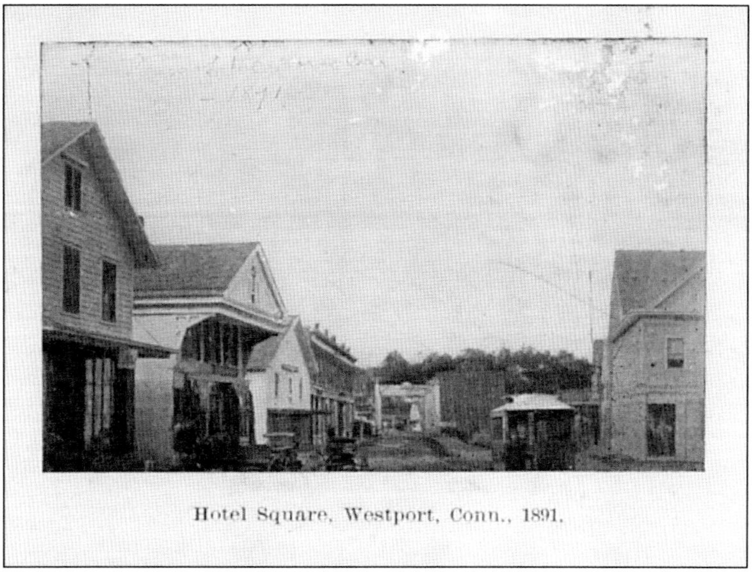

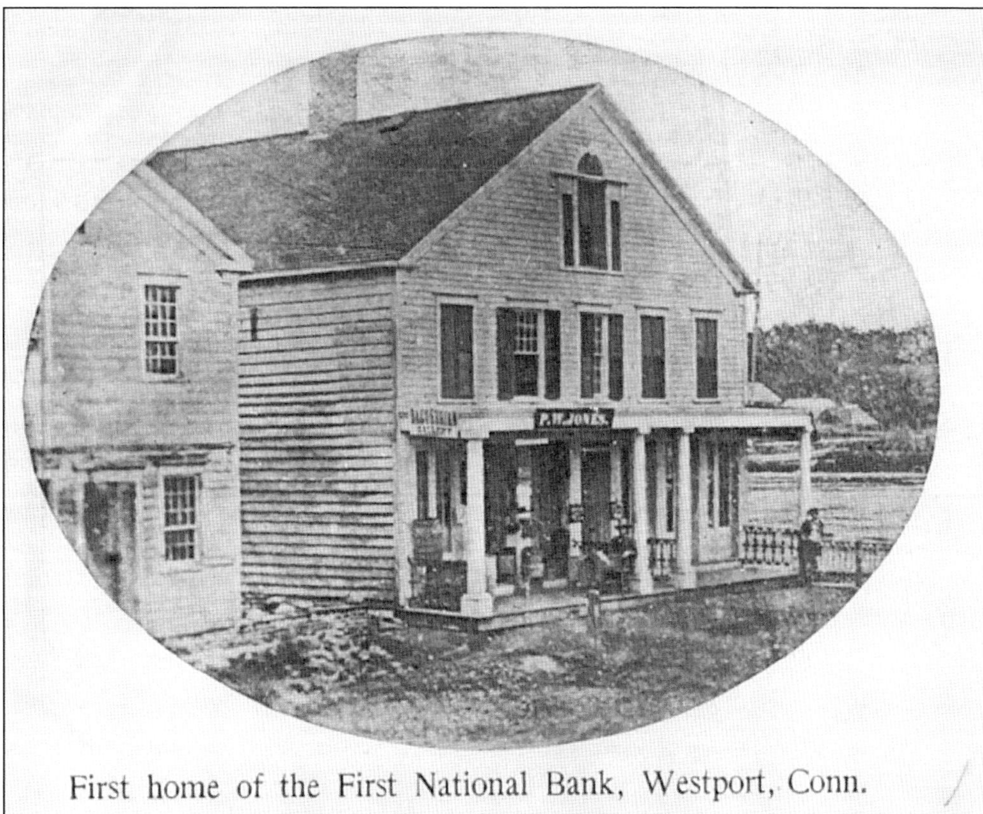

This building stood on the west bank of the Saugatuck, where National Hall is in the 1990s.

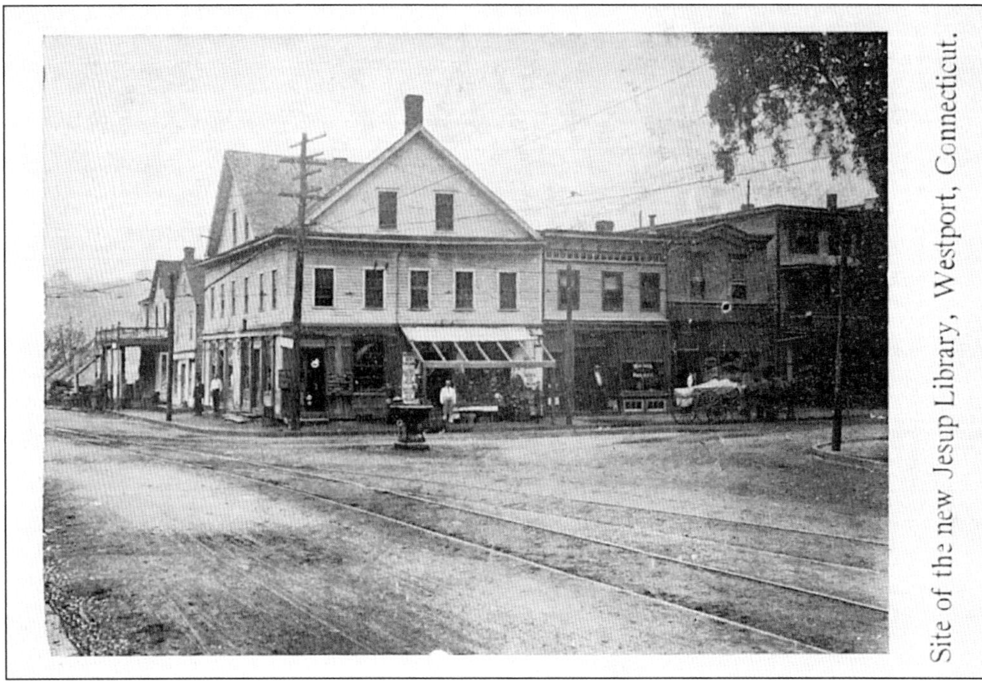

Mr. Jesup's library site, just before . . .

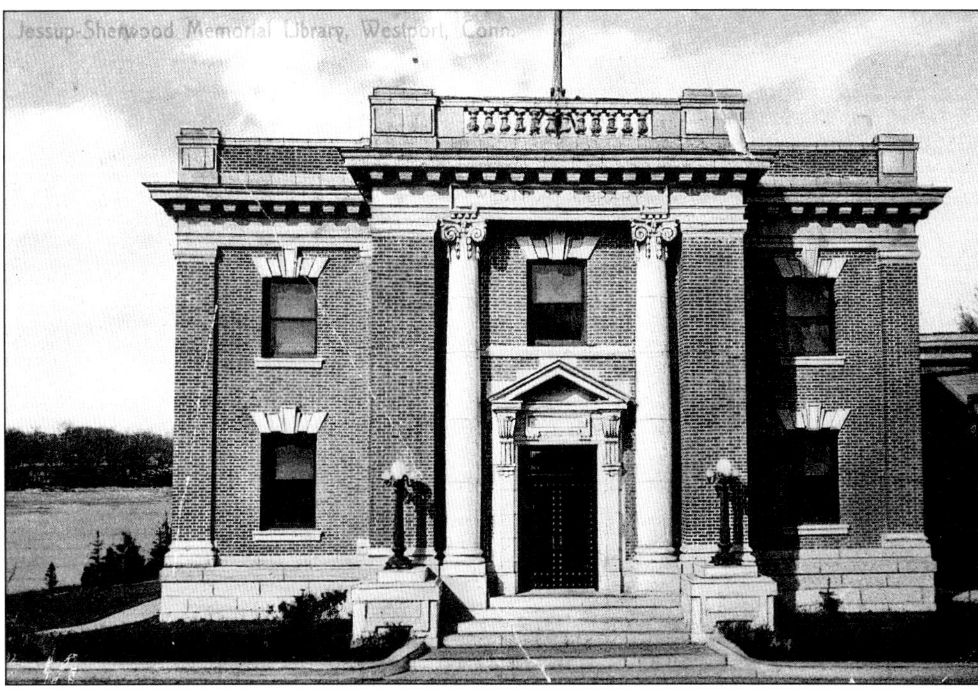

. . . and just after its construction in 1908.

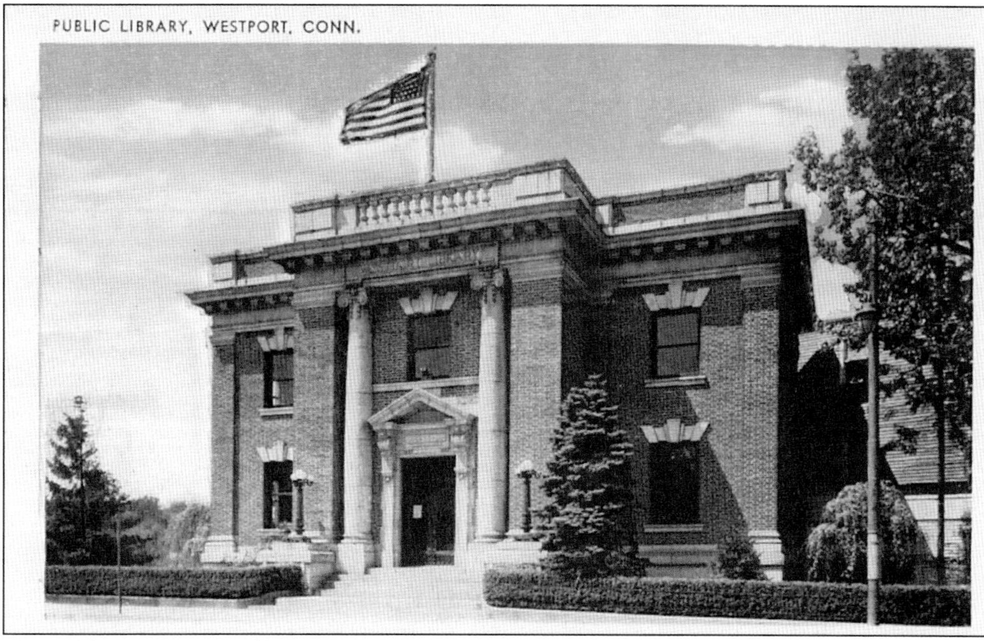

The "old" library was still on this postcard in March 1957 . . .

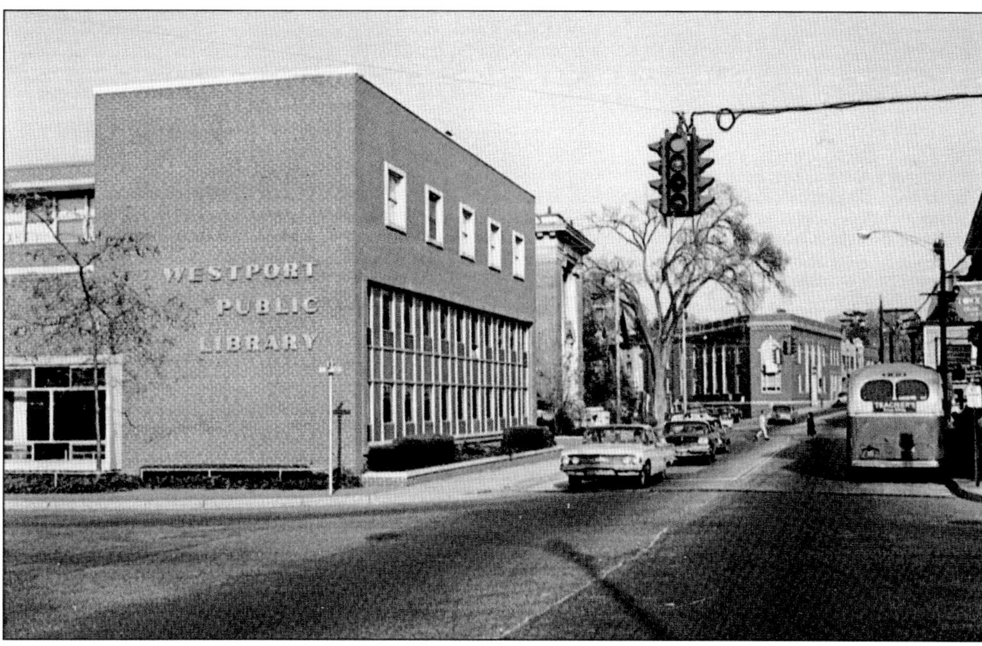

. . . and was added on to shortly thereafter.

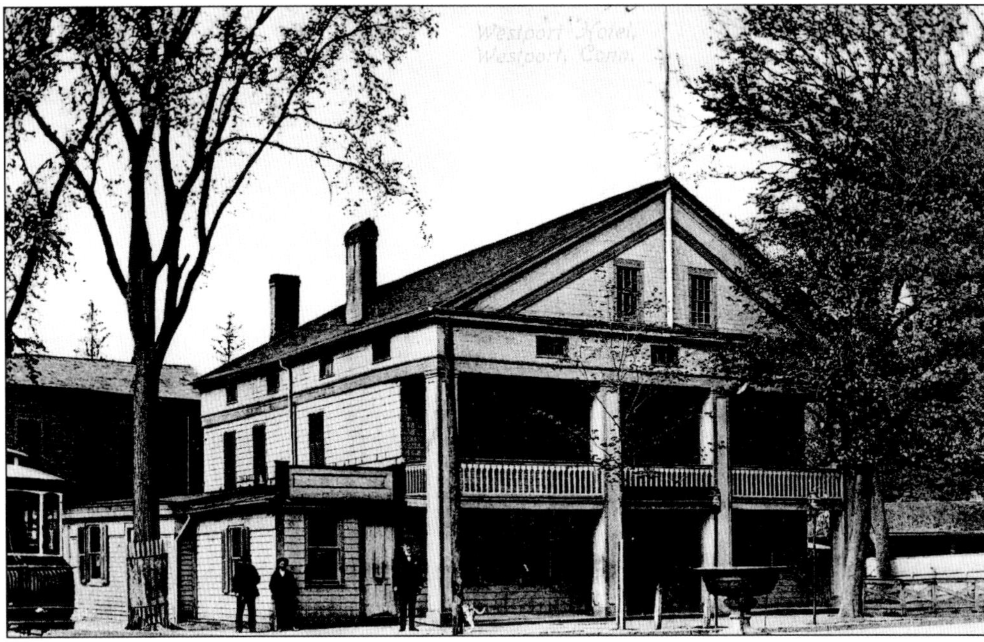

The Westport Hotel stood, at the turn of the century, where the YMCA stands in the late 1990s. The electric trolley (far left) first ran in 1896, past a horse watering trough.

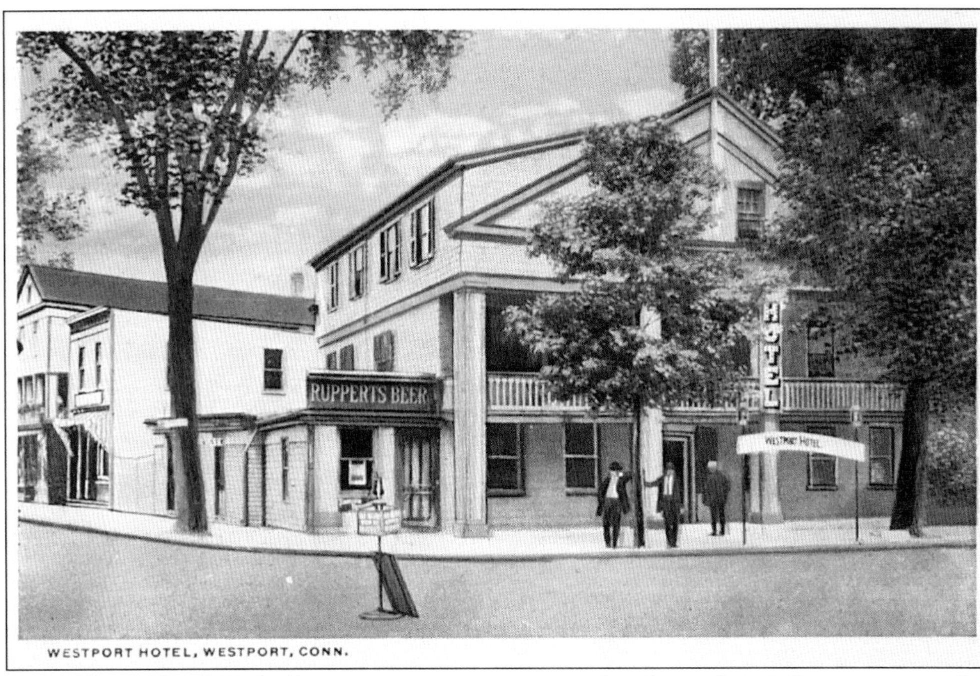

Legend has it that E.T. Bedford, too young to enter, stood in front of the billiard rooms in this hotel, vowing to build a facility that all could use . . .

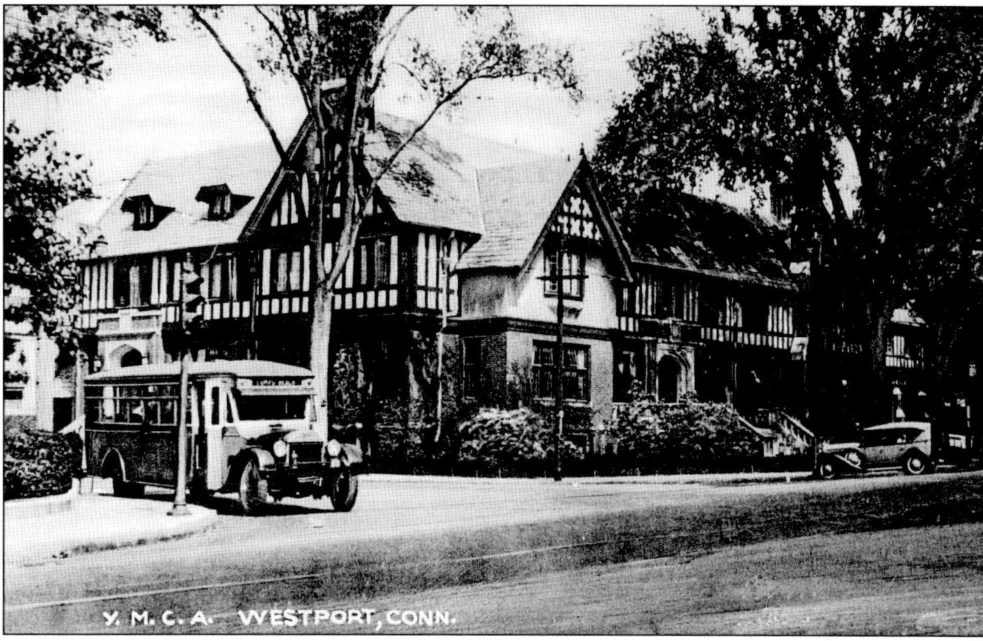

. . . which he did, in 1923, by underwriting the construction of the YMCA on this site. The YMCA is shown here when it was new, early in the 1920s.

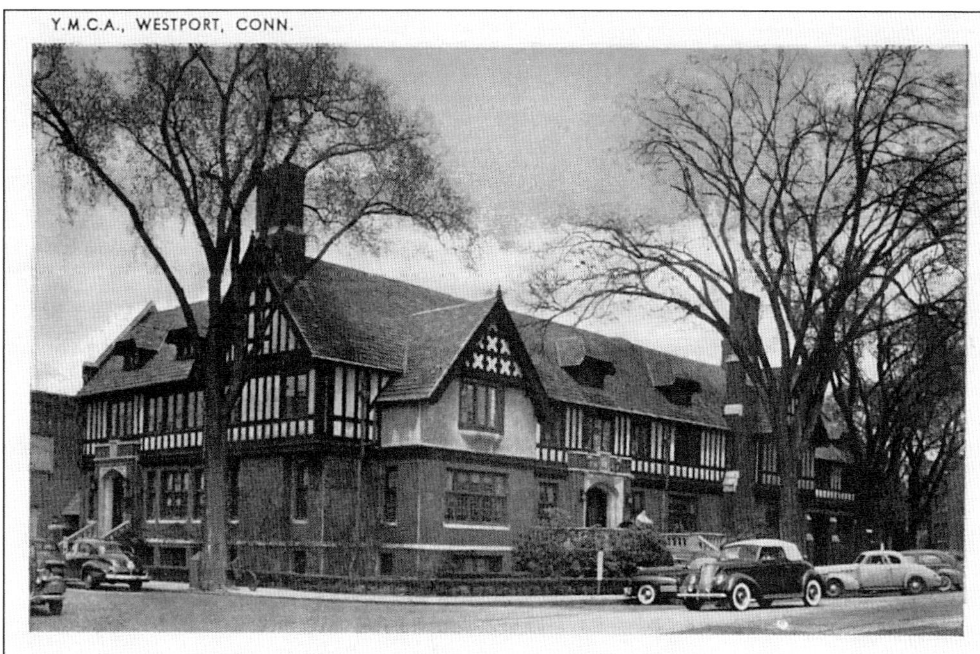

This is the same building the way it appeared 25 years later.

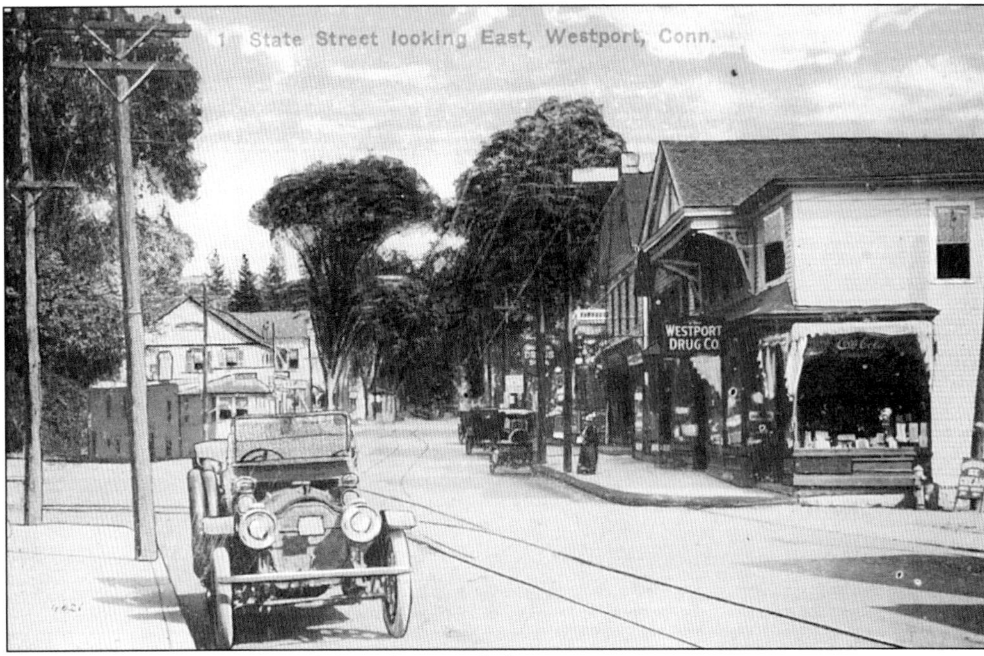

Looking east on the Post Road from the river *before* . . .

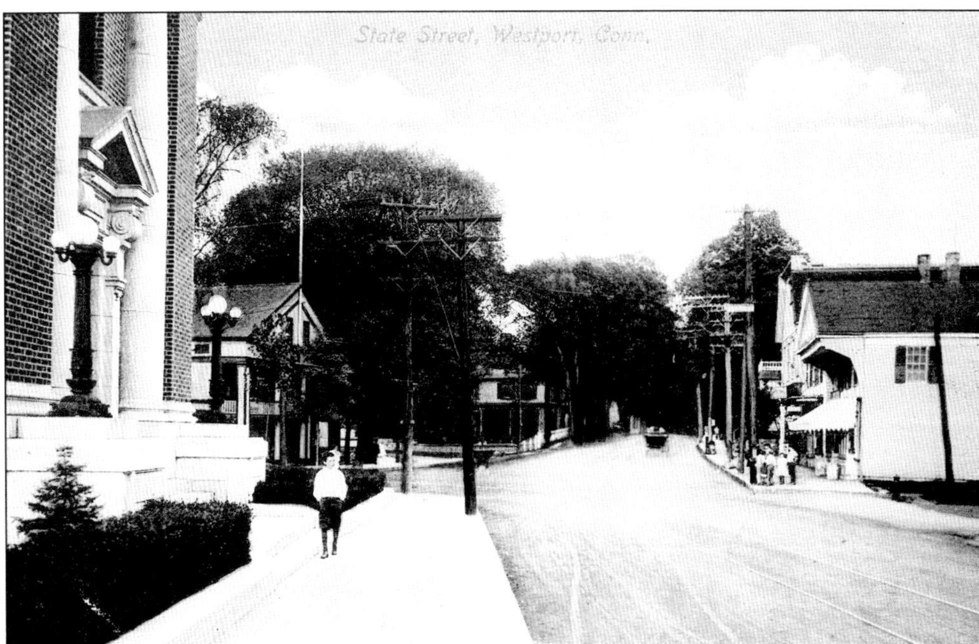

. . . and *after* Mr. Jesup's library was built in 1908.

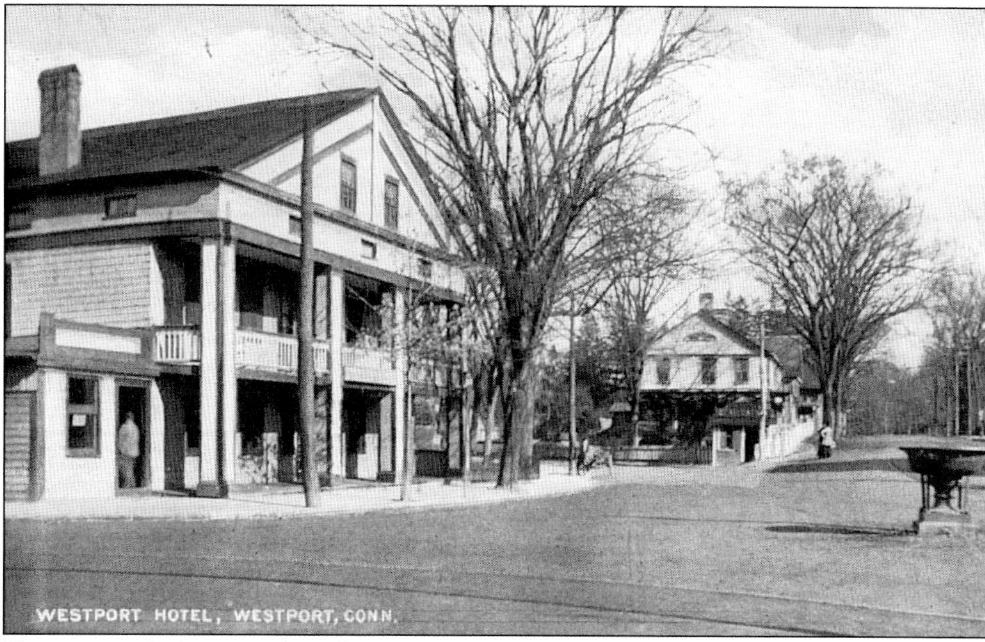

This is a view looking east from the intersection of the Post Road and Main Street. The building seen in the middle distance was replaced by the Westport Bank and Trust Company building.

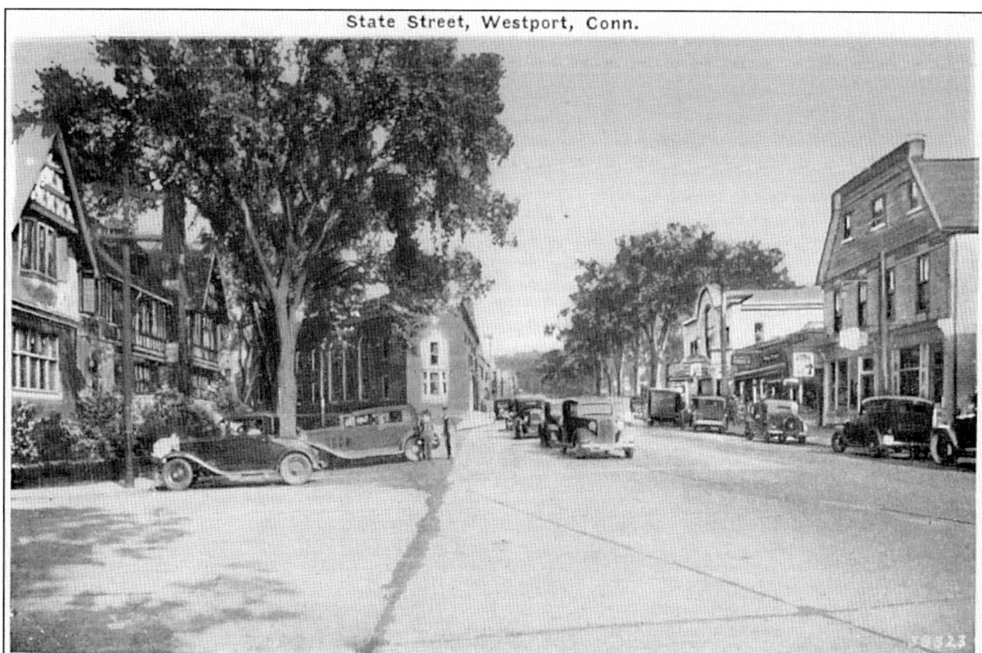

A similar view, taken about 1937, after the bank building was built, shows the Toquet Opera House (in the 1990s a teen center) in the building on the near right. The Fine Arts Cinema, the building with the rounded roof, is still a movie house in the 1990s.

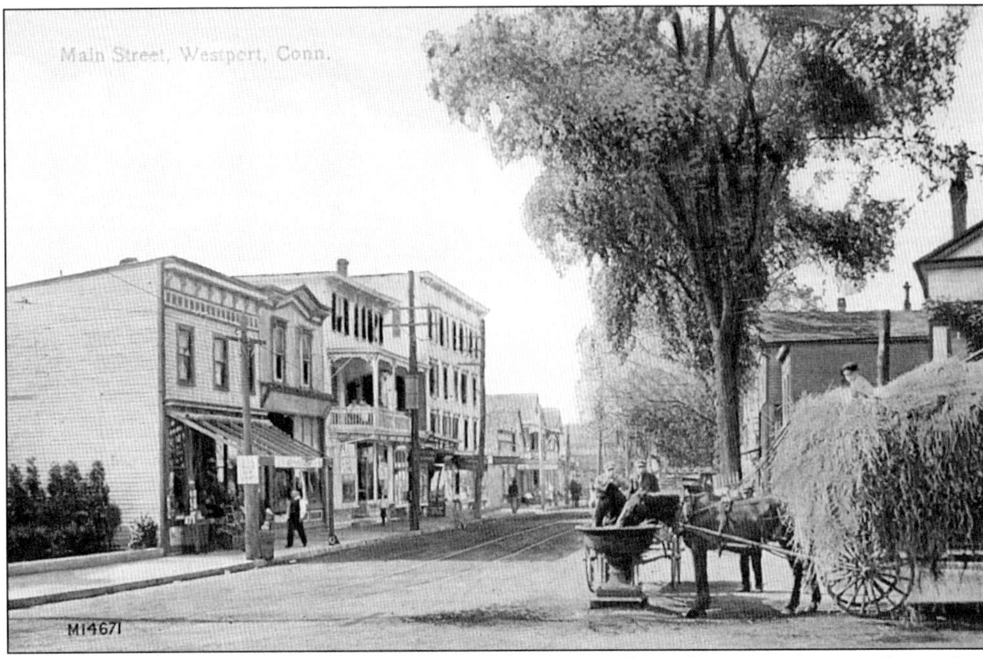

These shots of Main Street, taken around 1900, look north from the intersection with the Post Road, showing hay wagons . . .

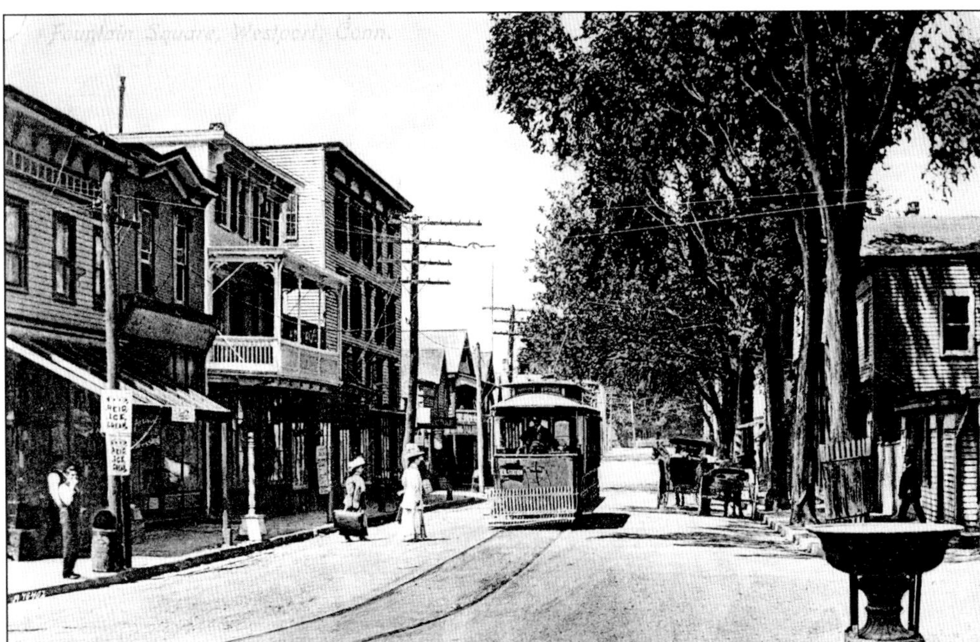

. . . and the trolleys which ran from downtown to neighboring towns and Compo Beach.

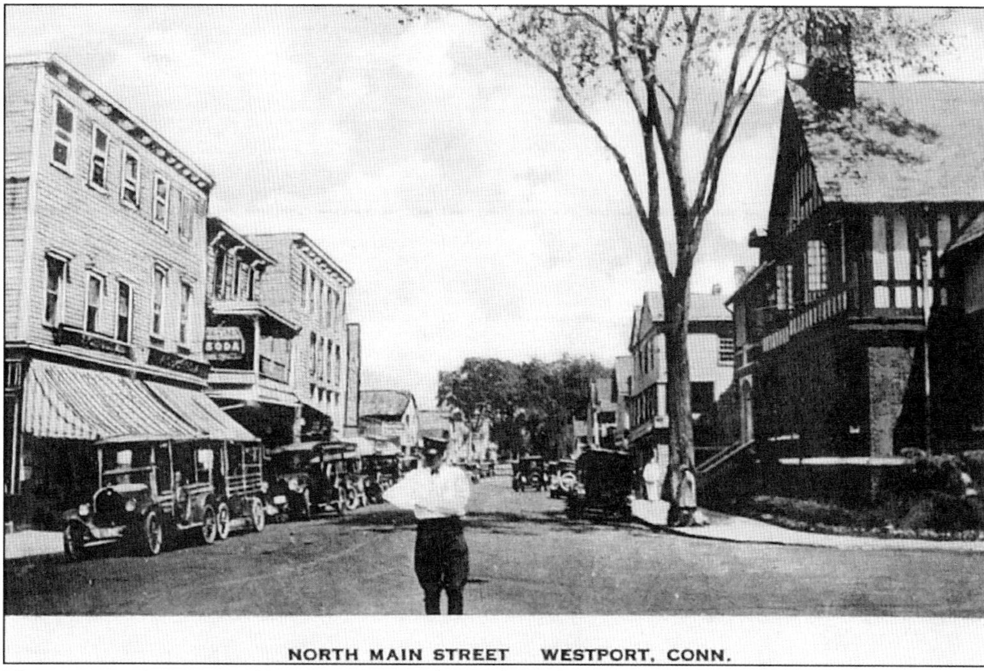

Here are similar views of Main Street in the early 20th century . . .

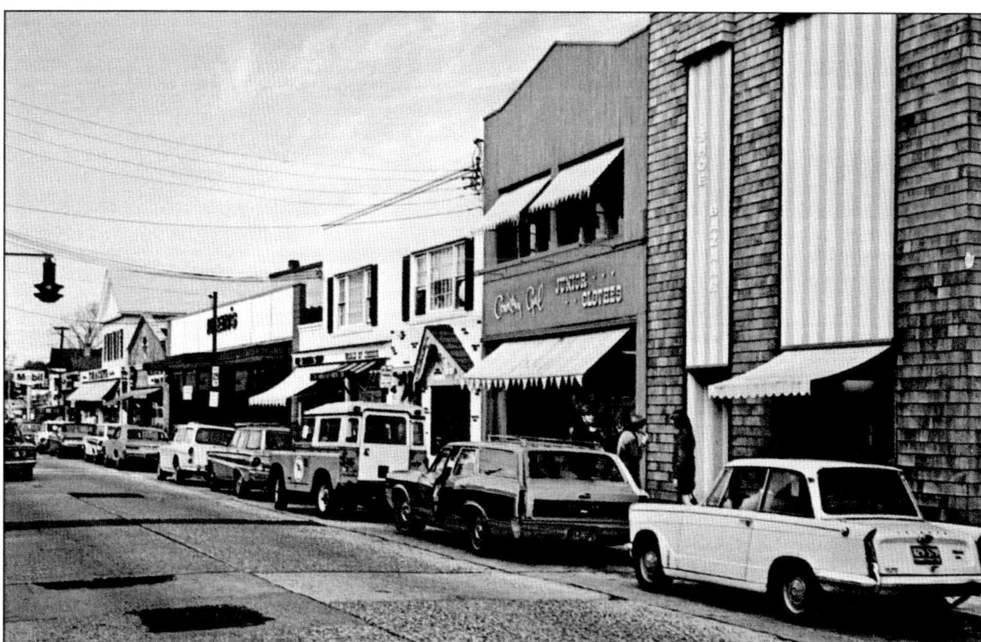

. . . and in the mid-20th century.

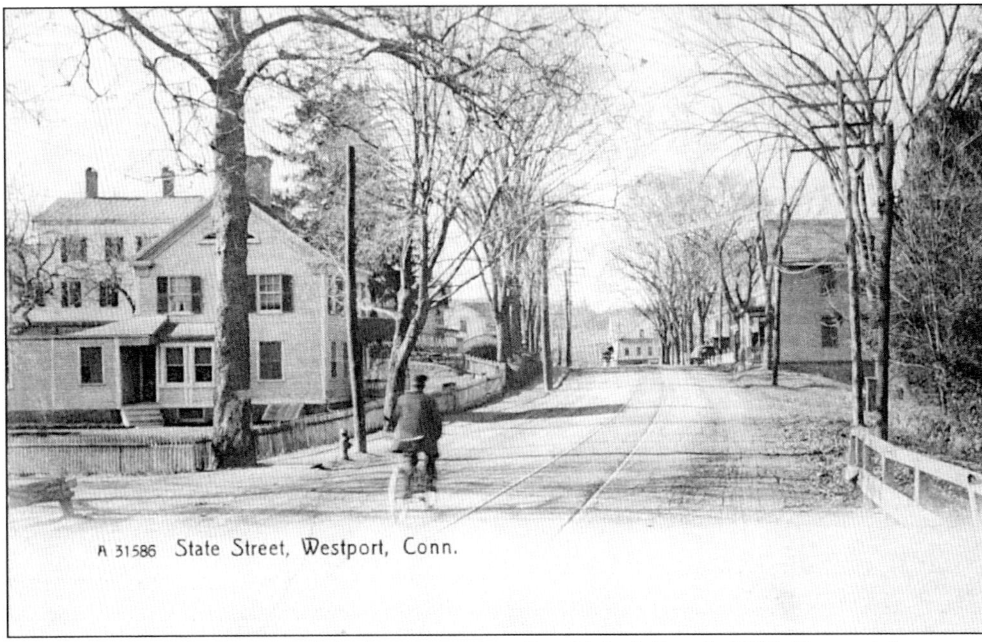

This card shows the Post Road, looking west from Dead Man's Brook. F.W. Kemper's house, on the left, was demolished to make room for the post office.

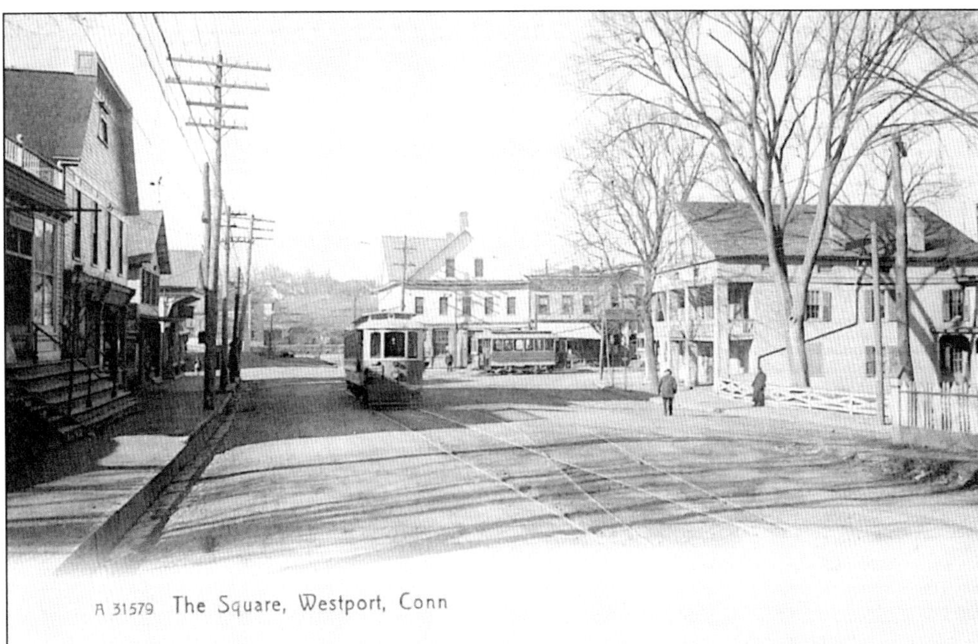

Here we see the Post Road, looking west from the future site of the Westport Bank and Trust Company building, sometime before 1908.

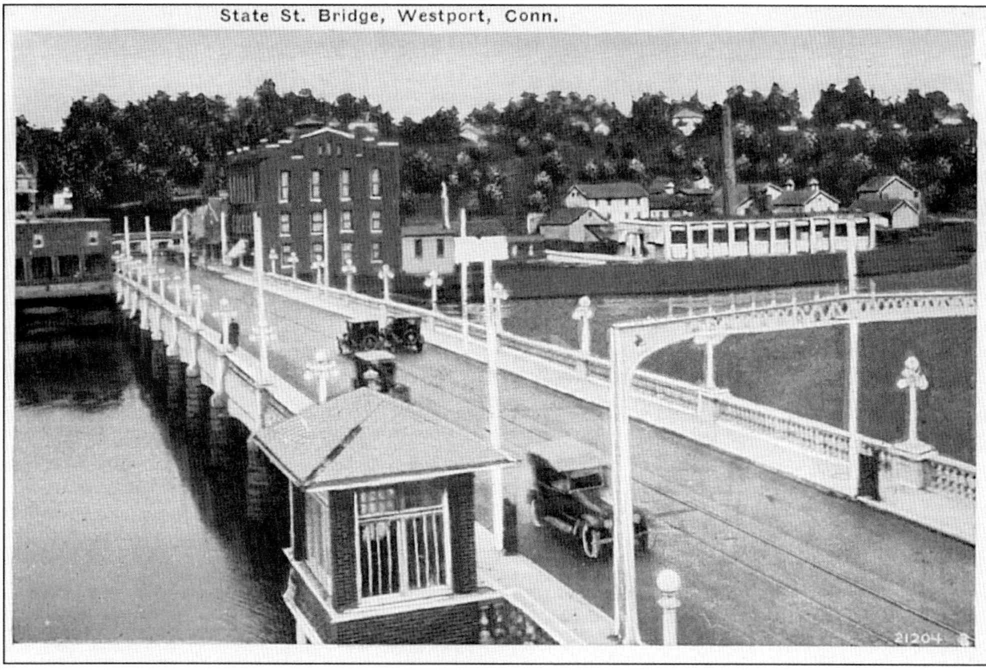

By the 1920s the Post Road bridge was elaborate, and National Hall, built in 1870 by Horace Staples as a bank, was visible on the west shore.

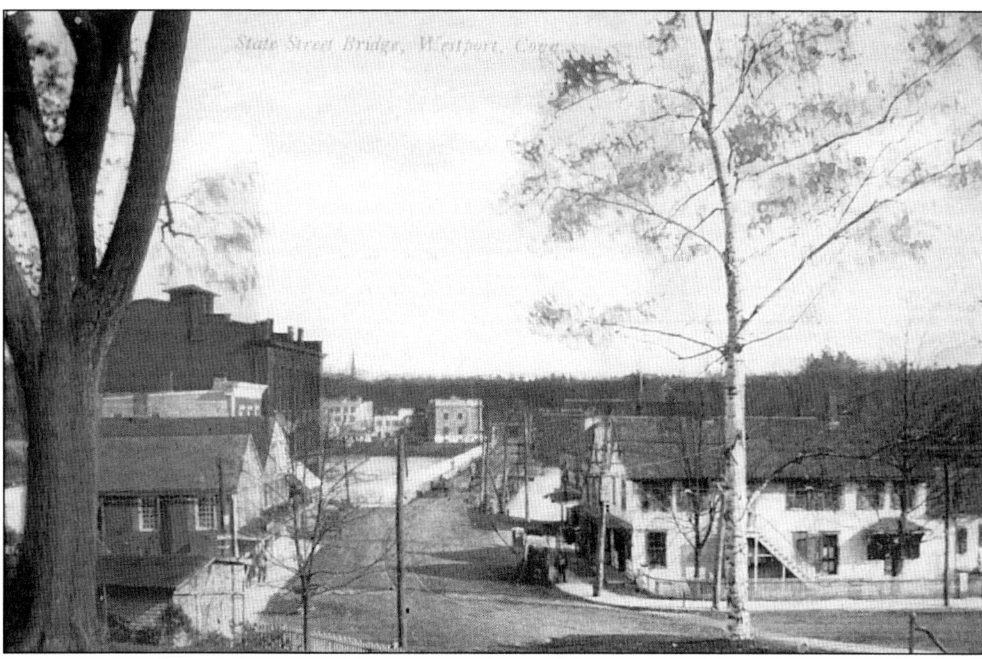

Looking east, about 1910, one can see Morris Jesup's library on the far side of the river.

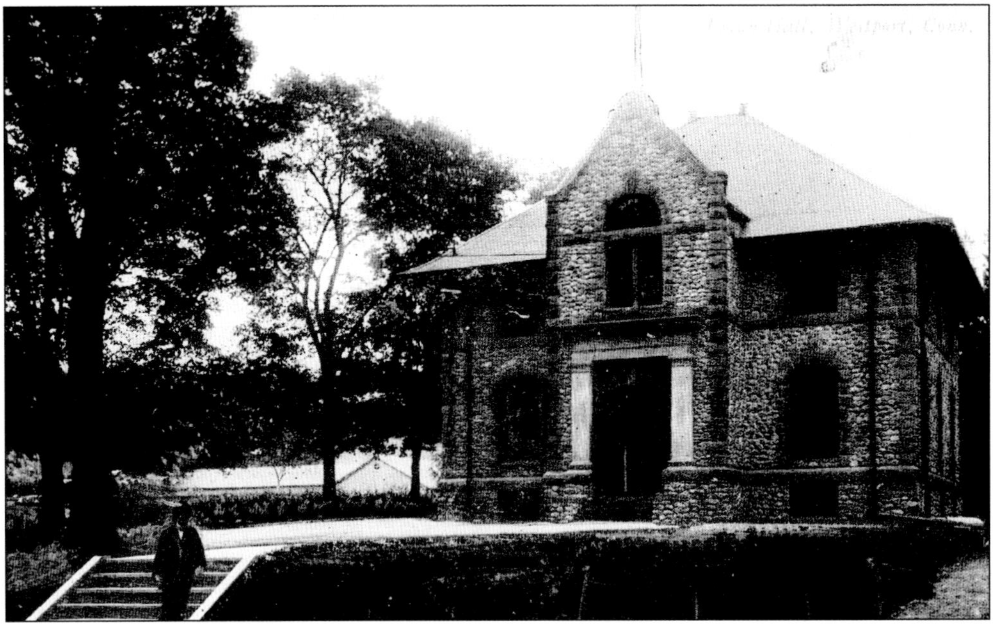

Town hall was built in 1909 on Main Street property costing $4,500 (the building cost $17,000), and served as the center of government until 1979, when the building was sold for $2 million.

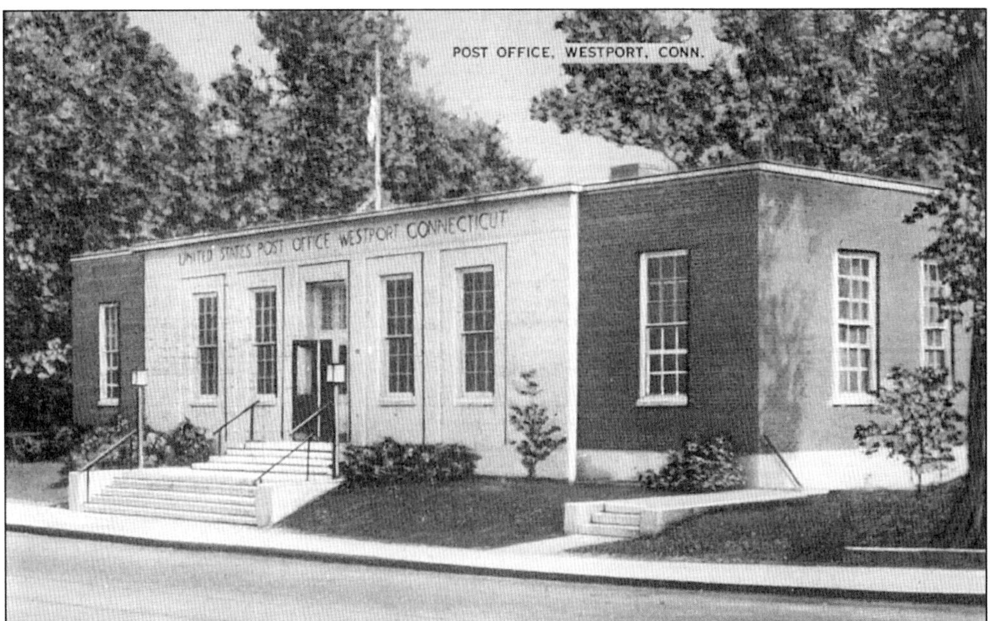

The current post office, seen here on a card mailed on March 13, 1942, sits on the corner of the Post Road and Bay Street.

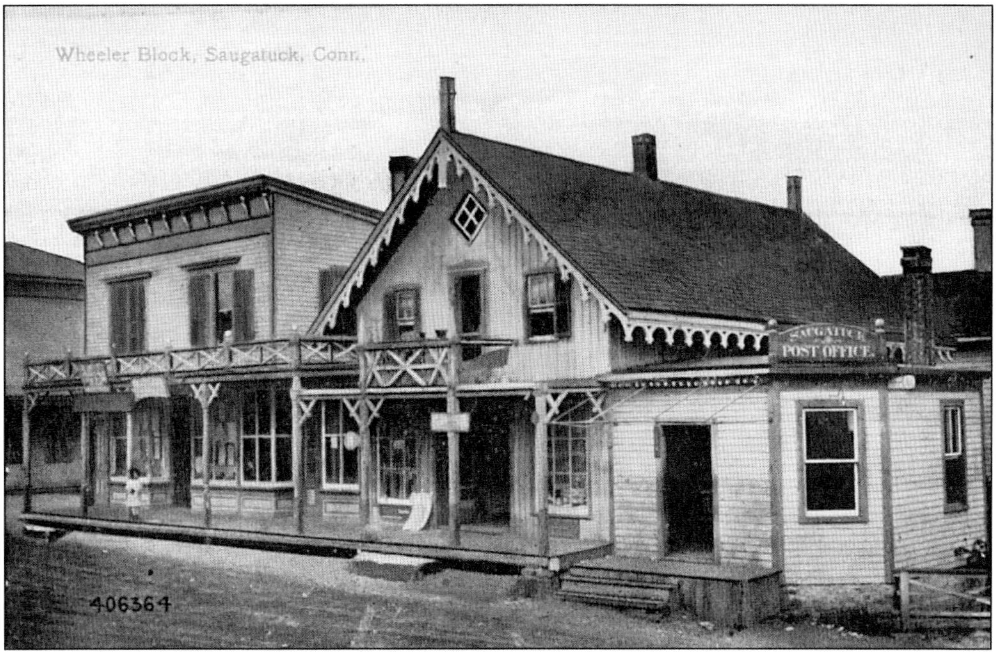

The Saugatuck Post Office, seen here on a card mailed November 2, 1915 . . .

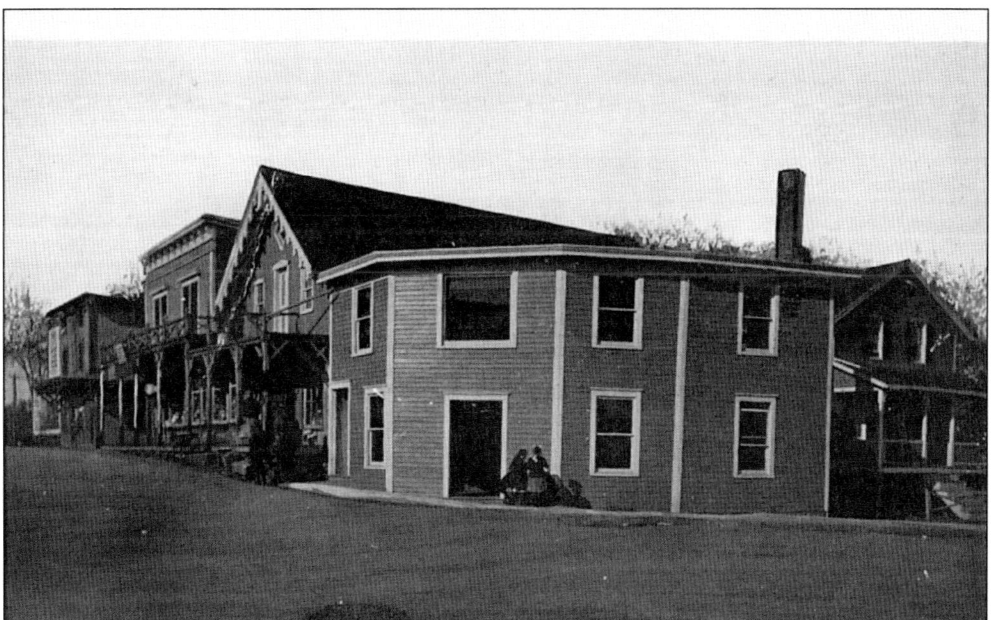

POST OFFICE & R. R. PLACE, Saugatuck, Conn.

. . . looked like this when renovated, before moving across the street to its present location.

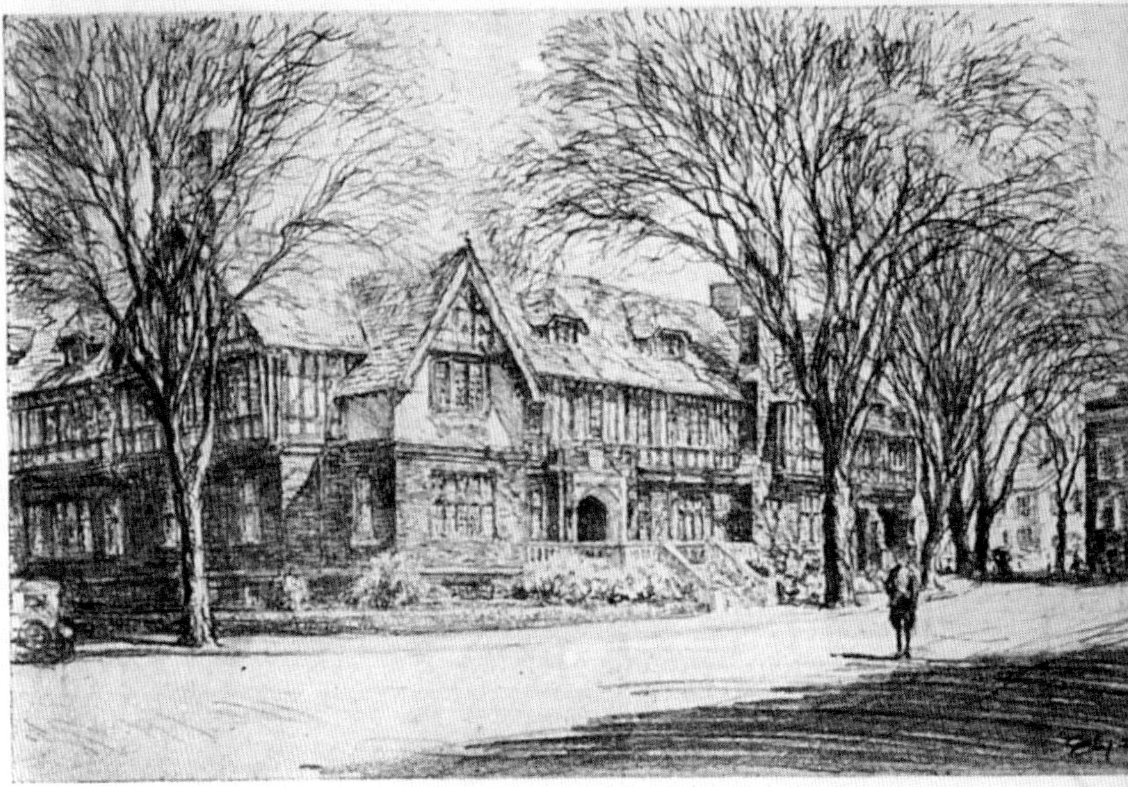

Y. M. C. A., WESTPORT, CONN.

Two

COMMERCIAL WESTPORT:

BUSINESSES AND FACTORIES

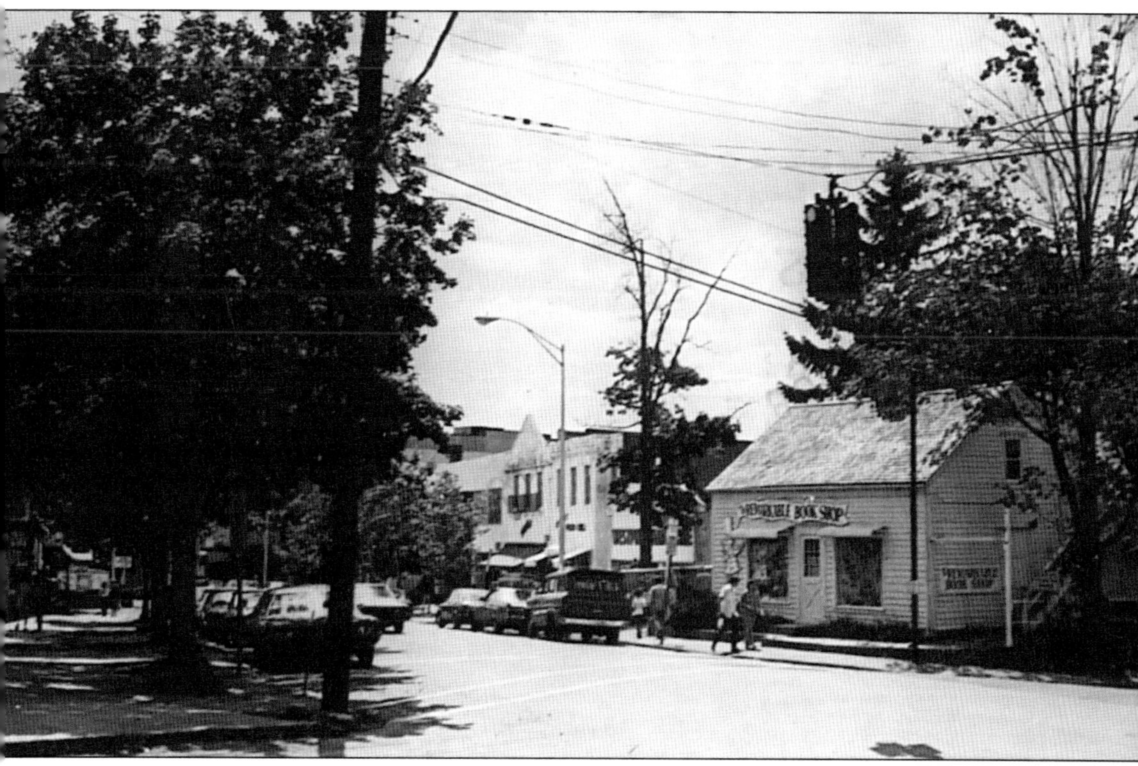

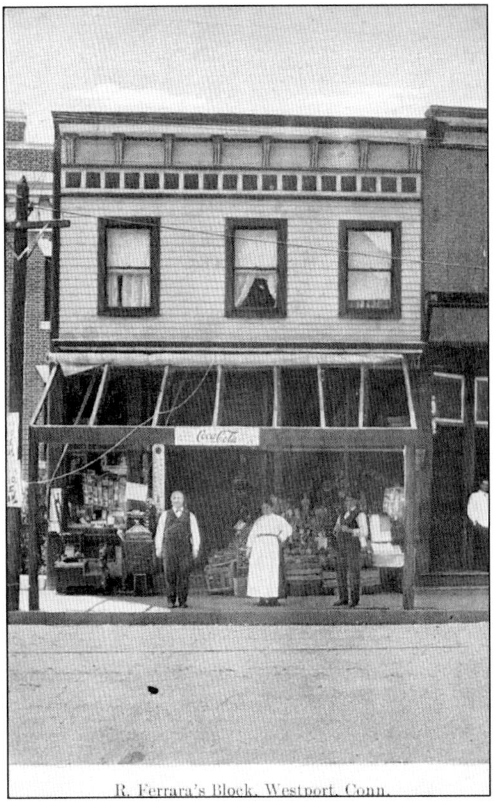

This building at 7 Main Street is still a store in the 1990s, but it carries shoes instead of Coca Cola.

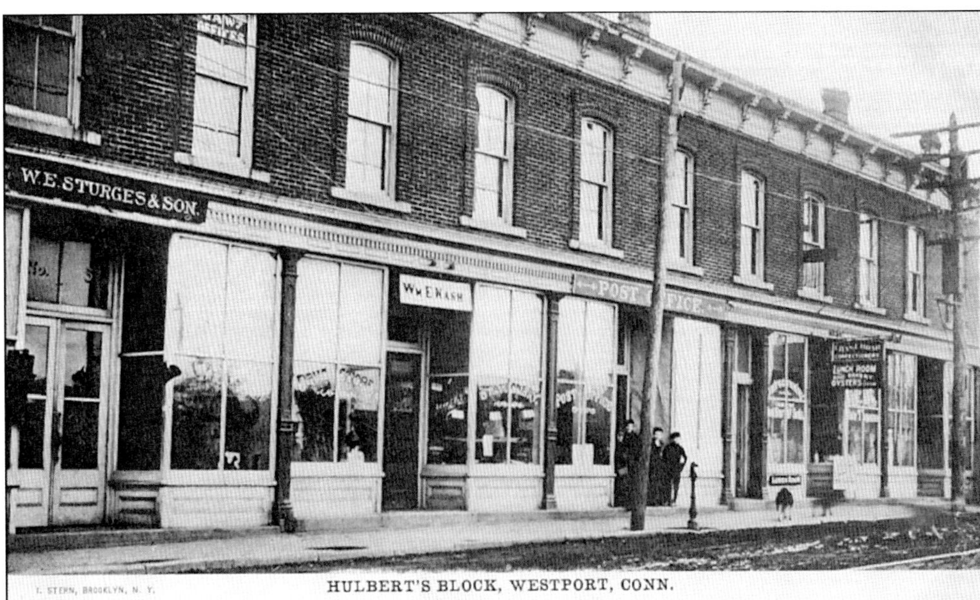

Mr. Hurlbutt (not "Hulbert") owned the future site of the Gault Building East, shown here about 1874. Note the Westport names of Sturges and Nash.

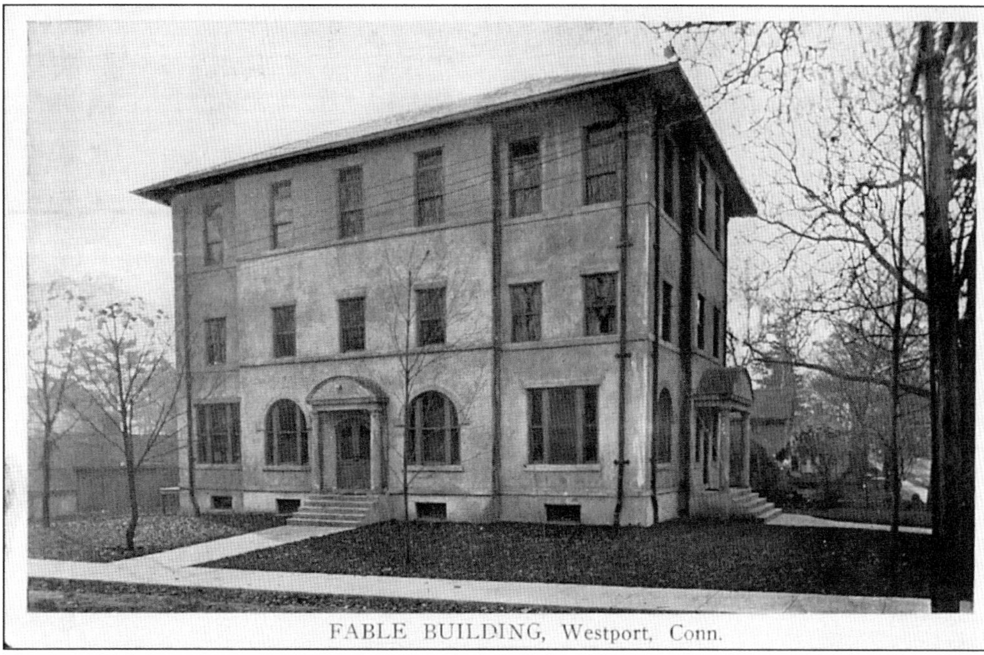

On the southwest corner of the intersection of the Post Road and Imperial Avenue, another old Westport family built a building, which is used in the 1990s as a funeral home on the third floor, and the home of Masonic Lodge Temple No. 65; in the 1870s, the Masons were in National Hall.

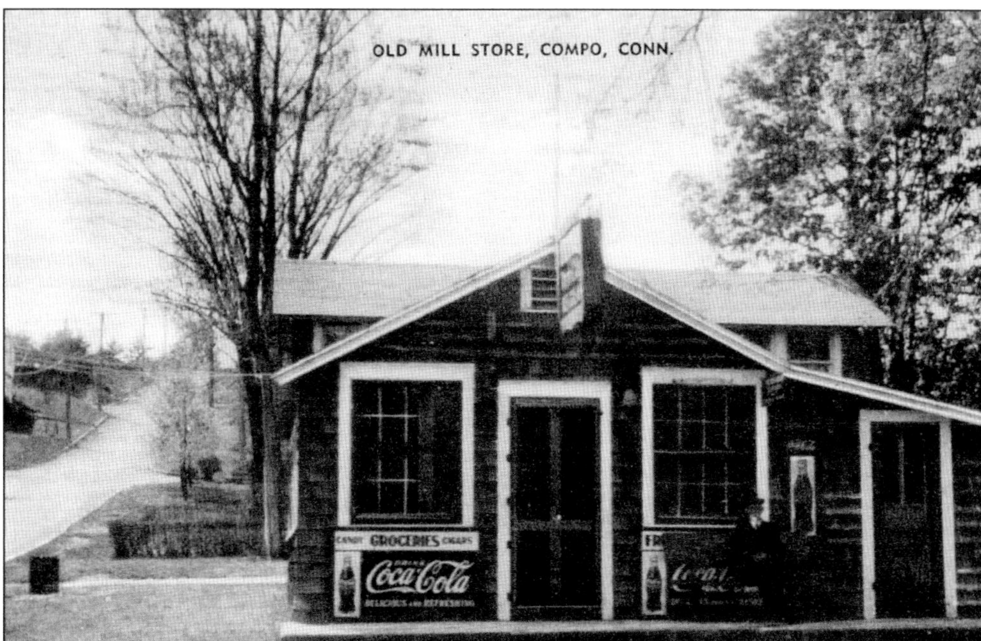

The store shown here, located on Hills Point Road at the base of Compo Hill, is largely unchanged from this 1935 view.

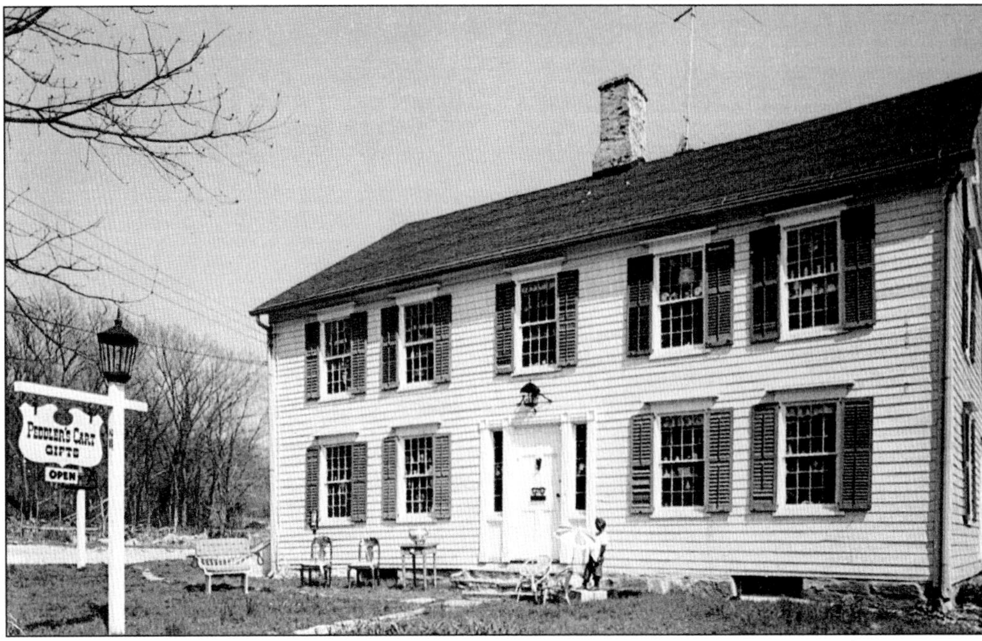

Many shops were simply recycled homes, which made a fine picture for a postcard.

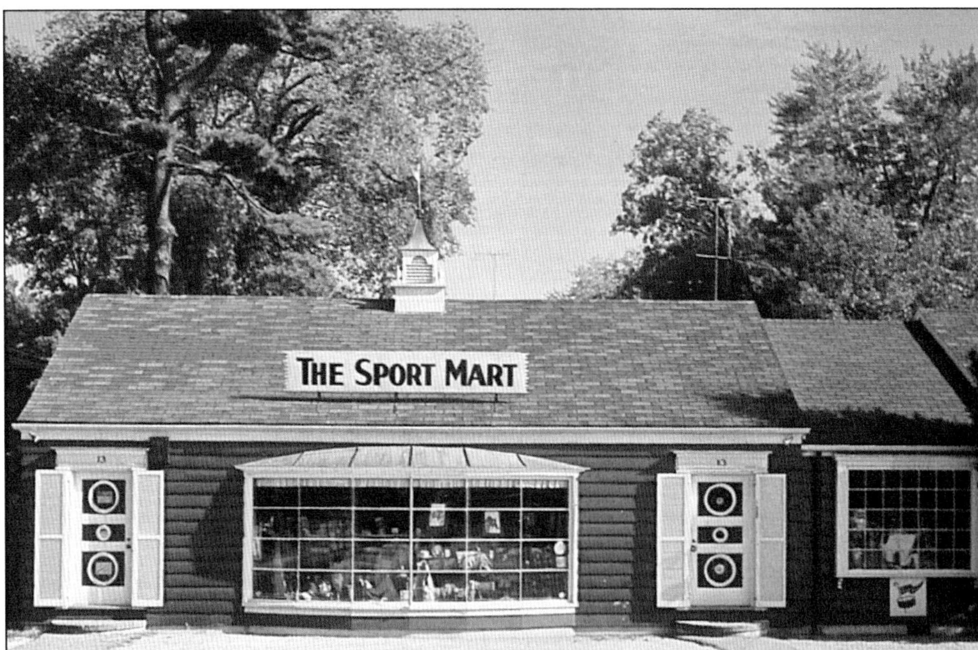

A Westport institution now on Main Street, the Sport Mart was previously located in what is Sconset Square in the 1990s.

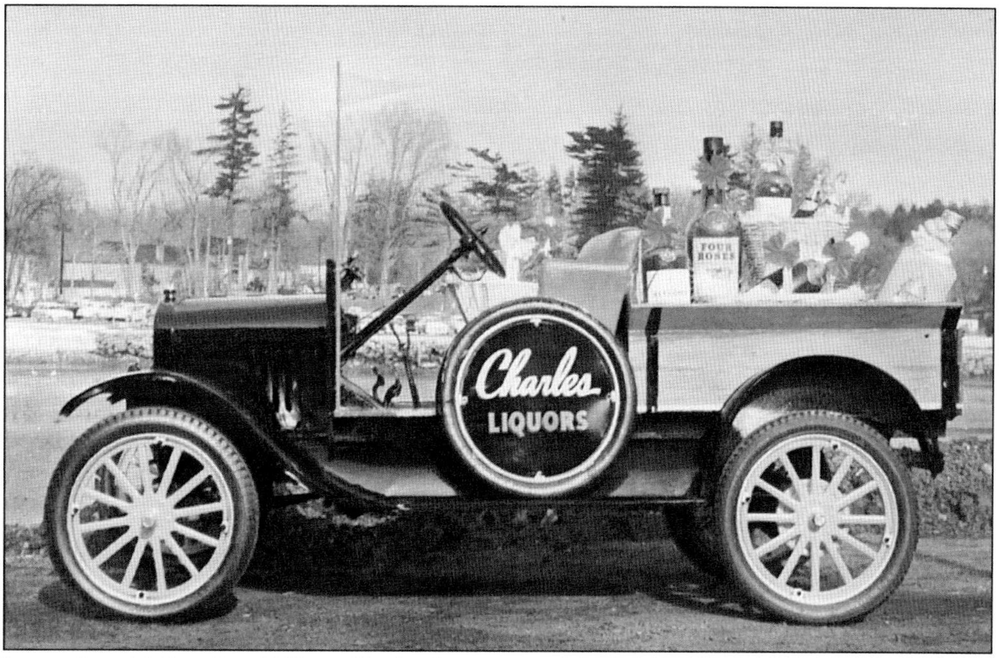

Located at 19 Post Road West, Charles Liquors used "we deliver" as a slogan and advertised with this postcard.

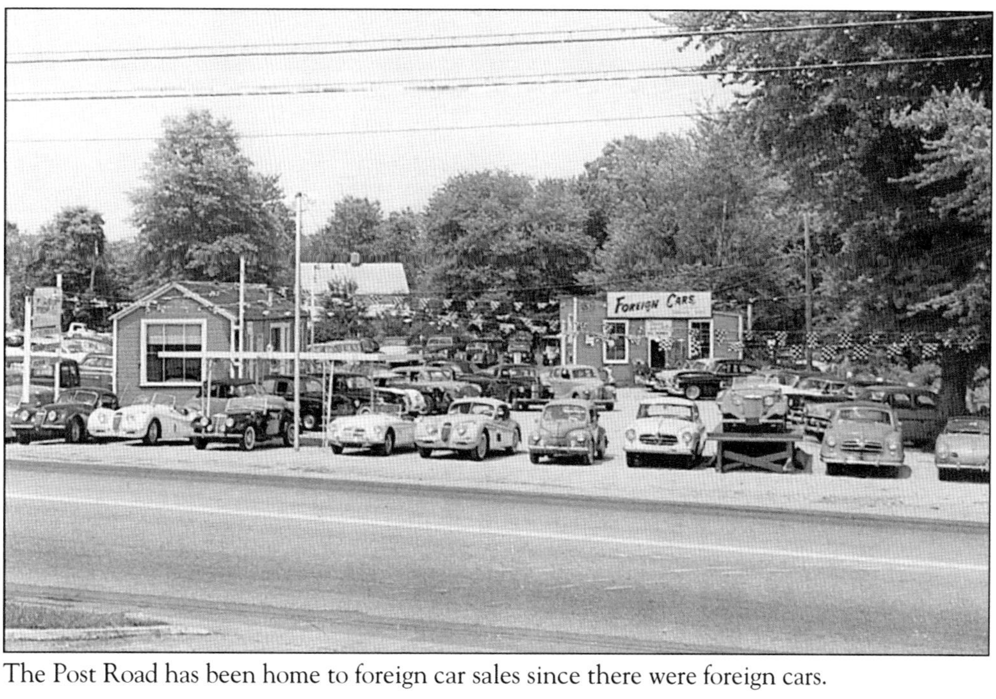

The Post Road has been home to foreign car sales since there were foreign cars.

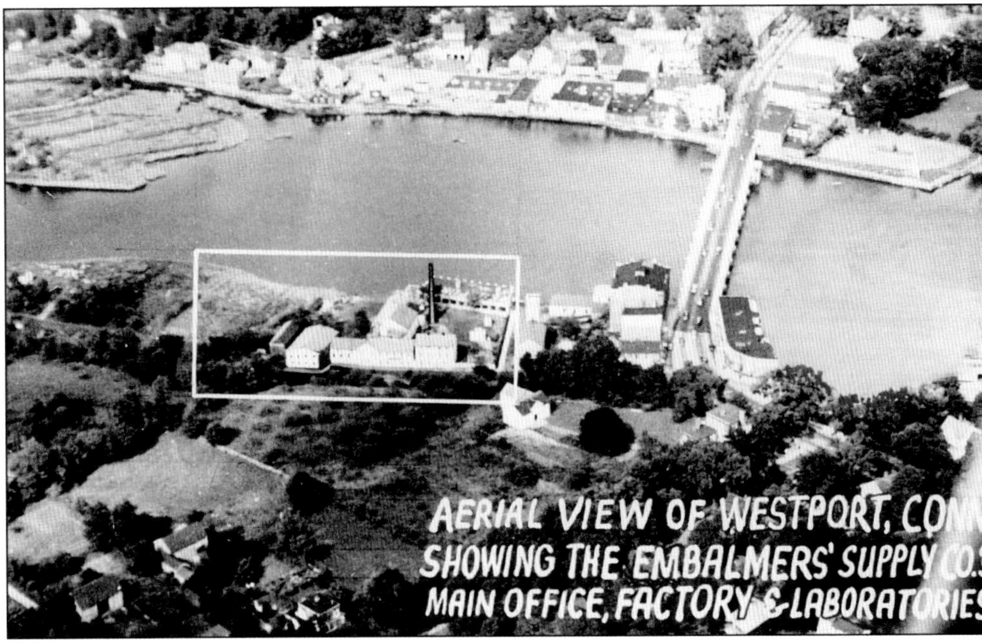

A factory makes an unlikely subject for a postcard, though almost any commercial activity is suitable for advertising. This site is located where Save The Children is in the 1990s.

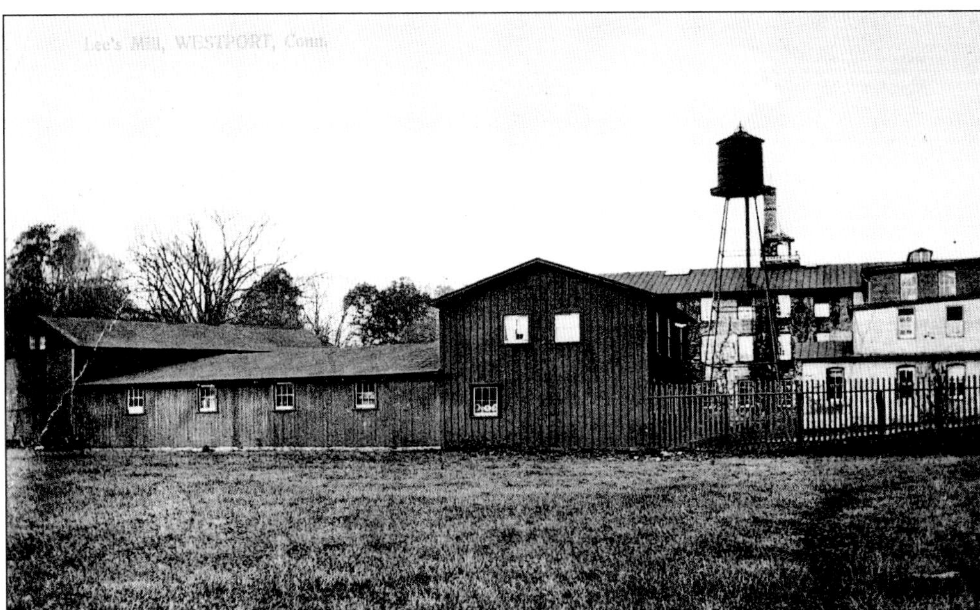

Lee's Mill, on Richmondville Avenue, manufactured cotton items such as lamp wicks and twine. This card was mailed in 1909.

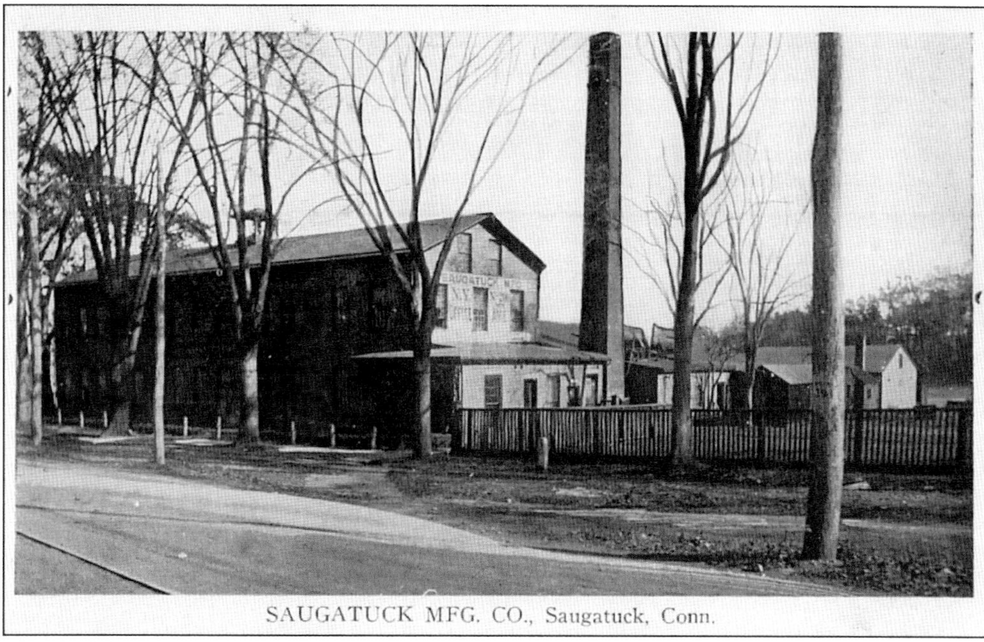

This building, built in 1848 as a foundry, is still standing as the year 2000 approaches, and is located to the left of the Saugatuck Post Office. The Saugatuck Manufacturing Company was a button manufacturer.

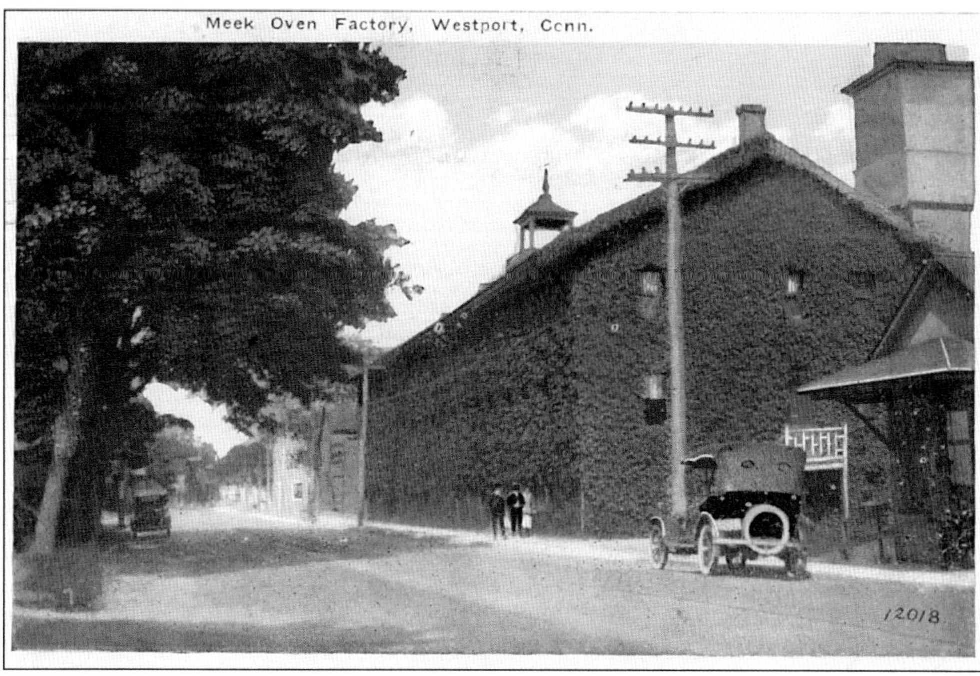

This card was sent on October 10, 1923. Meek Oven operated for a few years in the early 1920s.

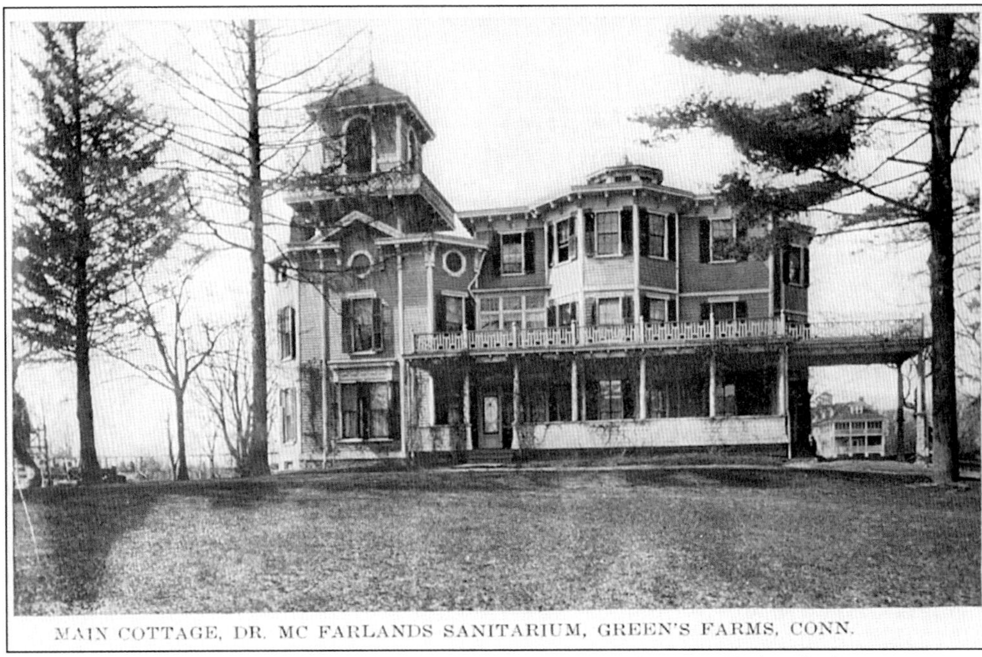

Before it was Hall-Brooke, the building at 47 Long Lots Road was McFarland's Sanitarium.

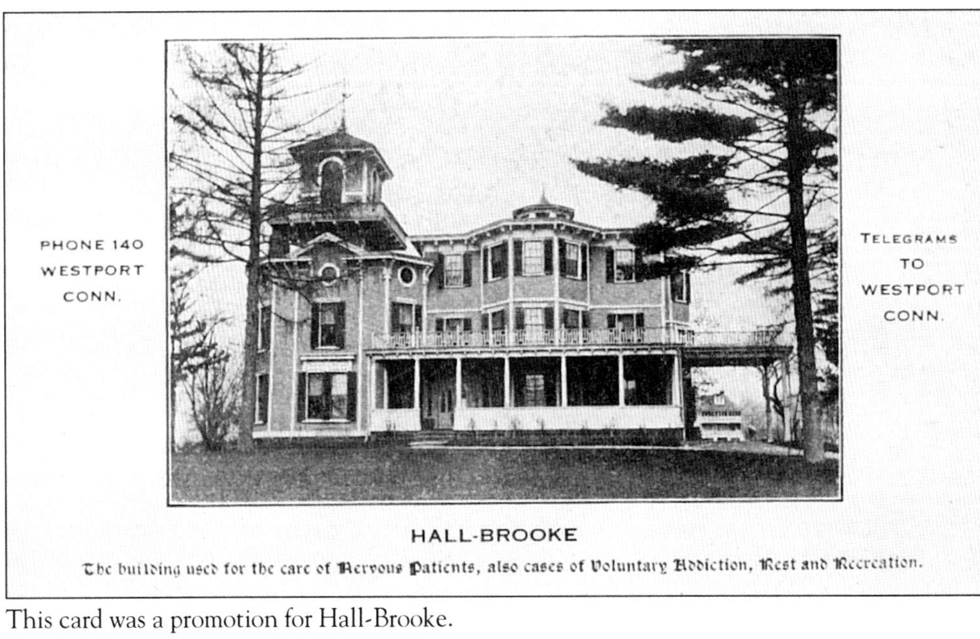

This card was a promotion for Hall-Brooke.

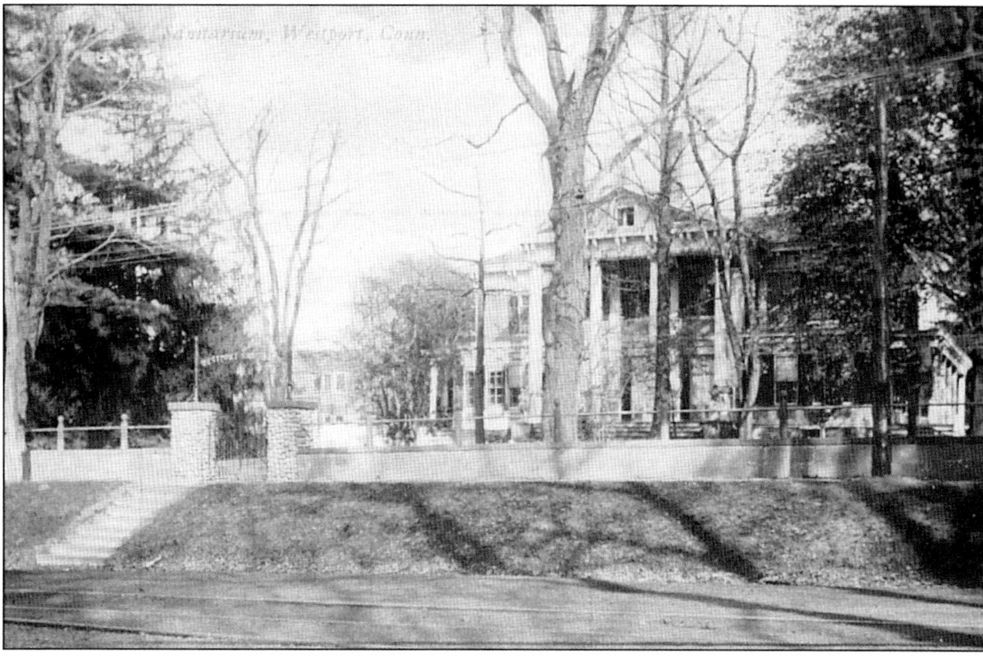

"Compo House," which stood at the northwest corner of Compo Road North and the Post Road, was acquired by Richard Winslow in 1853; it became a sanitarium after 1861 and was demolished on August 18, 1973. It is now the site of Winslow Park.

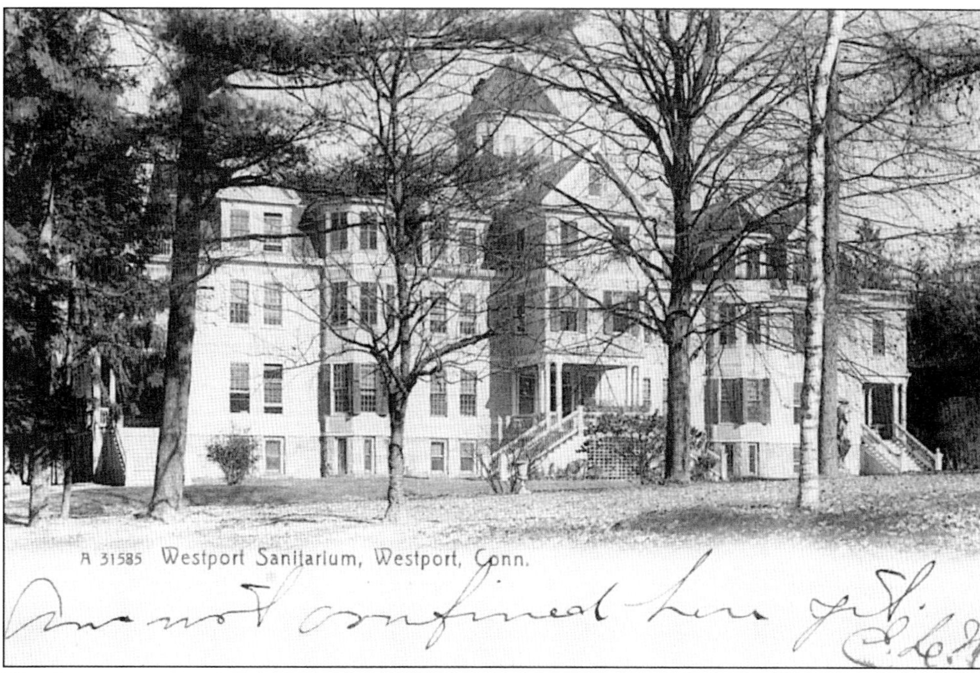

This large structure, behind "Compo House," was an annex to the sanitarium.

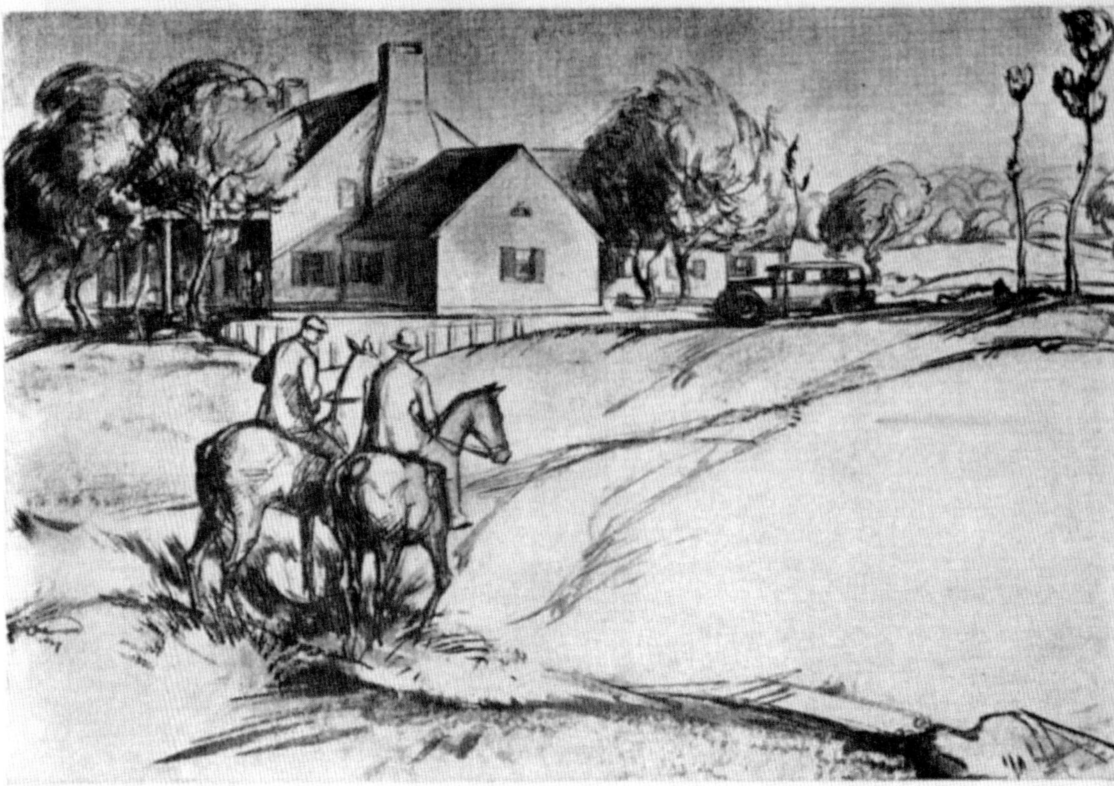

FAIRFIELD COUNTY HUNT CLUB © 1927

Three

Residential Westport: Houses and Street Scenes

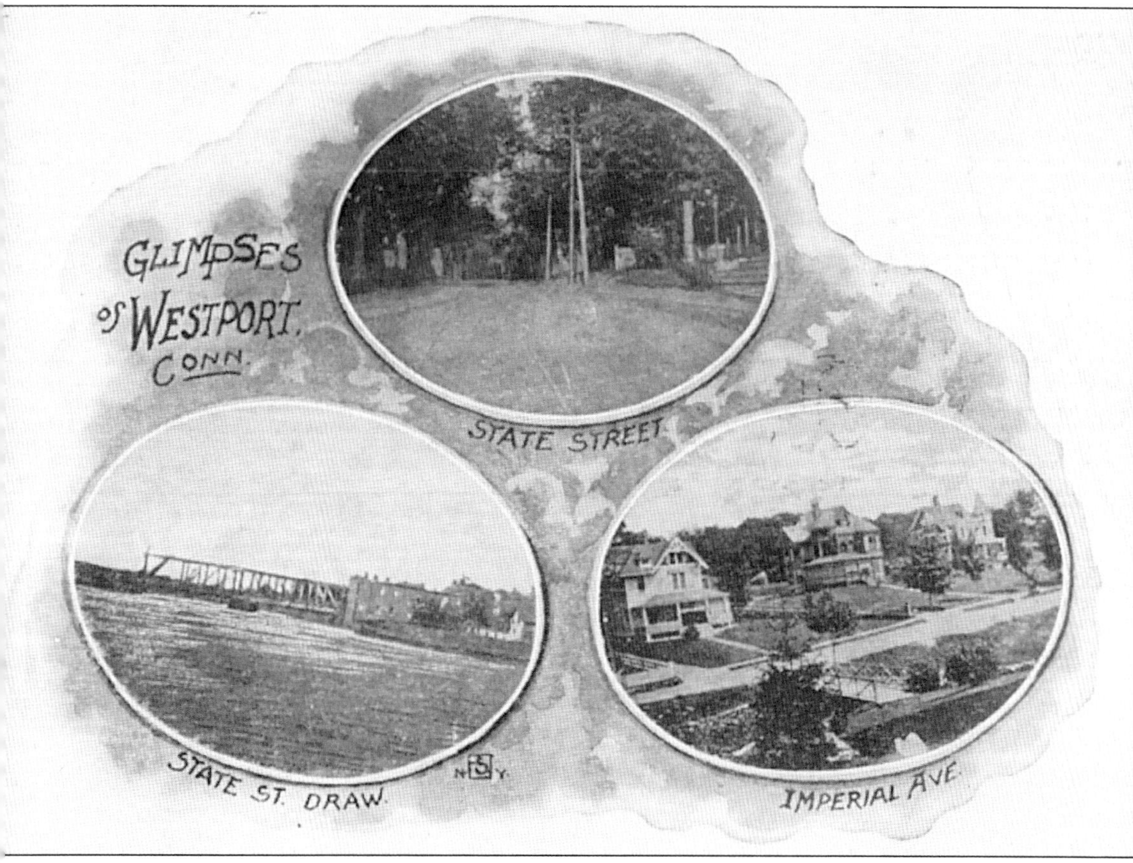

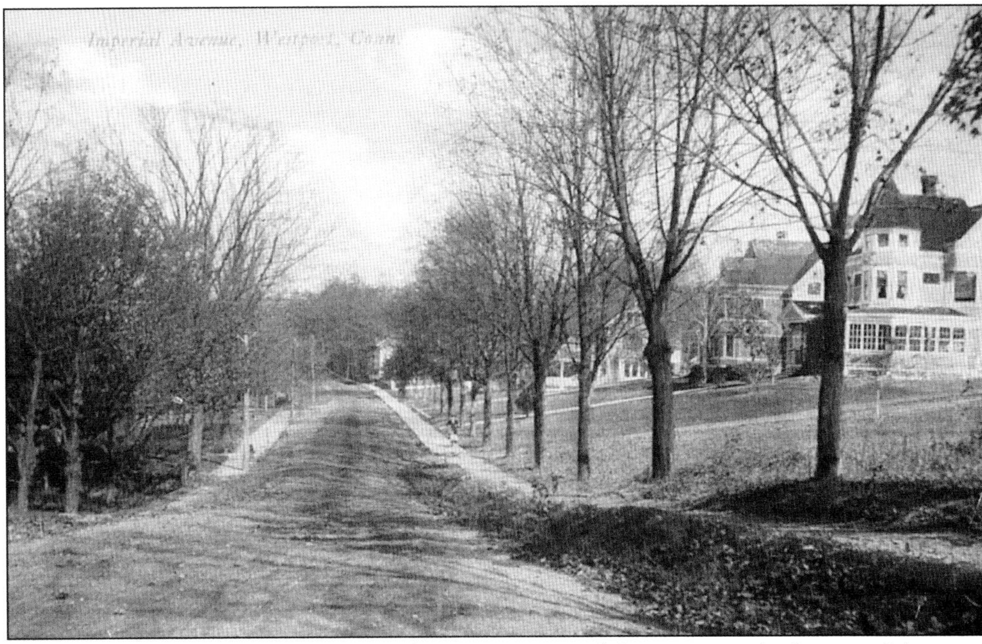

A street of law firms and businesses in the 1990s, Imperial Avenue once had views of the river.

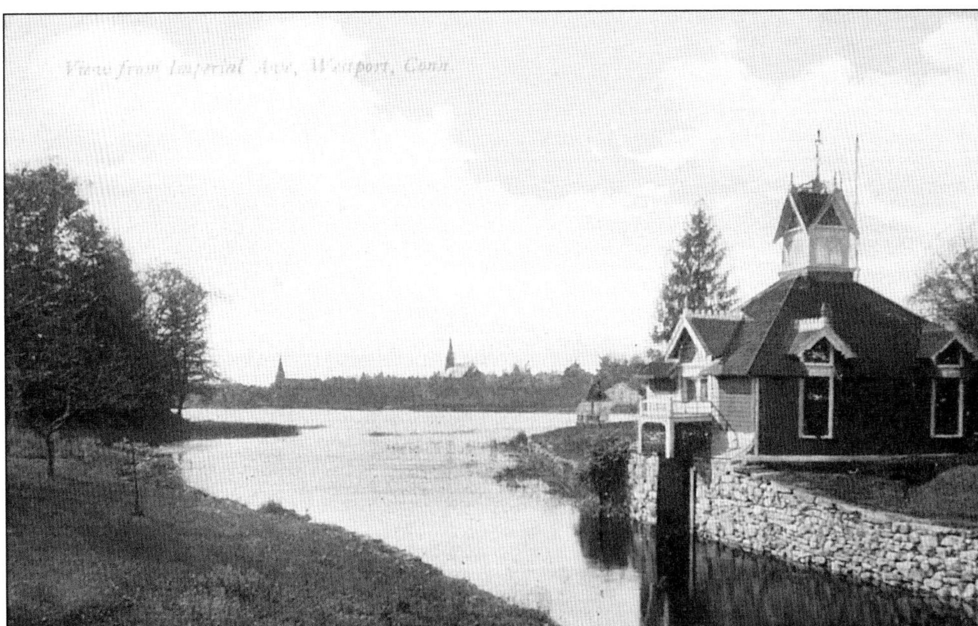

Since moved to 244 Greens Farms Road, the Godillot boathouse originally was across from 32 Imperial Avenue on Dead Man's Brook.

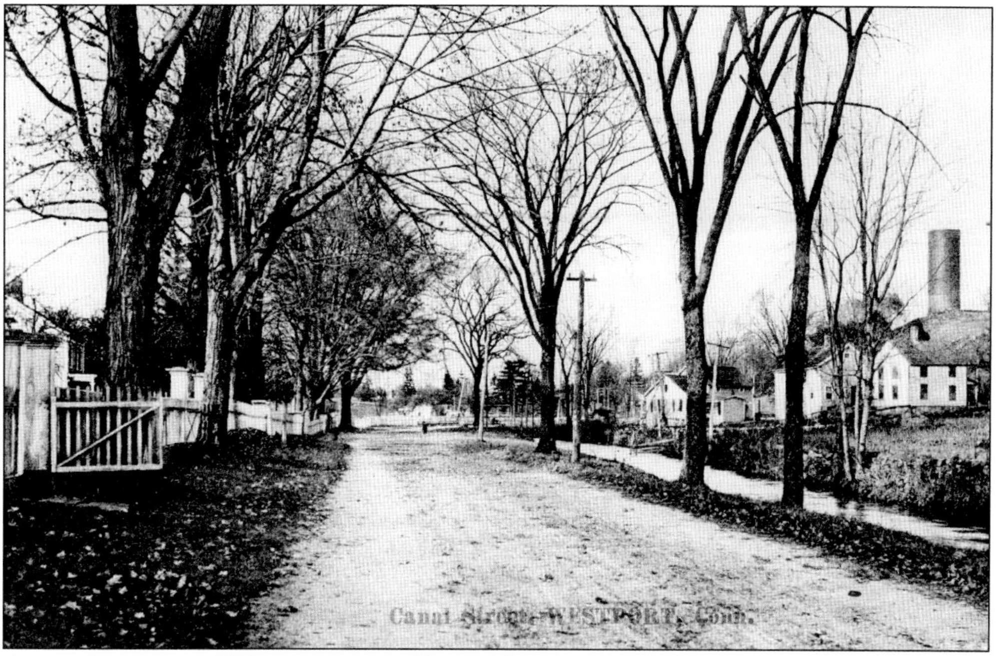

As you drive around Westport, it is still possible to recognize these streets by the remaining houses . . .

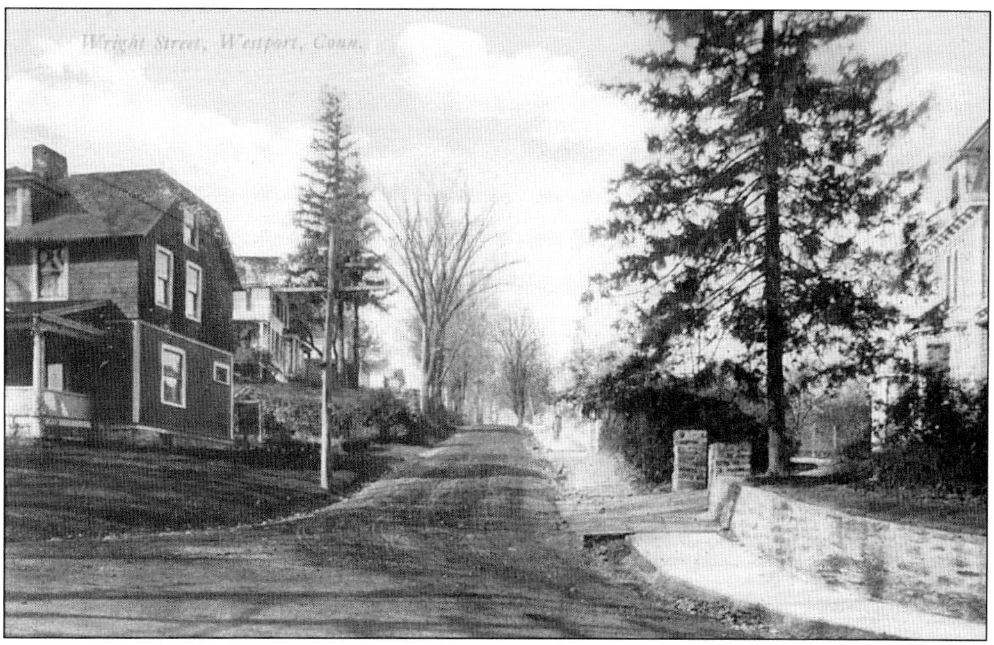

. . . sandwiched between office buildings, new houses, and, of course, much more traffic.

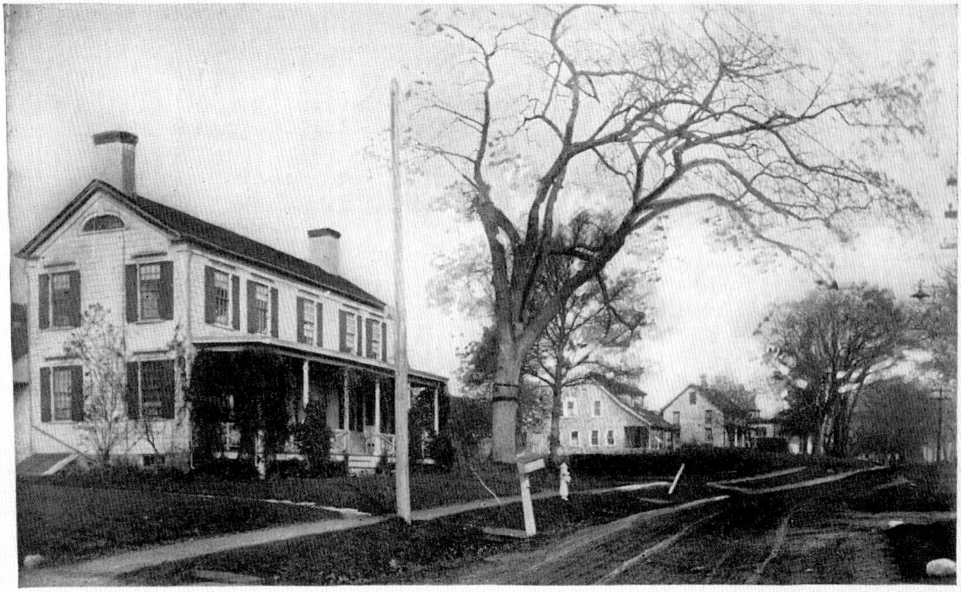

VIEW ON KING ST., WESTPORT, CONN.

In the 20th century, 57 Kings Highway North was the home of, variously, a drama critic for the *New York Daily News*, a New York City real estate developer, and a political pollster.

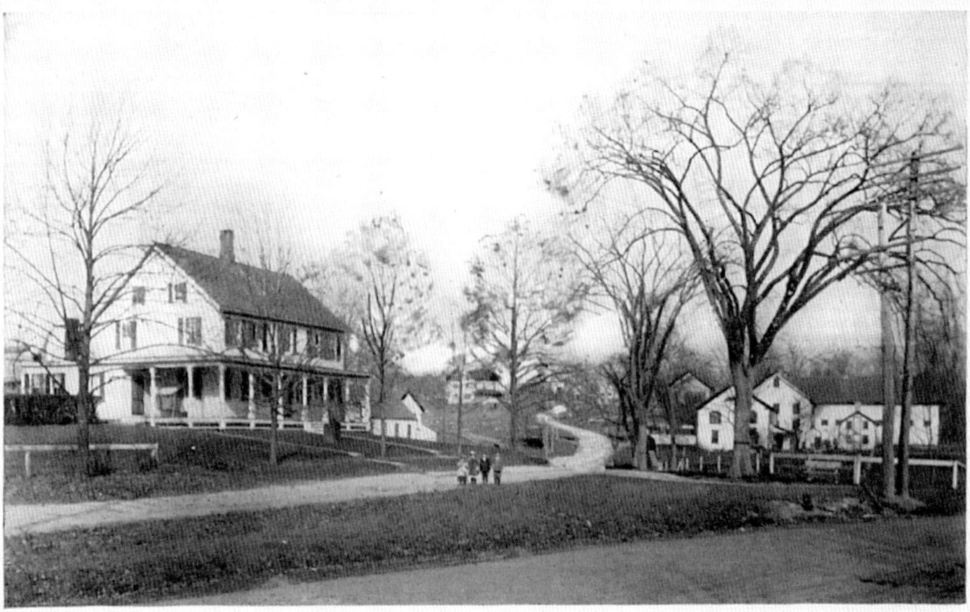

KING ST. FROM STATE ST., WESTPORT, CONN.

The building at the corner of Kings Highway North and the Post Road is currently surrounded by commercial buildings.

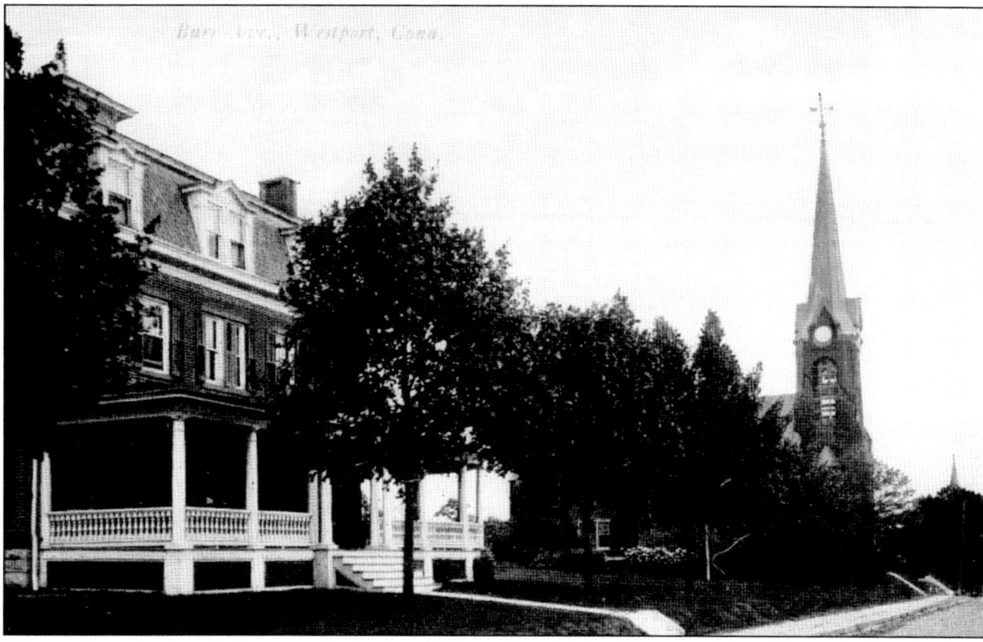

Elegant houses lined the main streets of Westport, often close to churches like this one near Christ Church.

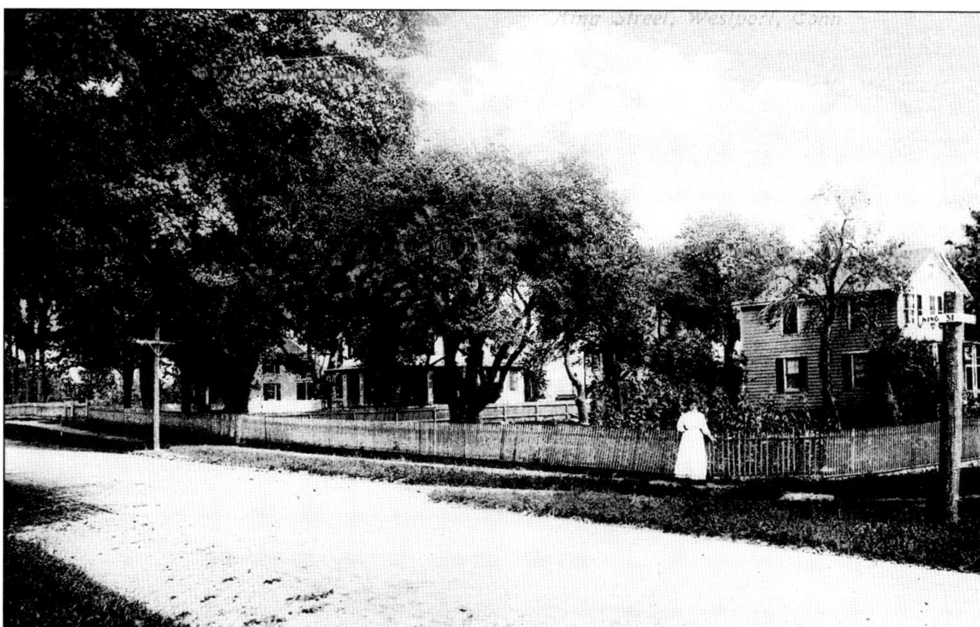

This card shows a woman strolling in what is now the Kings Highway Historic District.

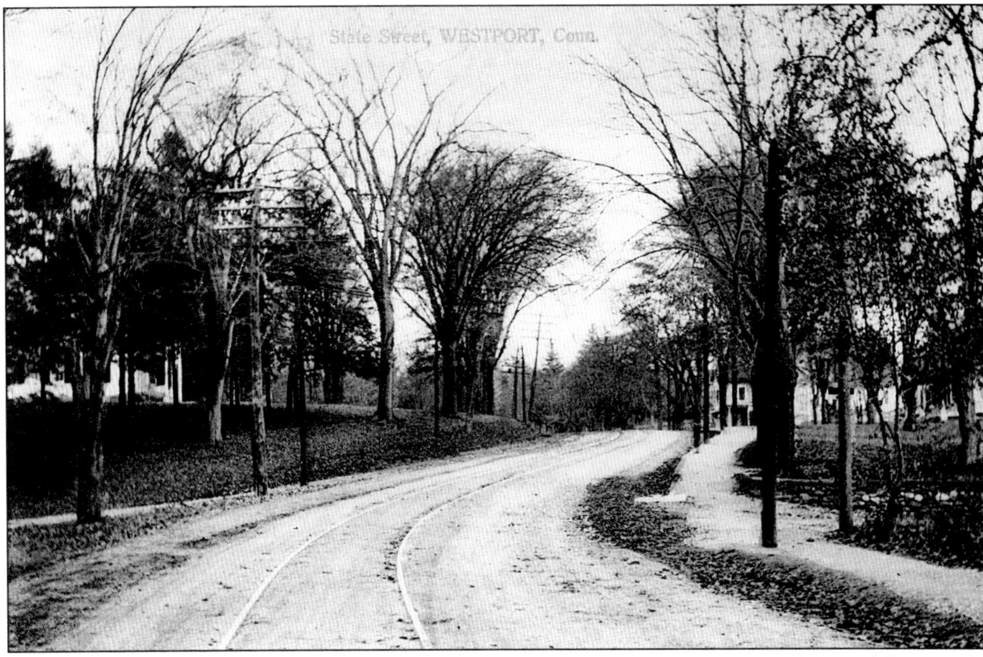

In this quiet scene, the only sign that the Post Road was an important thoroughfare is the trolley tracks.

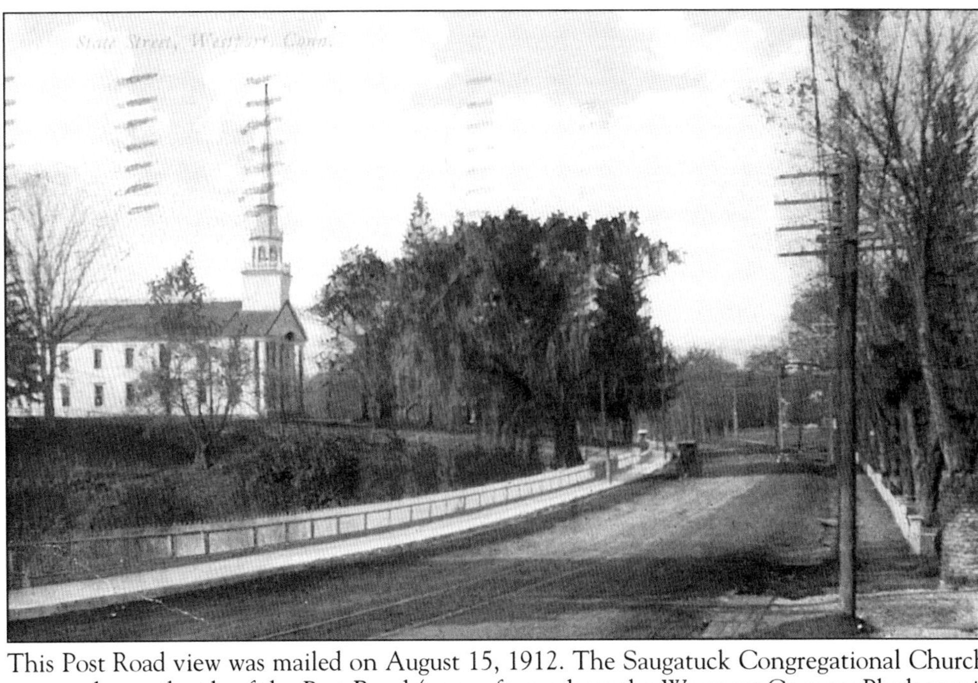

This Post Road view was mailed on August 15, 1912. The Saugatuck Congregational Church was on the south side of the Post Road (across from where the Westport Country Playhouse is in the 1990s) until it was moved in the 1950s.

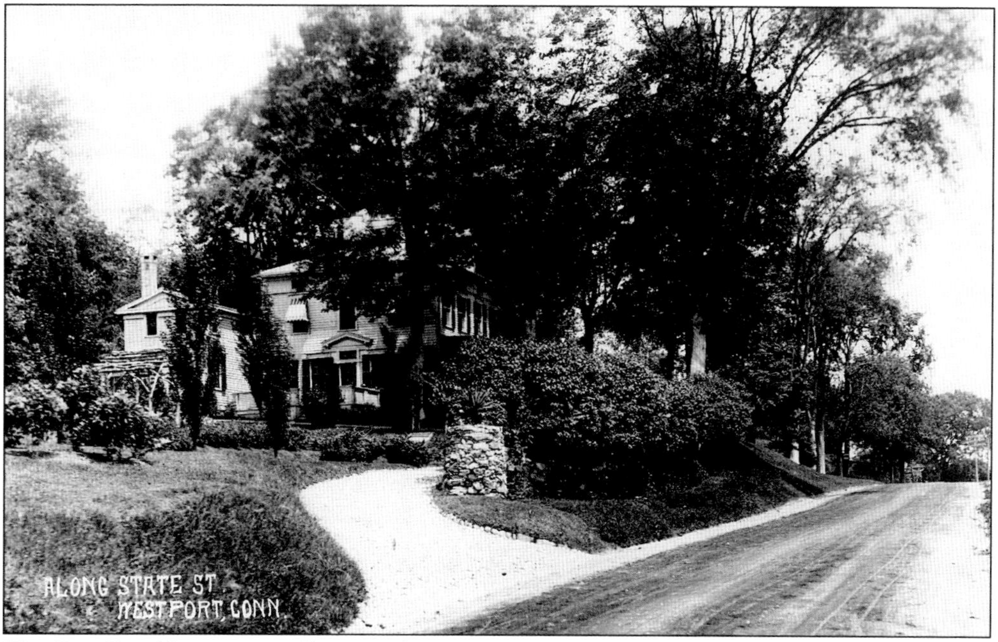

This Post Road house, at Ludlow Road, was near King's Highway School.

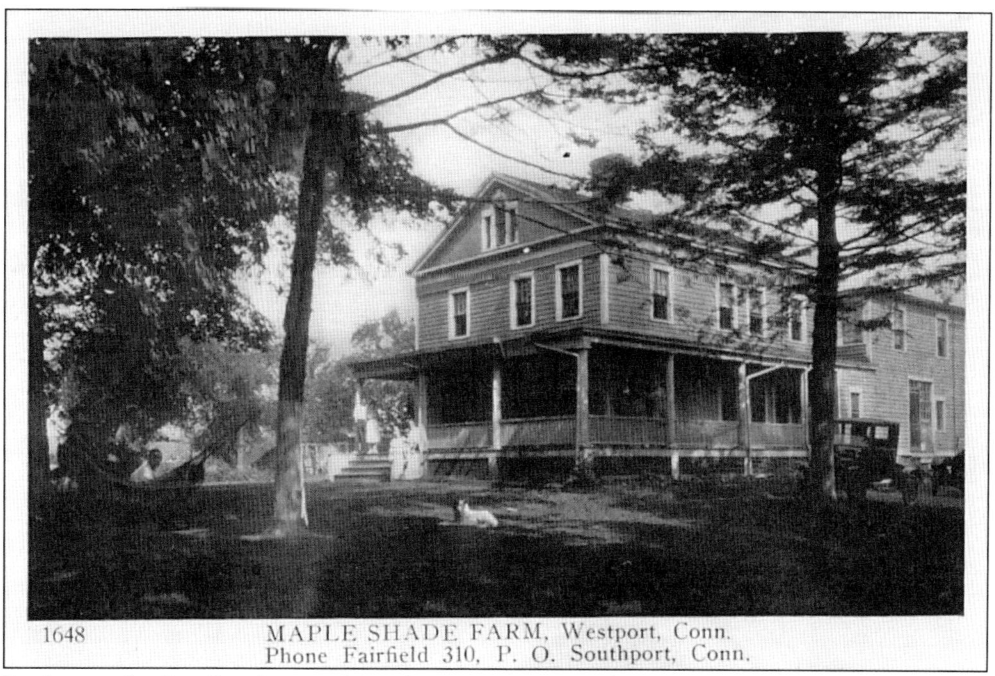

Further up the Post Road, toward Southport, were more substantial houses and farms.

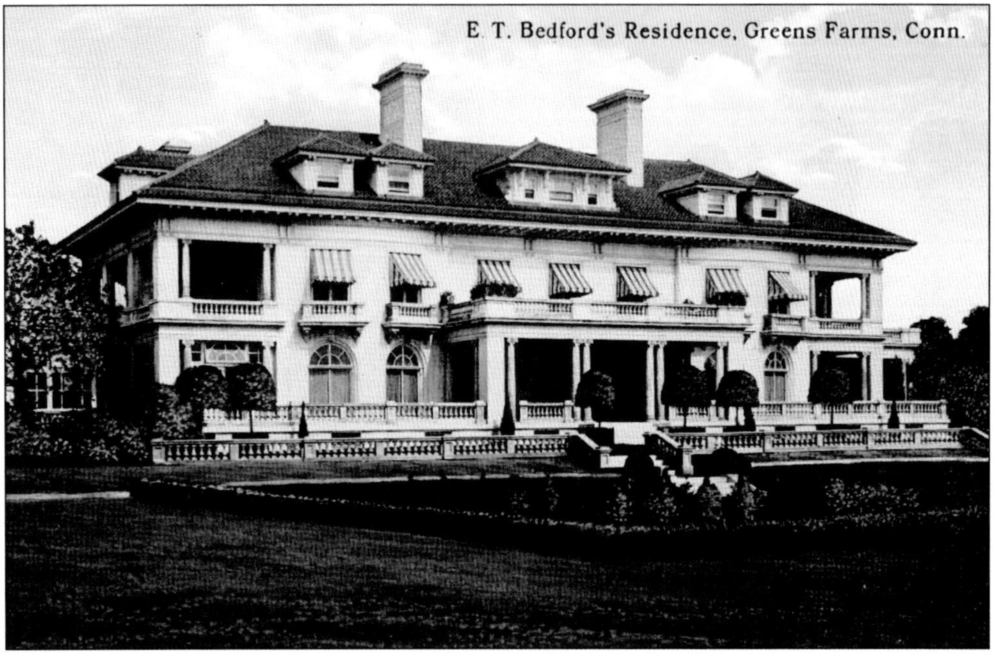

Then, as now, some of the most beautiful houses were found in Greens Farms . . .

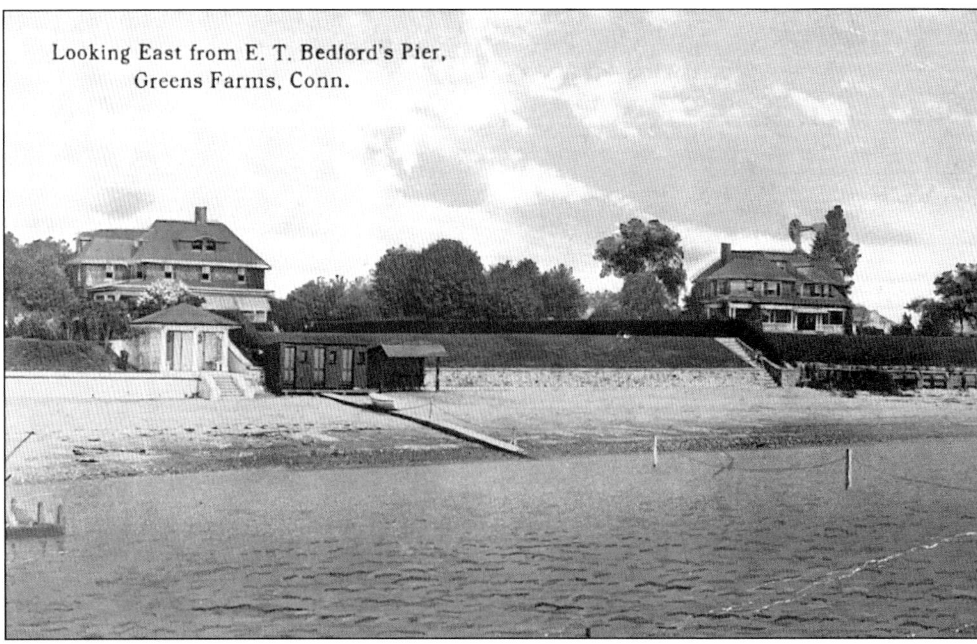

. . . including that of Mr. Bedford, one of Westport's most significant benefactors.

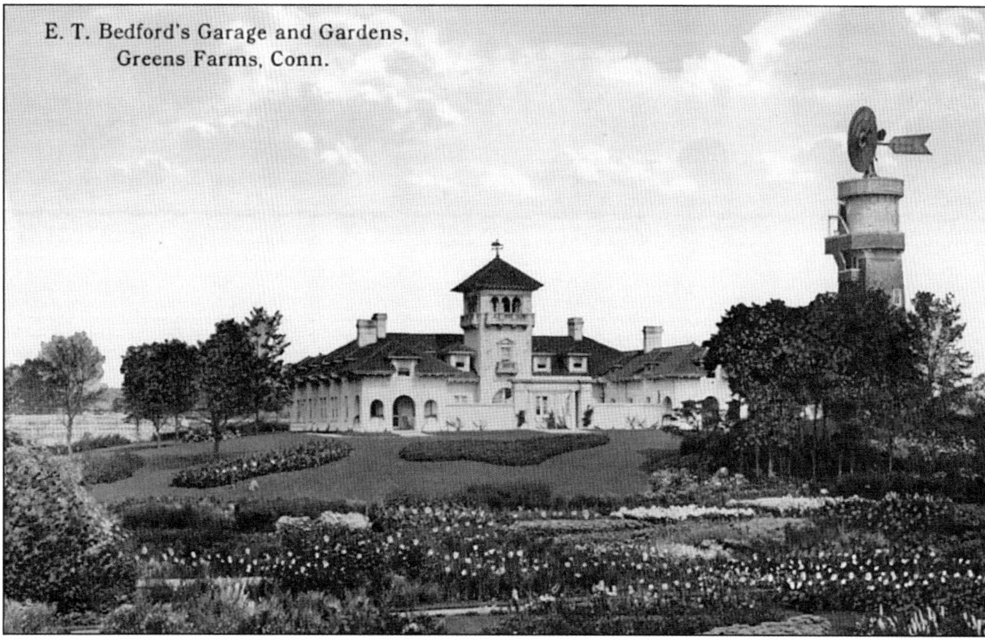

Tourists came to see his gardens from miles away . . .

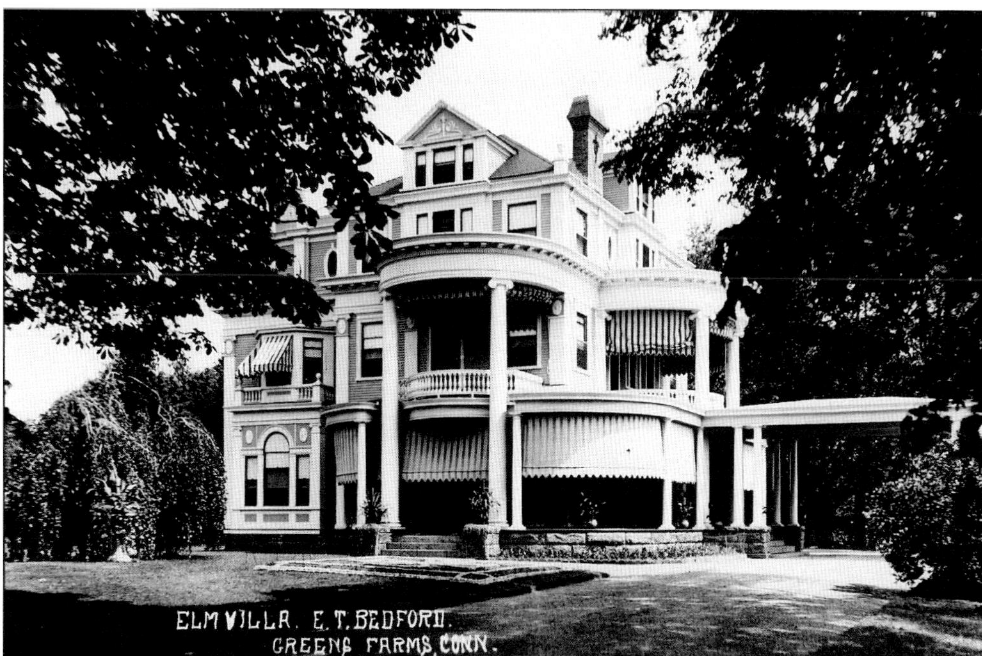

. . . and sent home postcards showing the "mansions' and villas of Westport.

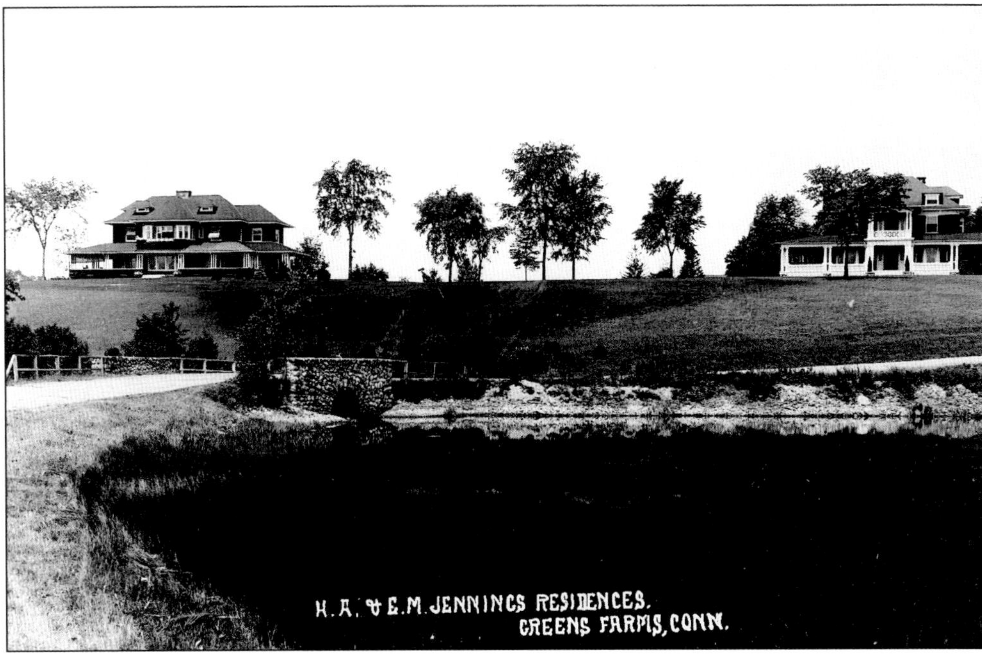

These pages show a range of architectural styles from 19th-century Westport. The Jennings family was based in Greens Farms, with several residences located there.

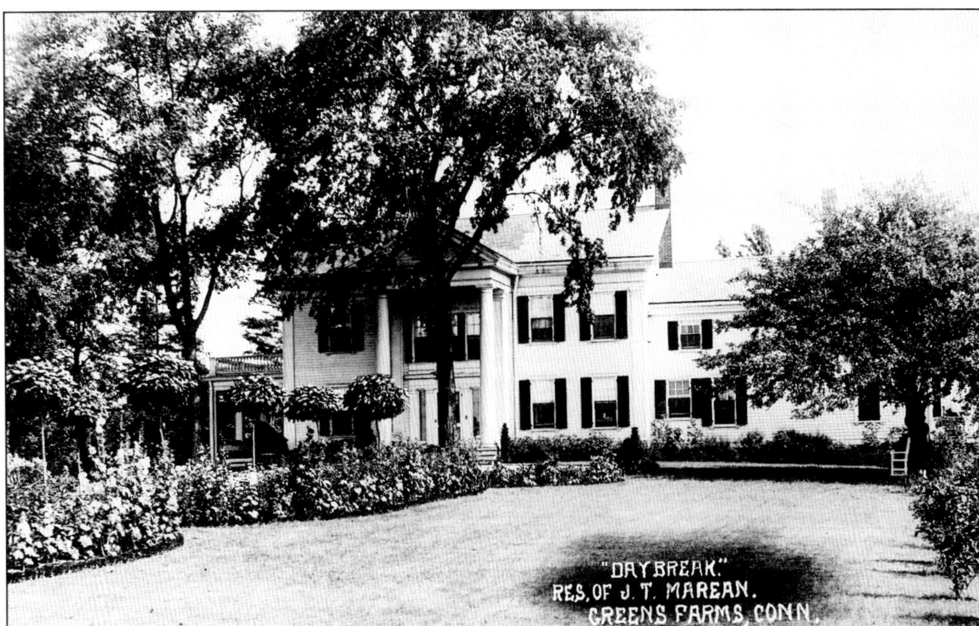

"Daybreak" still stands at 10 Prospect Street, although the property has been subdivided.

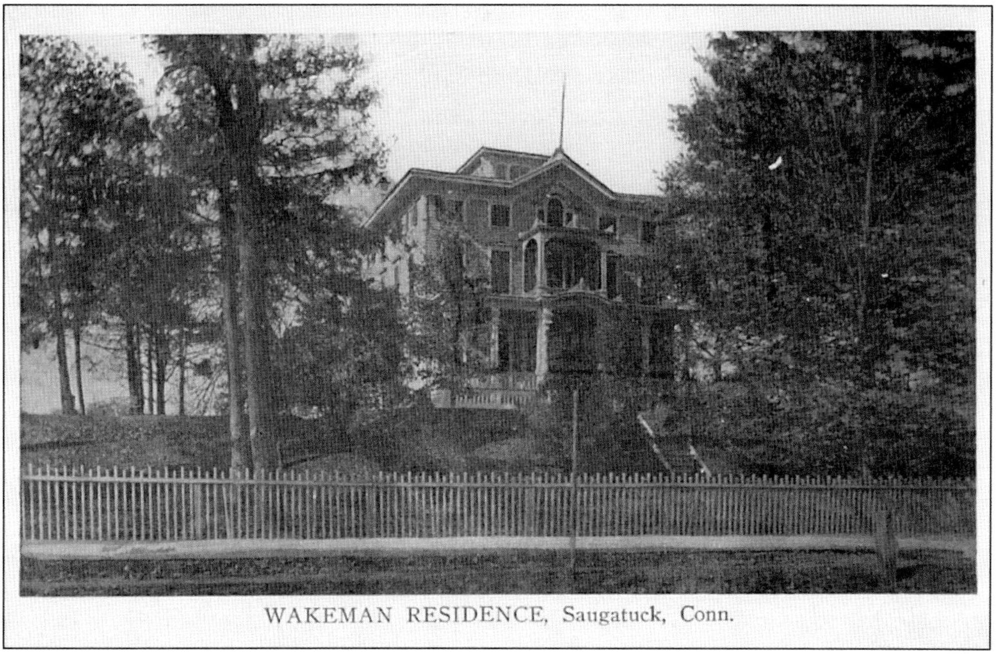

The Wakeman family residence proudly gives its address as Saugatuck . . .

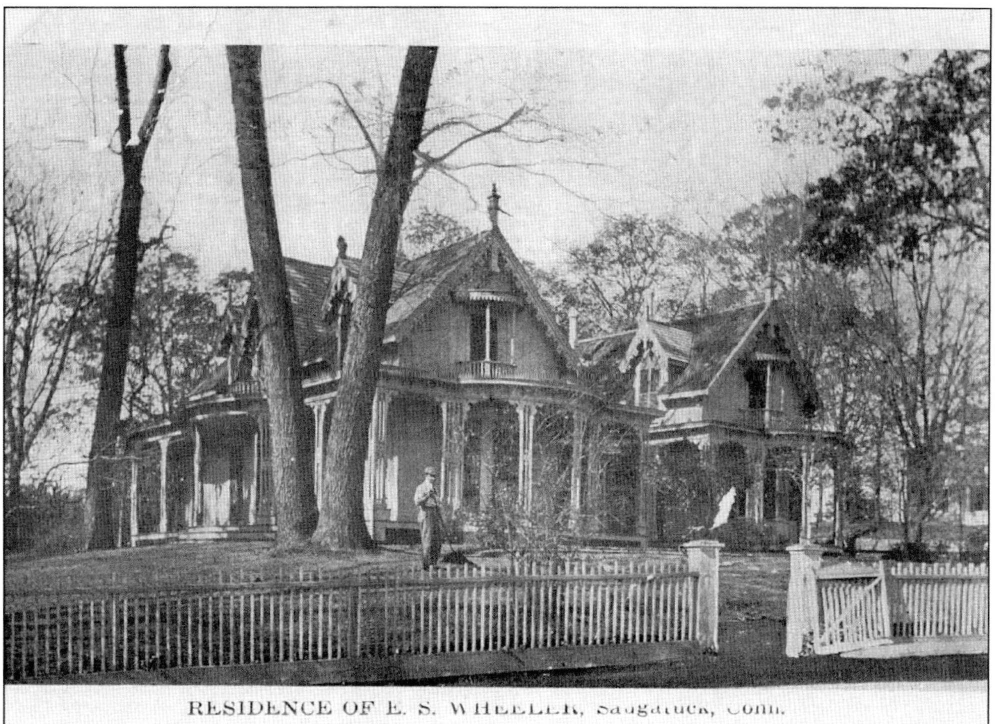

. . . as does this Wheeler house. Both families had members who lived in other parts of Westport as well.

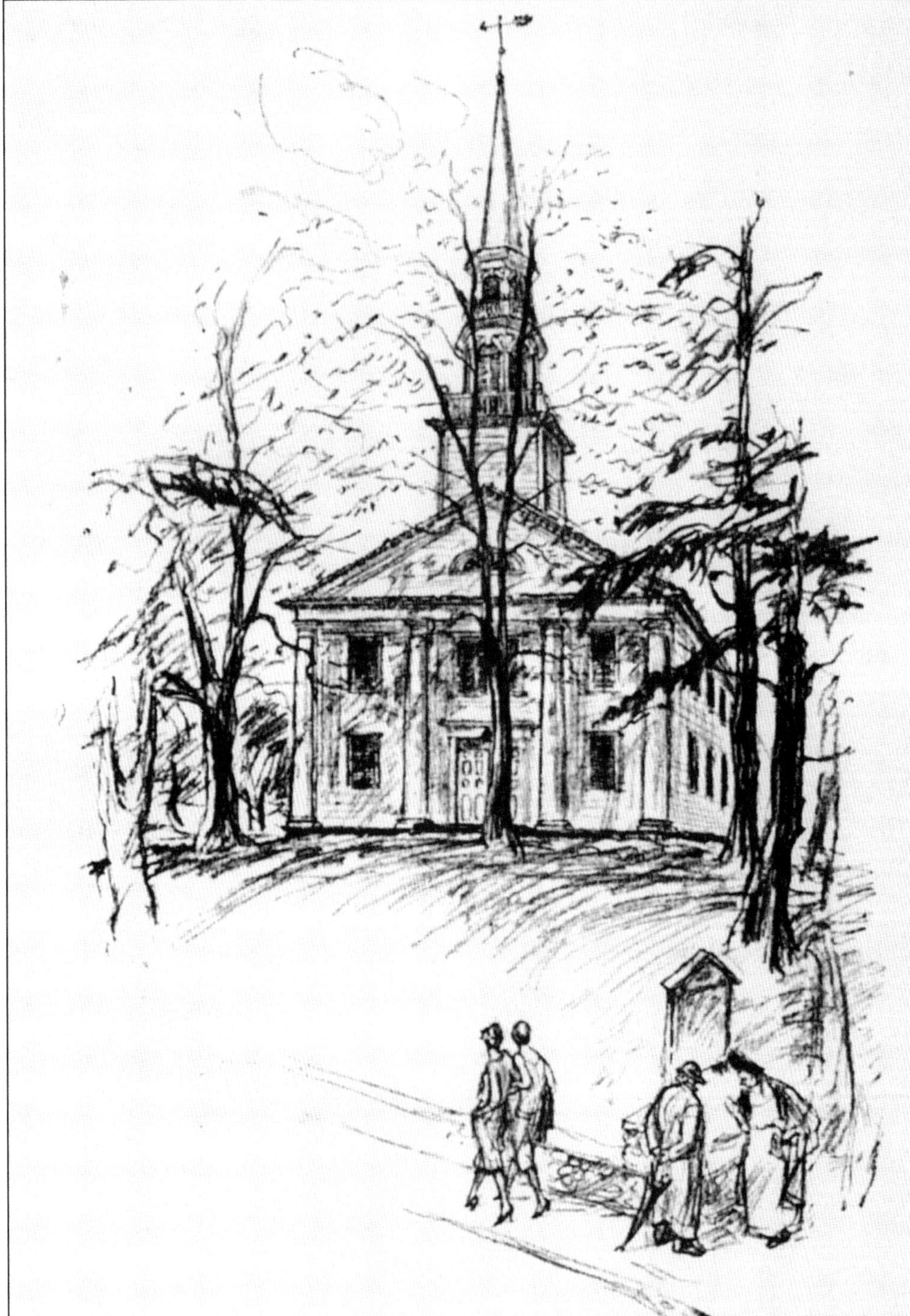

SAUGATUCK CONGREGATIONAL CHURCH
WESTPORT, CONN.

Four

Institutional Westport: Churches and Schools

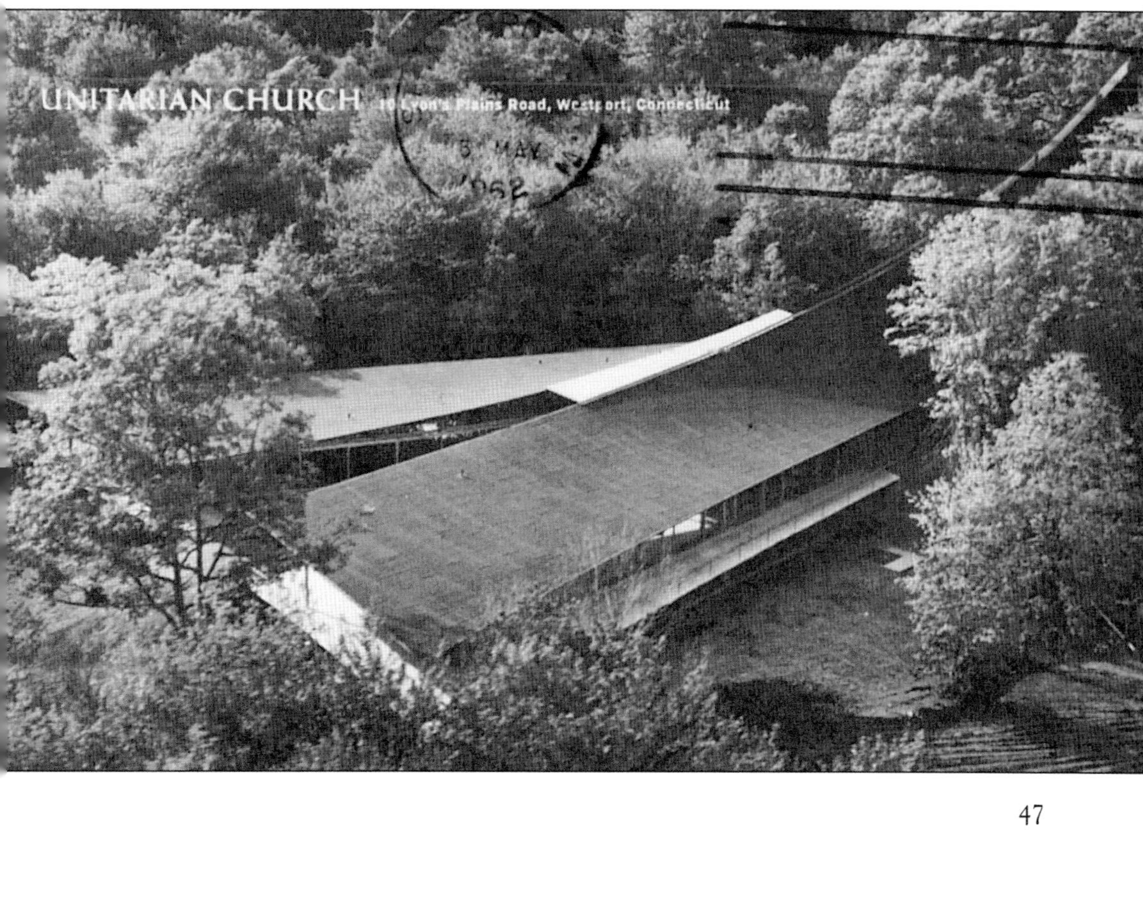

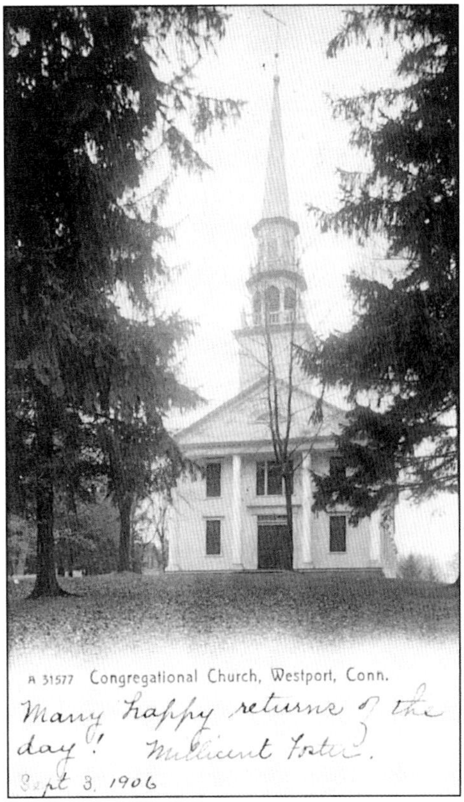

Founded in 1832, Saugatuck Congregational Church started life on the south side of the Post Road, across from the Westport Country Playhouse . . .

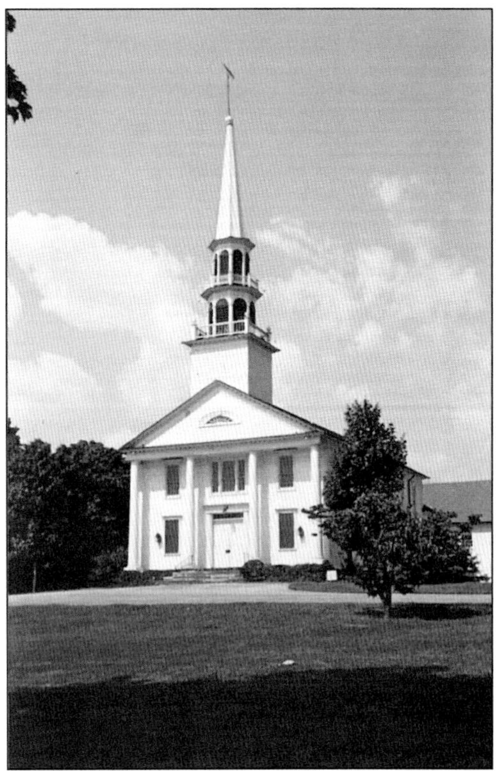

. . . moving across the street in 1950 to land donated in 1884 by Morris K. Jesup.

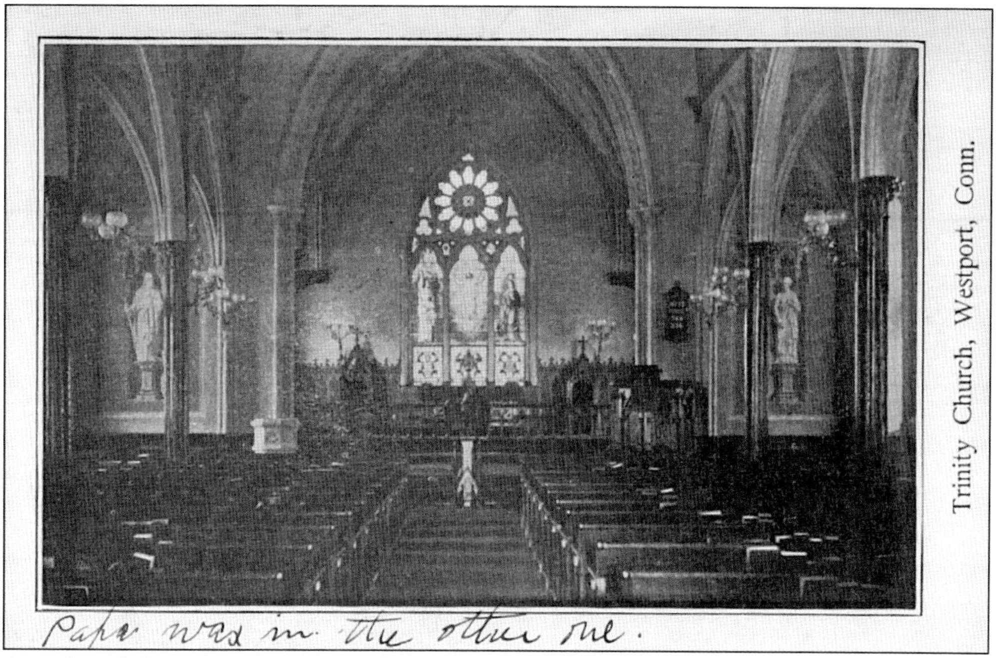

A card mailed on August 14, 1905, shows the interior of Holy Trinity Church.

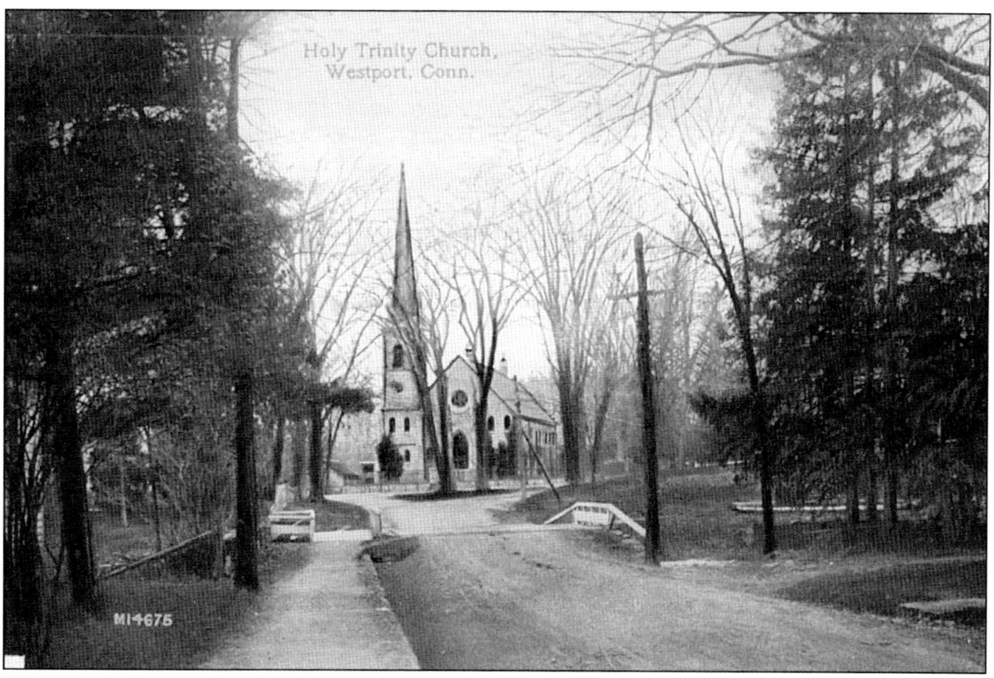

Merged with Christ Church in 1944, Holy Trinity Church is still in use at the intersection of Church Lane and Myrtle Avenue as Christ and Holy Trinity Church.

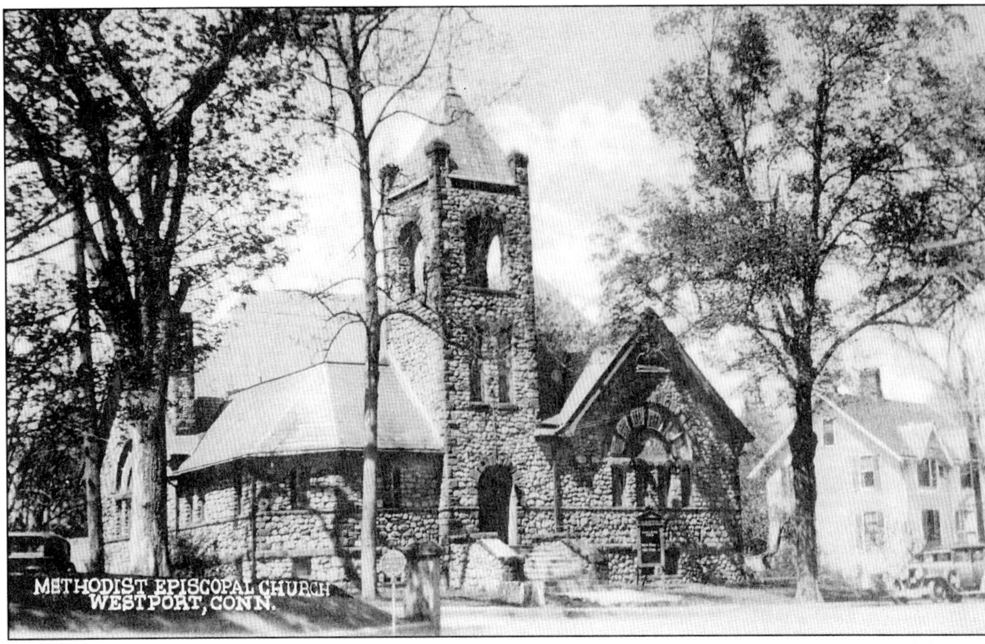

This Methodist church building served from 1907 to 1968, when it was acquired by neighboring Christ and Holy Trinity Church for $100,000.

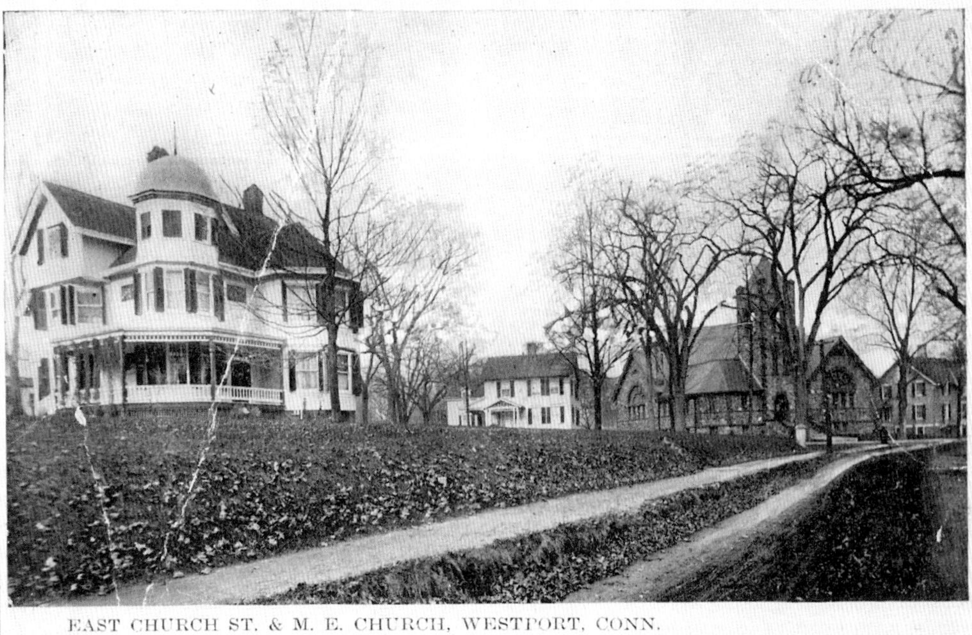

EAST CHURCH ST. & M. E. CHURCH, WESTPORT, CONN.

This card, mailed on July 7, 1914, shows the homes surrounding the Methodist church, visible in the distance.

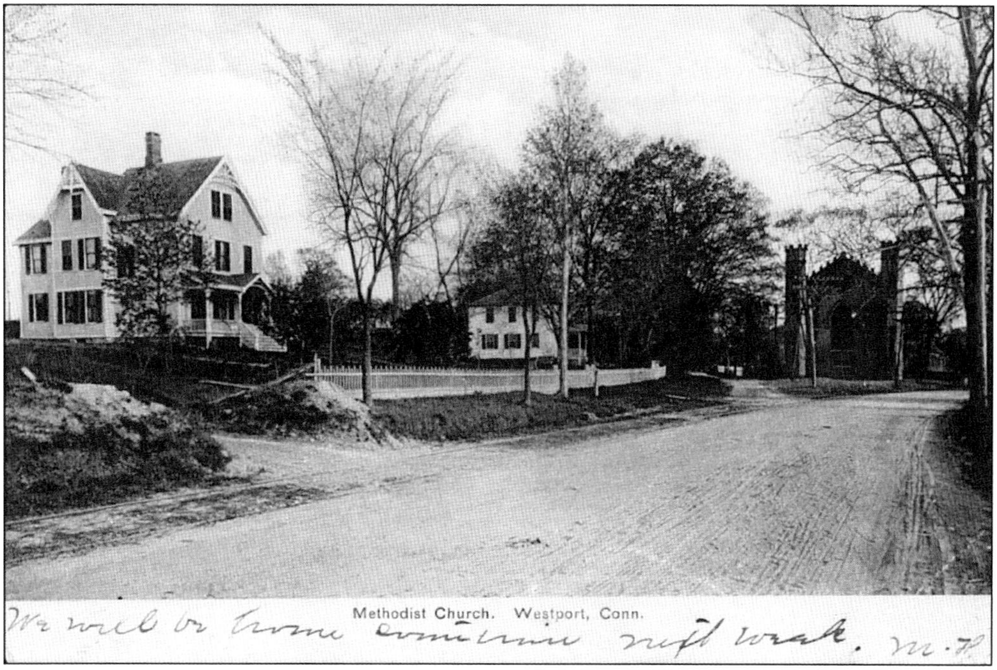

This card was mailed on September 28, 1907, and shows the Methodist church . . .

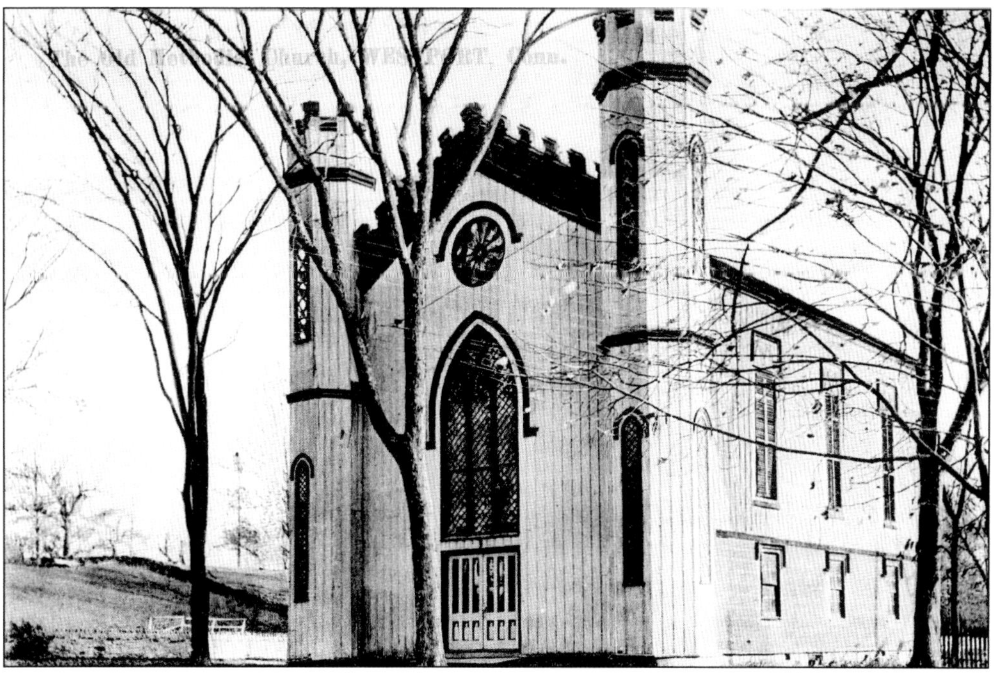

. . . located at 234 Main Street, where a law office is in the 1990s.

Built in 1900, Assumption Catholic Church (shown here on a card mailed July 20, 1933) . . .

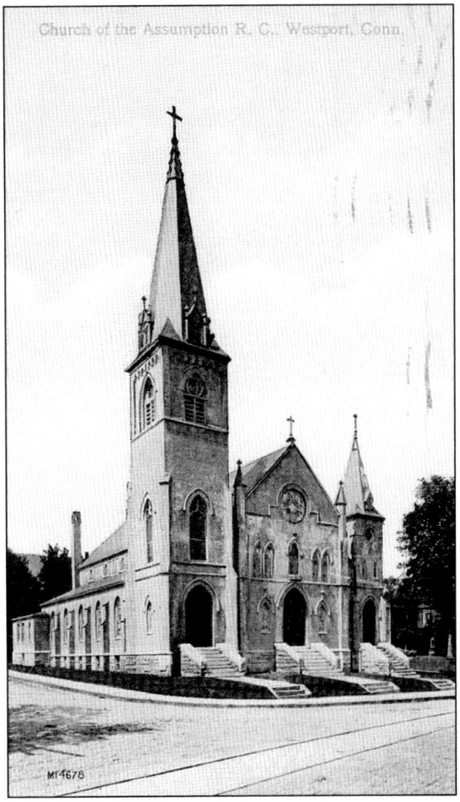

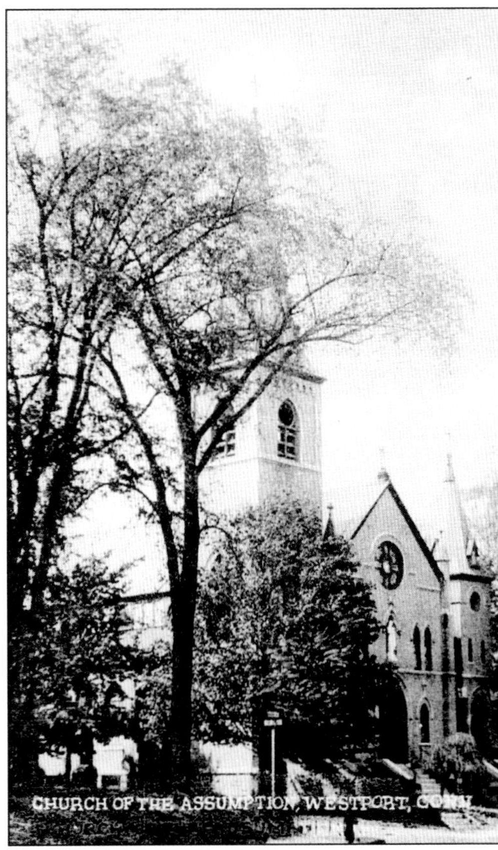

. . . still remains, at 98 Riverside Avenue.

Built in 1885, this Christ Church was on Burr Street at the Post Road and replaced the church's Ludlow Street frame building.

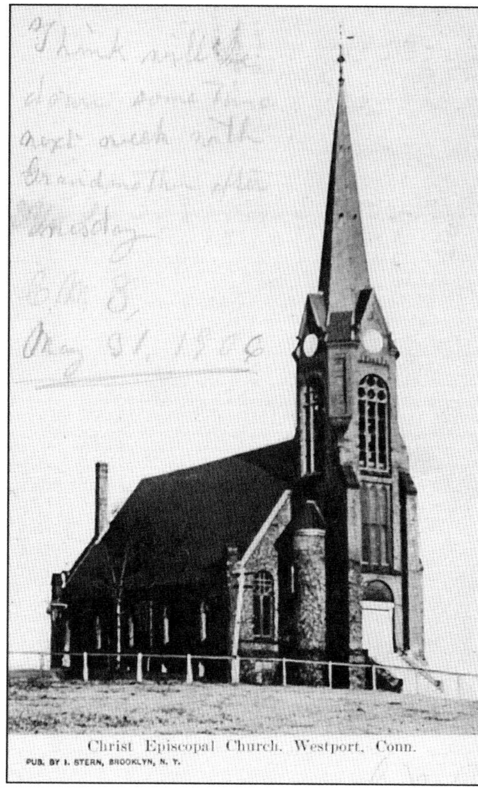

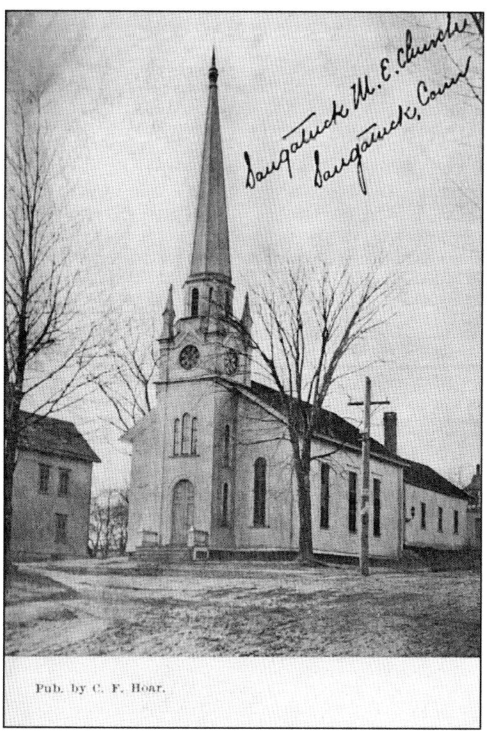

Built in 1853, the Saugatuck Methodist Church was demolished for the Connecticut Thruway; it stood on Saugatuck Avenue near West Ferry Lane.

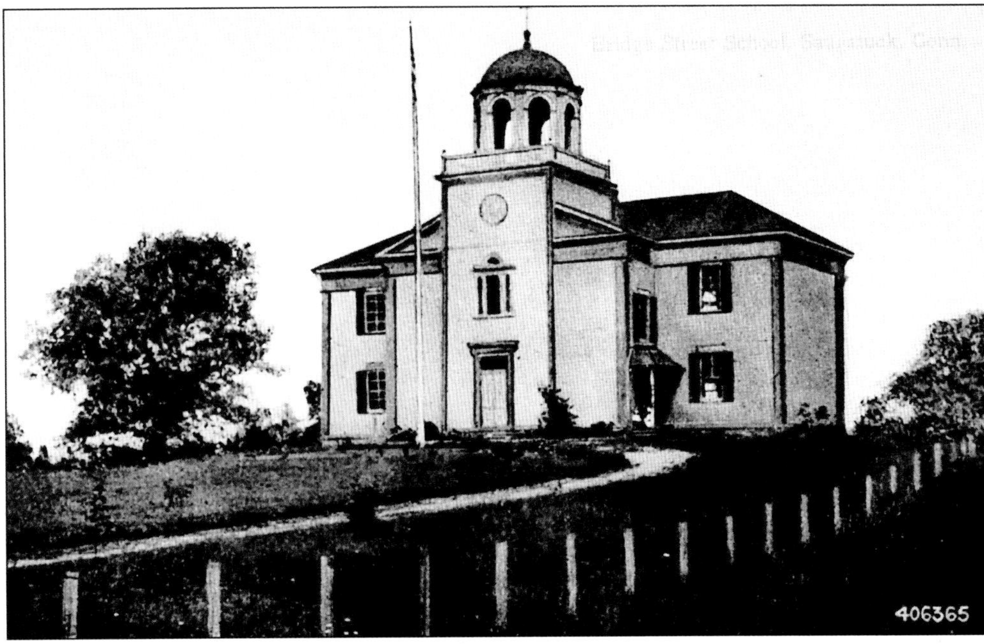

This Bridge Street school building was razed . . .

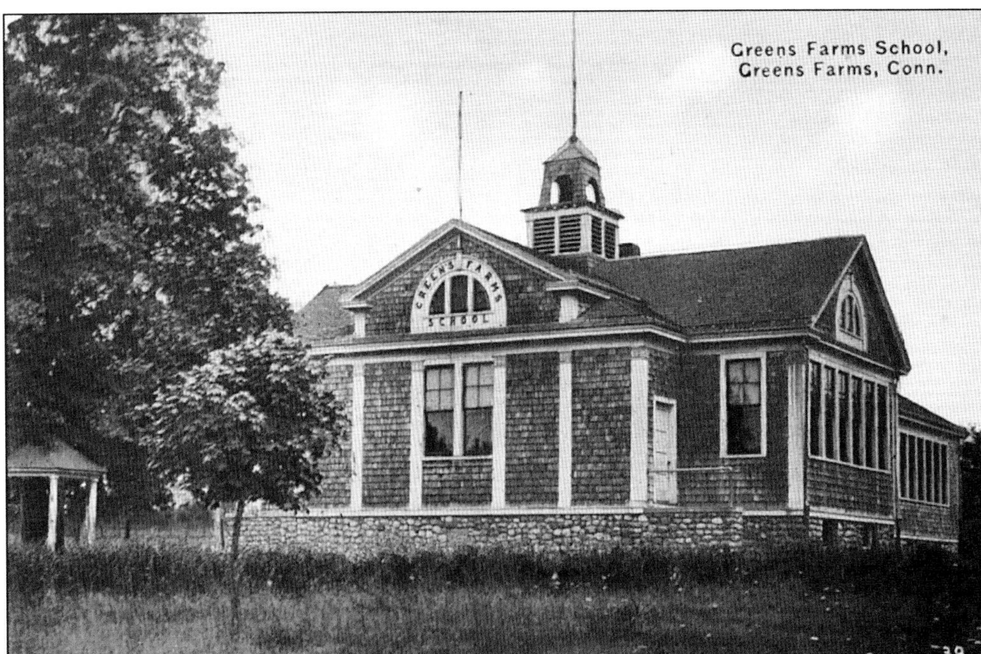

. . . but the Greens Farm School building remains, at 37 Clapboard Hill Road, as a private residence. The Greens Farm name was later used for a school at the intersection of the Post Road and Morningside Drive South.

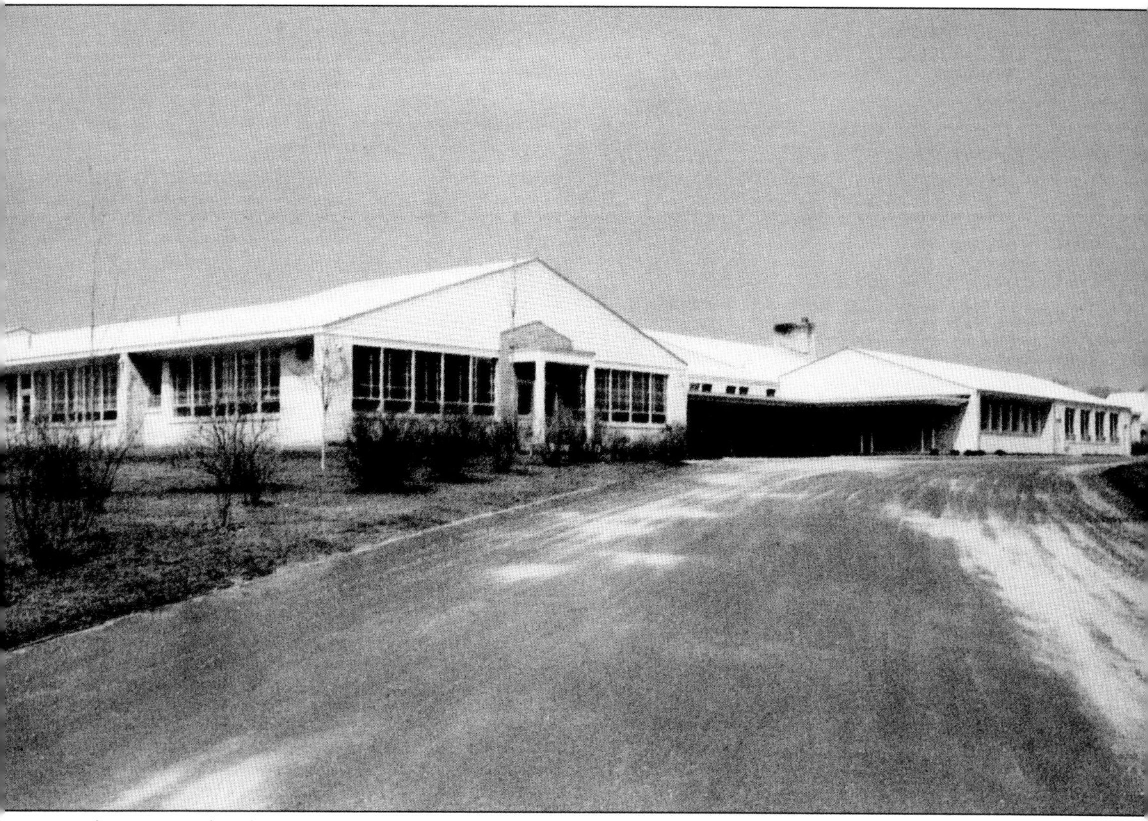

Coleytown School, named for the part of town populated by the Coley family, is, in the 1990s, largely the same as when it was built in 1953.

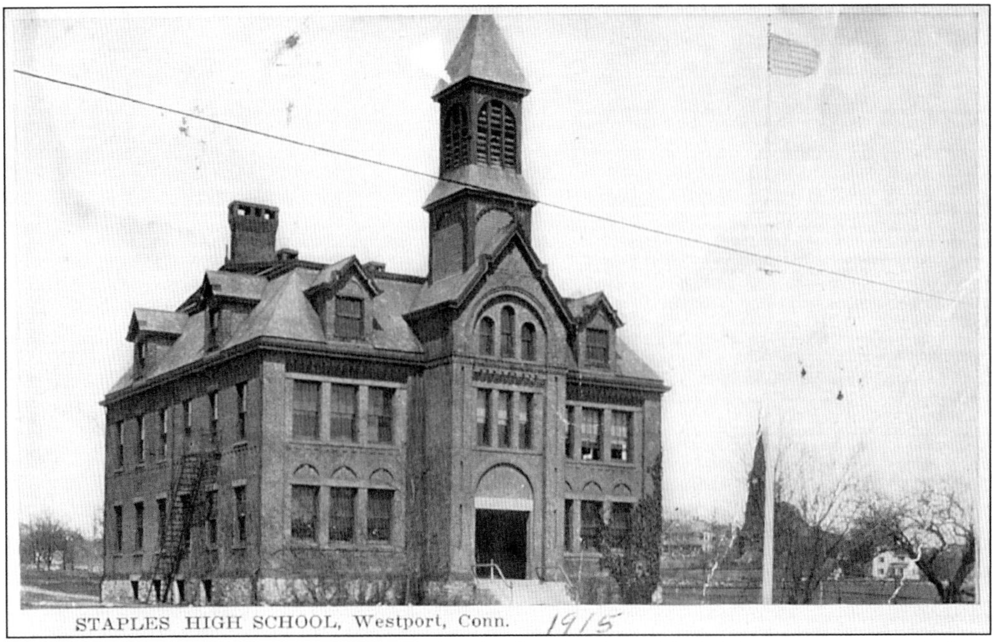

Horace Staples underwrote the town's first high school in 1884 (this card was mailed on August 7, 1915) . . .

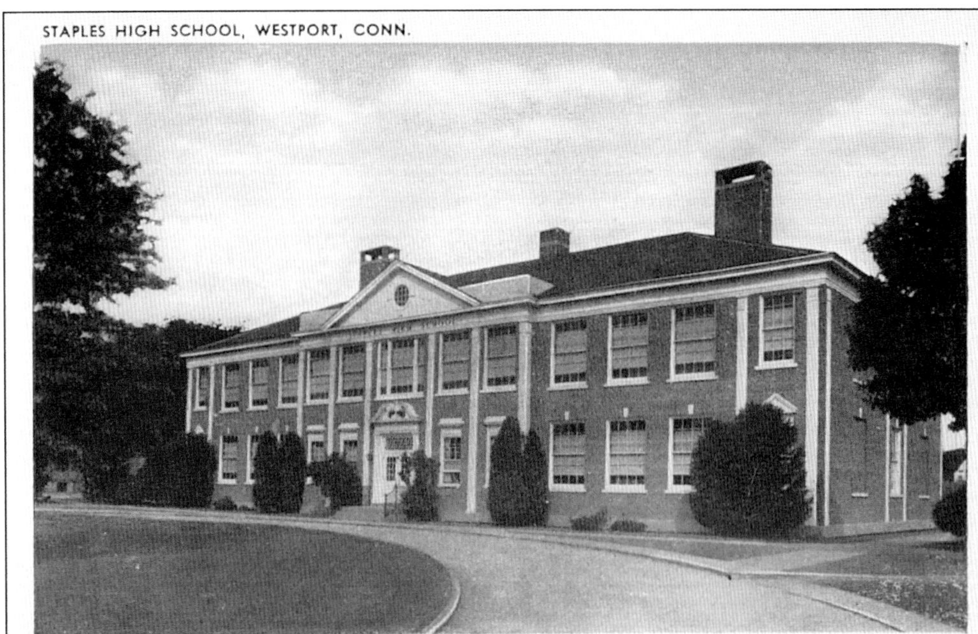

. . . but he would not recognize the building built on this site (Bedford Middle School in the 1990s) . . .

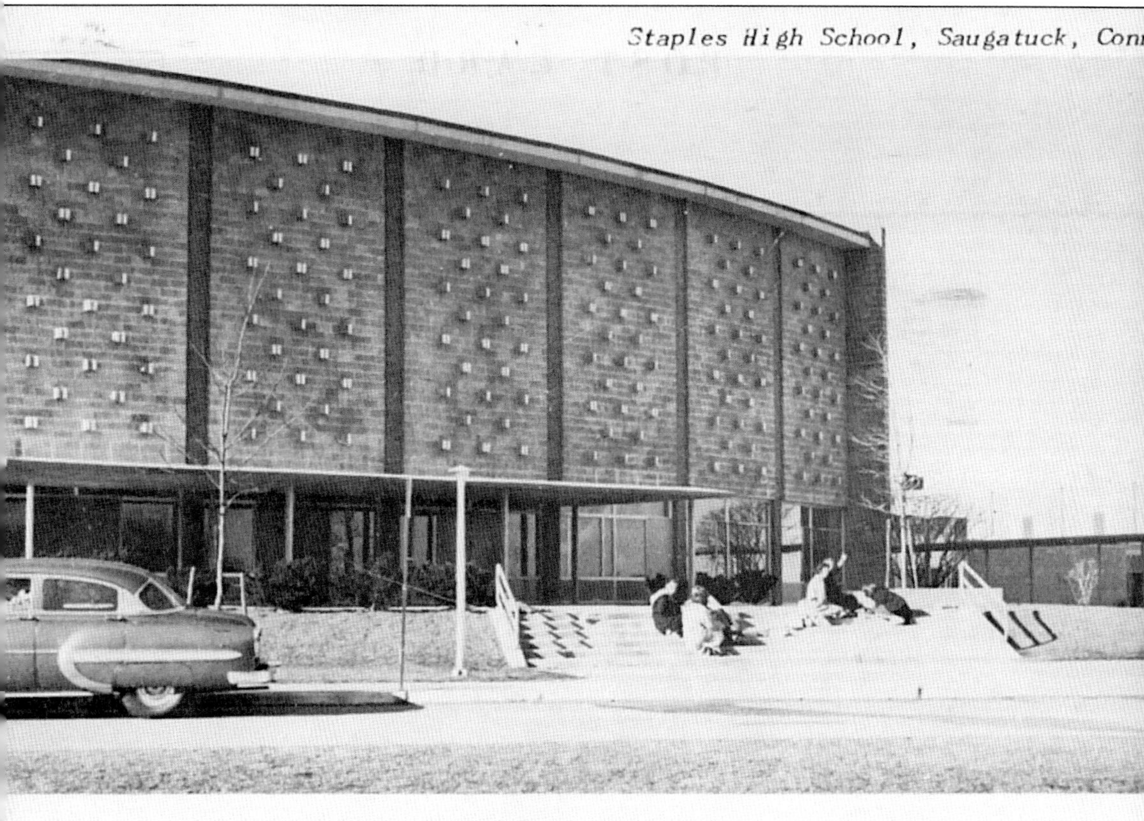

. . . or the building that currently bears his name on North Avenue, built in 1959.

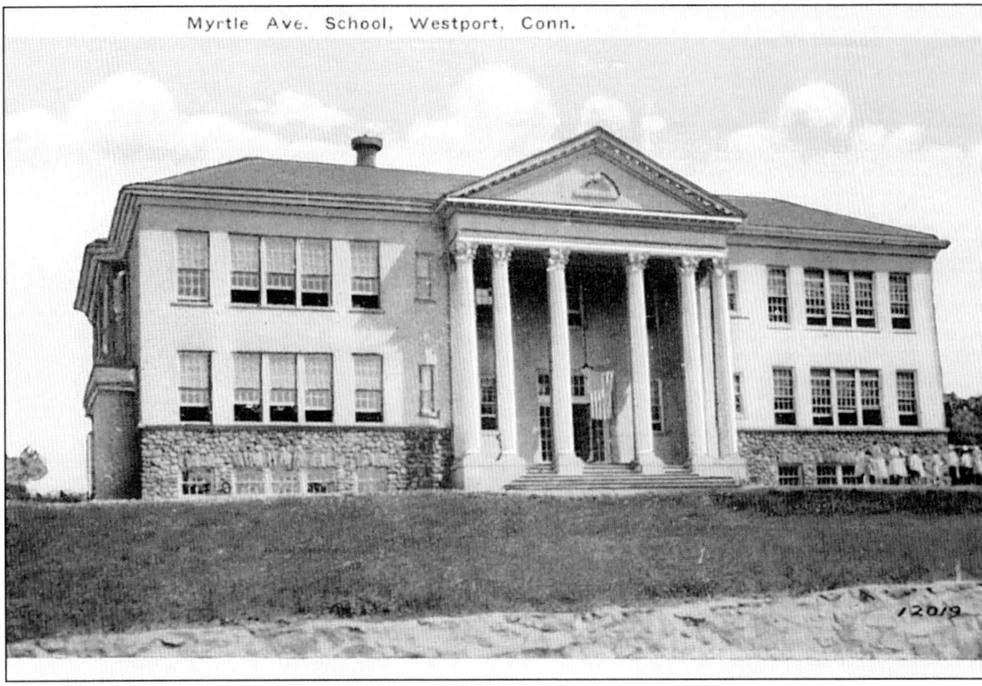

This school on Myrtle Avenue, built and paid for by the Bedford family, became . . .

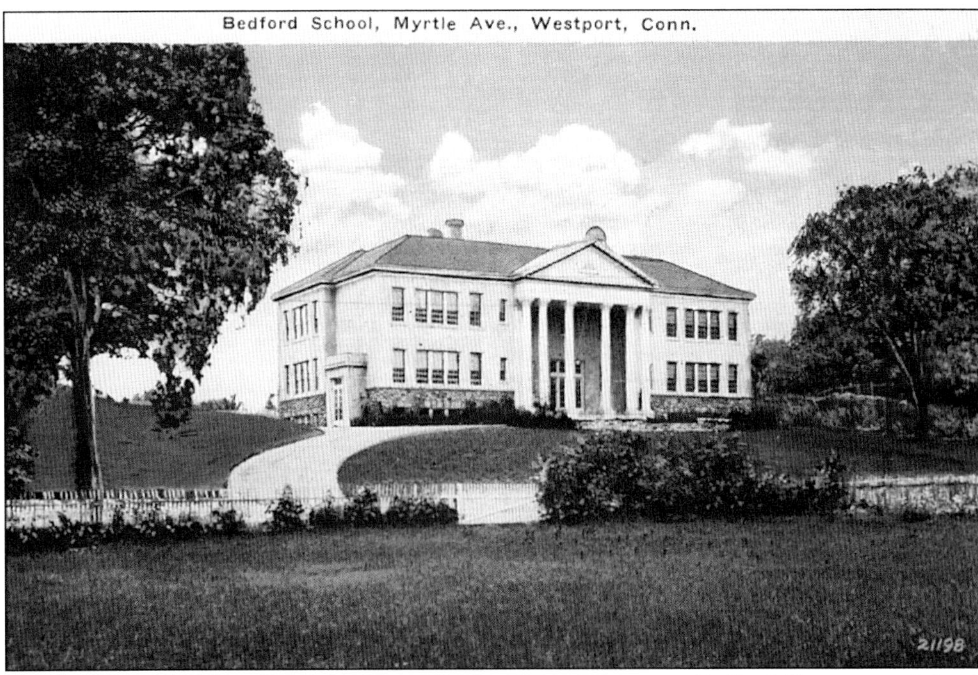

. . . Bedford Elementary School.

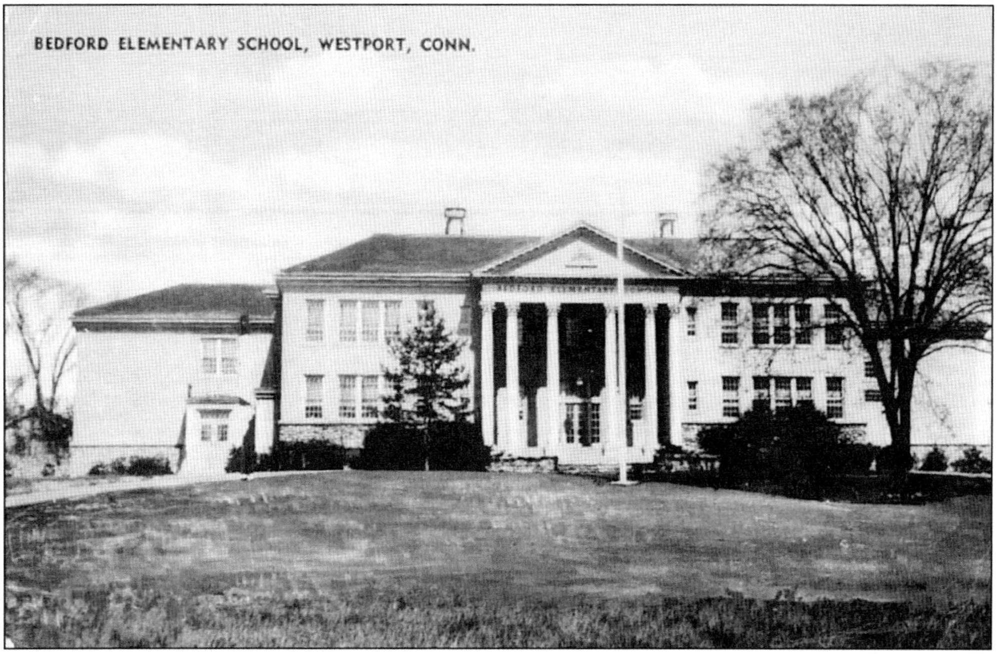

Seen here after being enlarged, this Bedford school became Westport's town hall, and the Bedford family name . . .

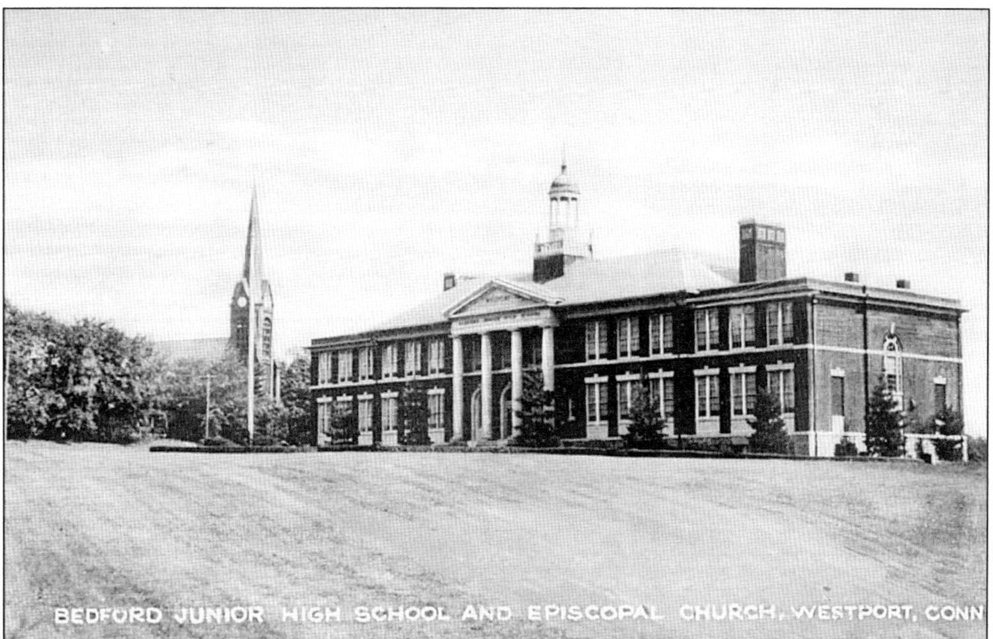

. . . was used on a junior high school, which later became Kings Highway Elementary School.

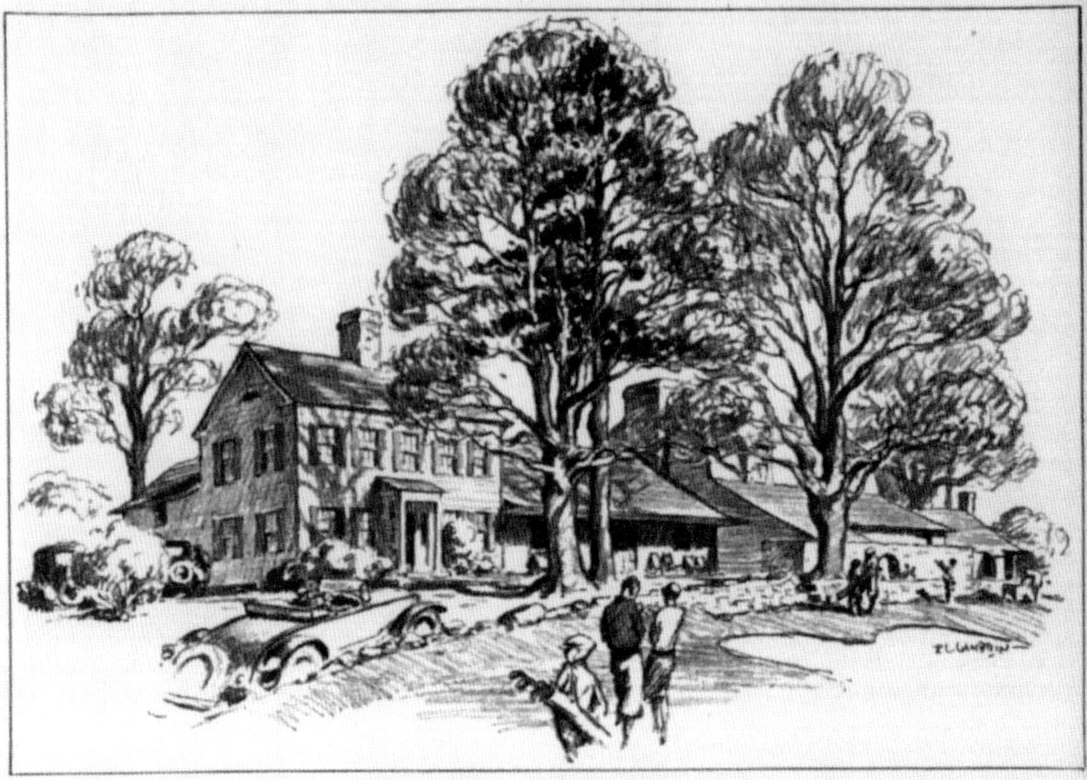

WESTPORT COUNTRY CLUB

Five

Tourist Attractions: Hotels, Restaurants, and Clubs

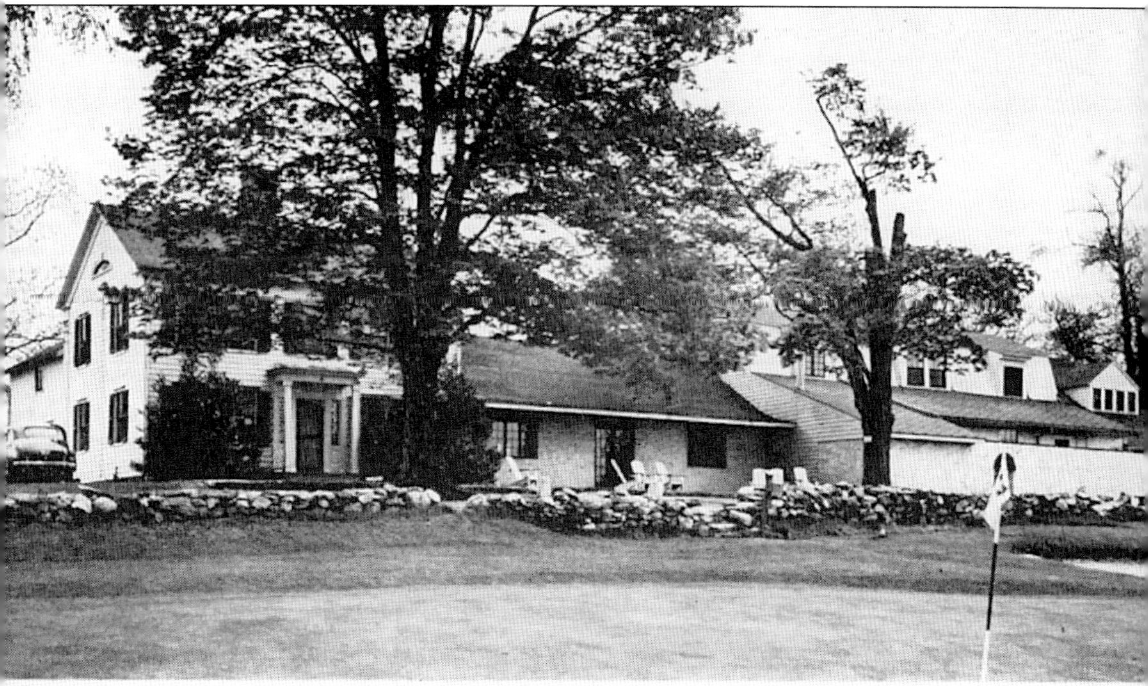

WESTPORT COUNTRY CLUB, WESTPORT, CONN.

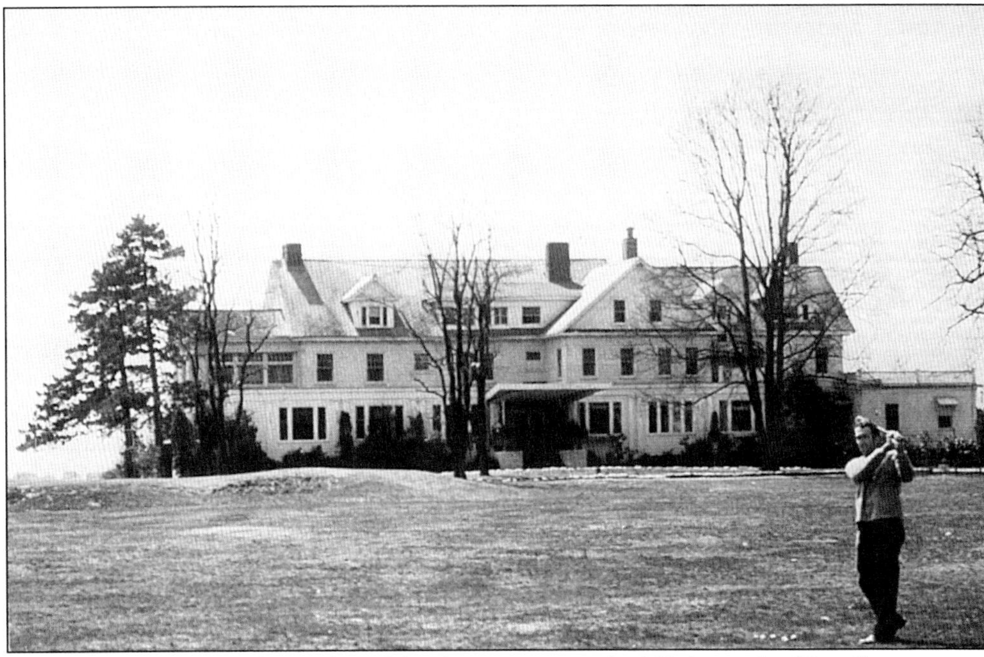

Longshore Country Club, purchased by the town around 1960 for under $2 million, was an extensive and elaborate private club, which included golf . . .

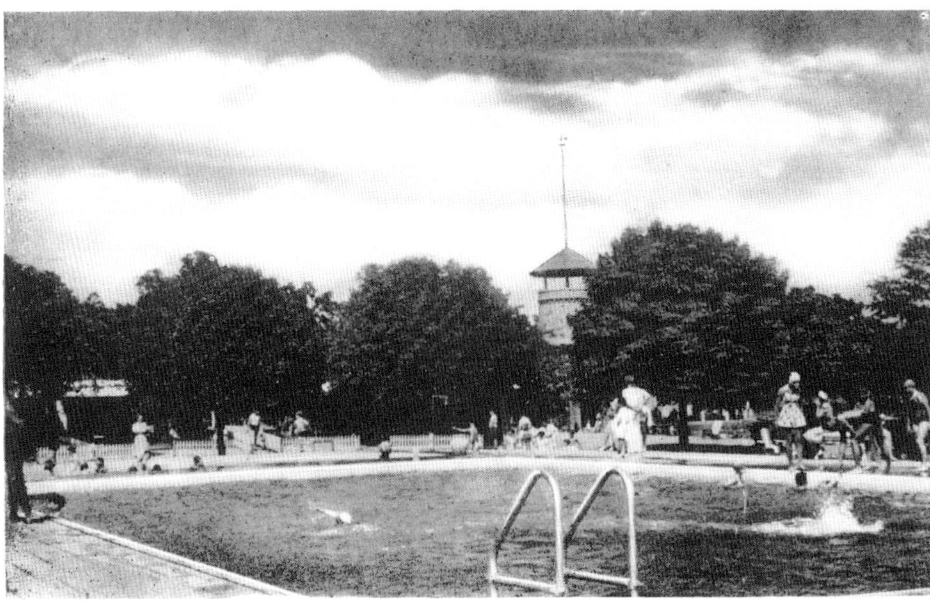

SWIMMING POOL, LONGSHORE CLUB, WESTPORT, CONN.

. . . swimming, tennis, and marina facilities.

Removed in the 1960s after the town acquired Longshore, this "play" lighthouse was situated adjacent to the bathhouse.

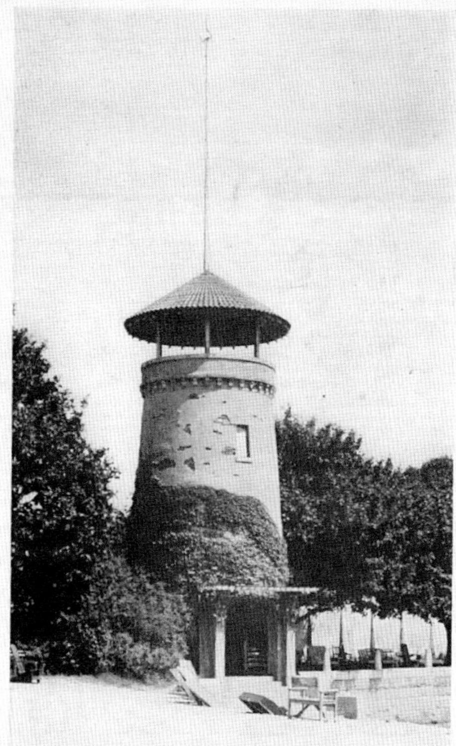

Lookout Tower, Long Shore Country and Beach Club, Westport, Conn.

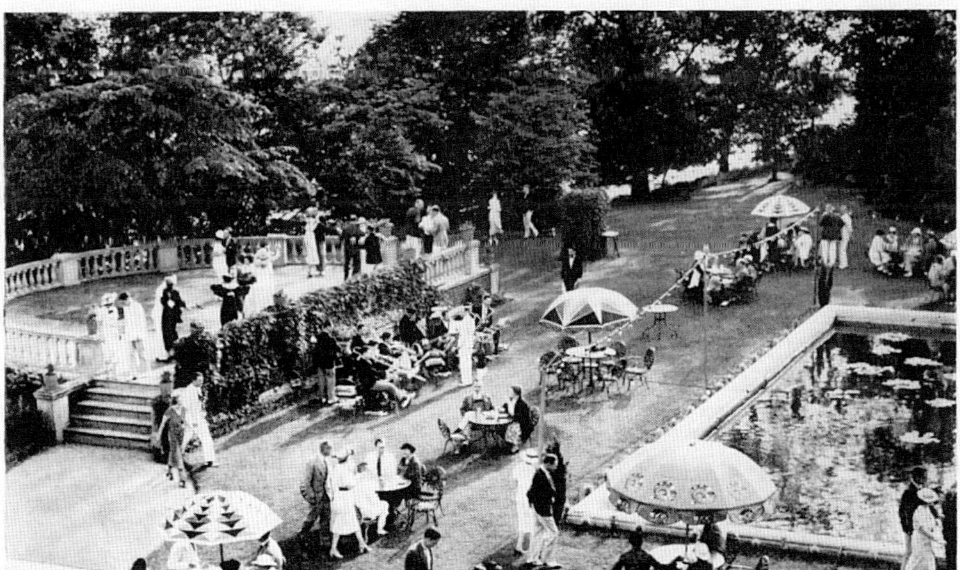

THE COCKTAIL HOUR ON THE LILY POND TERRACE, LONGSHORE CLUB, WESTPORT, CONN.

Then, as now, cocktails and gatherings outdoors were popular activities at Longshore.

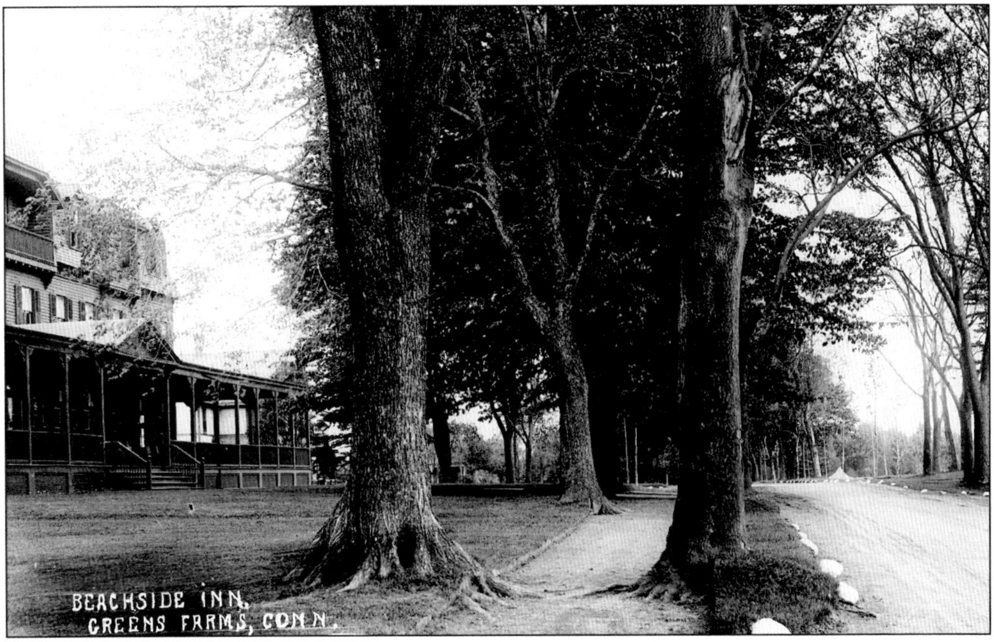

The Beachside Inn was a luxury resort. Formerly the house of Mrs. J.L. Phipps, the hotel had wide verandas . . .

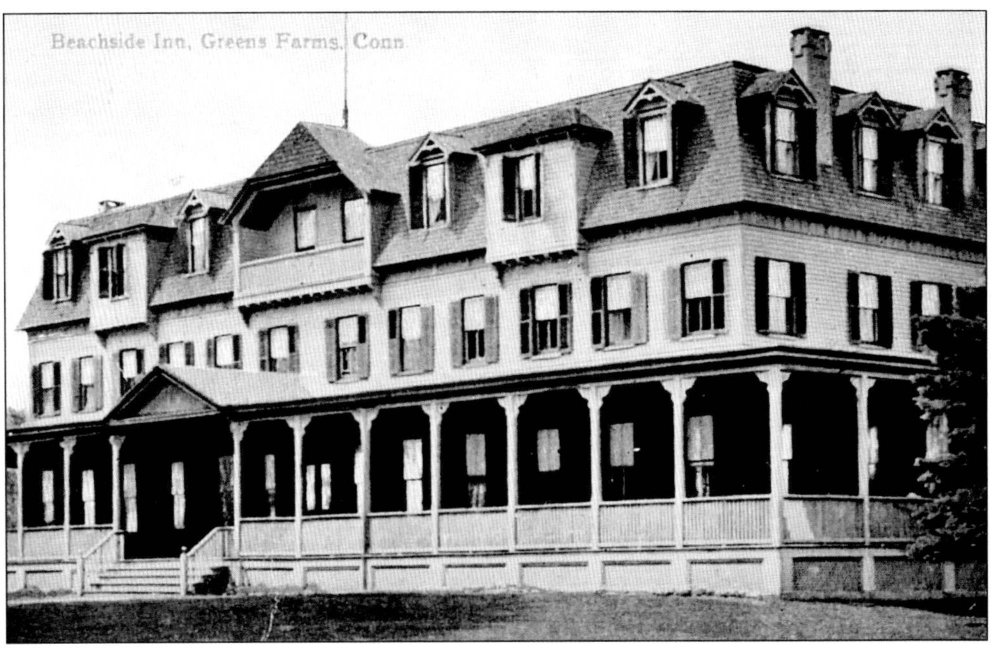

. . . and views of Long Island Sound.

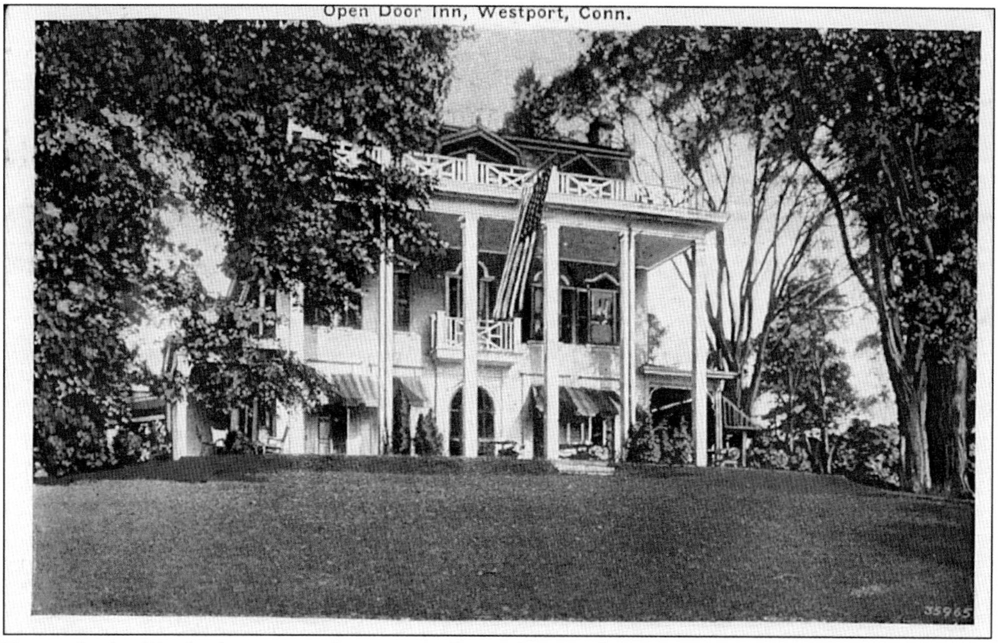

Formerly the Taylor home on what is now Jesup Green, the Open Door Inn . . .

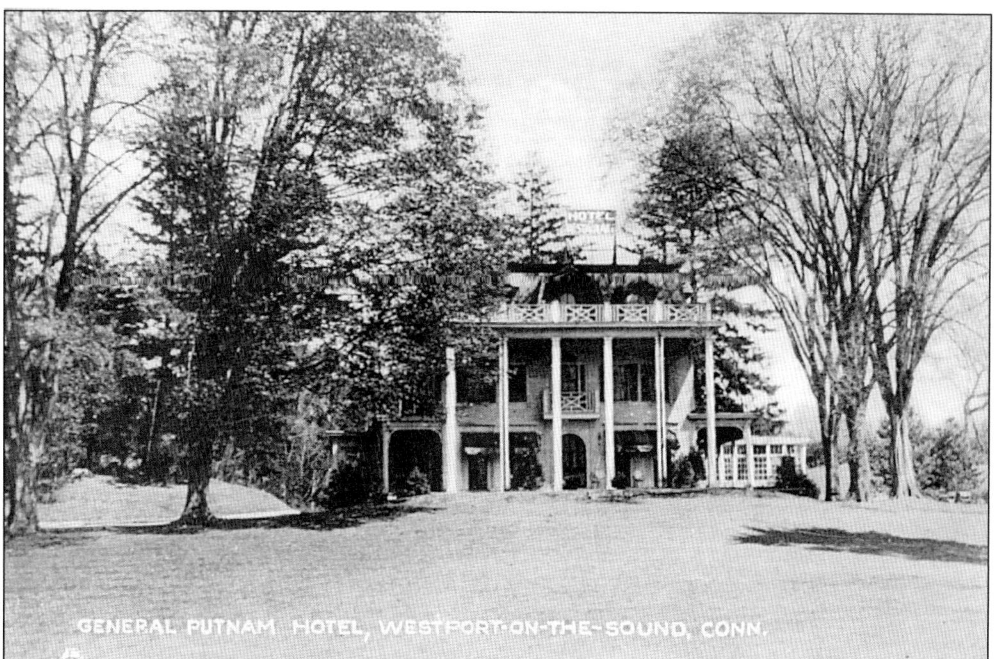

. . . later renamed the General Putnam Inn, was demolished for the current police station.

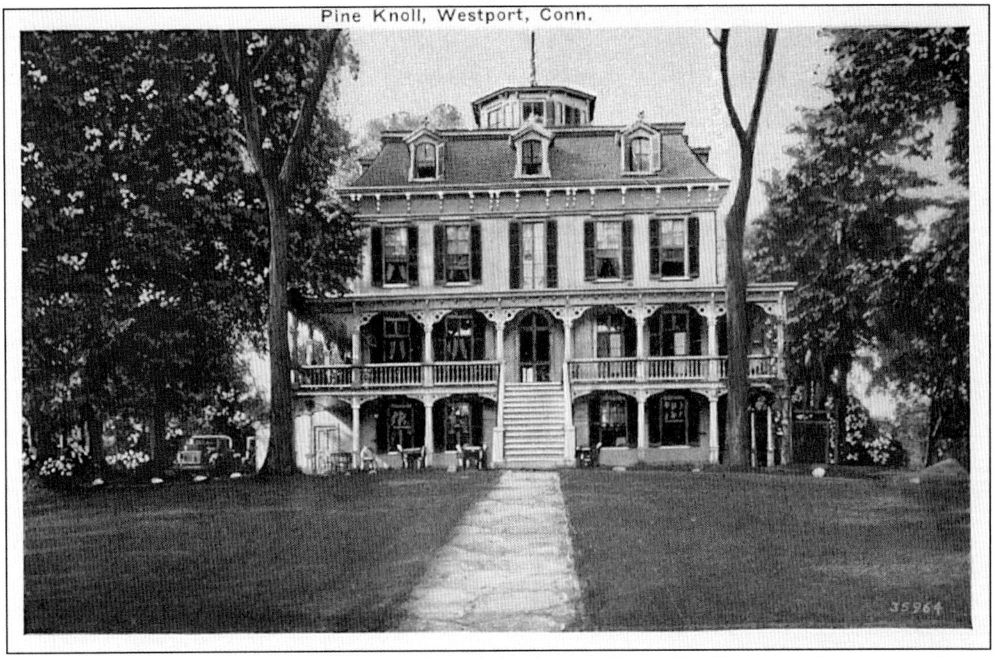

With a porch that surrounded three sides of the house, Pine Knoll was built as a residence by Charles Kemper in what is now Playhouse Square at 281 Post Road East. This card was mailed in the 1920s. The house, later an inn, was demolished in 1981 to make room for the Playhouse Condominiums.

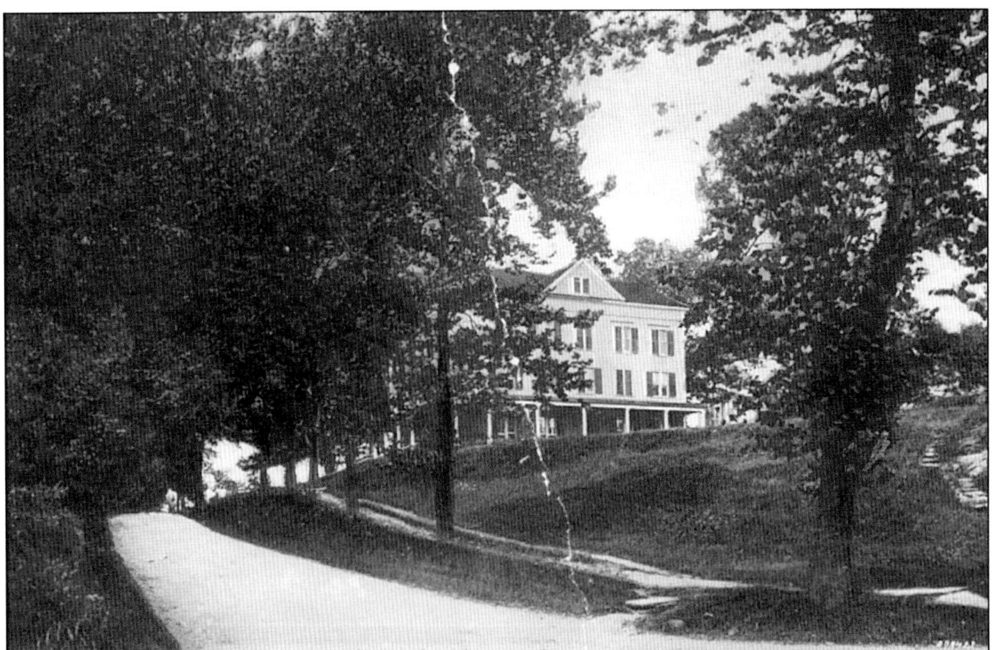

Another Westport hotel, later known as the Compo Inn, stood where Christ Church had been located. Edward Nash purchased the old Christ Church and converted it into a summer hotel. West Church Street is now known as Ludlow Road.

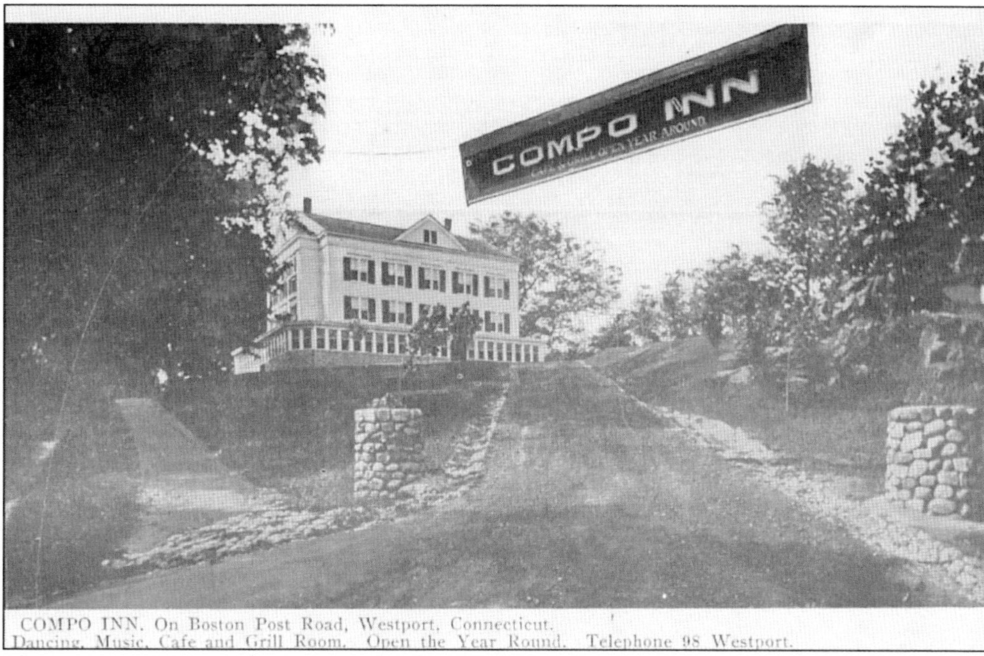

The Compo Inn catered in part to the theatrical crowd . . .

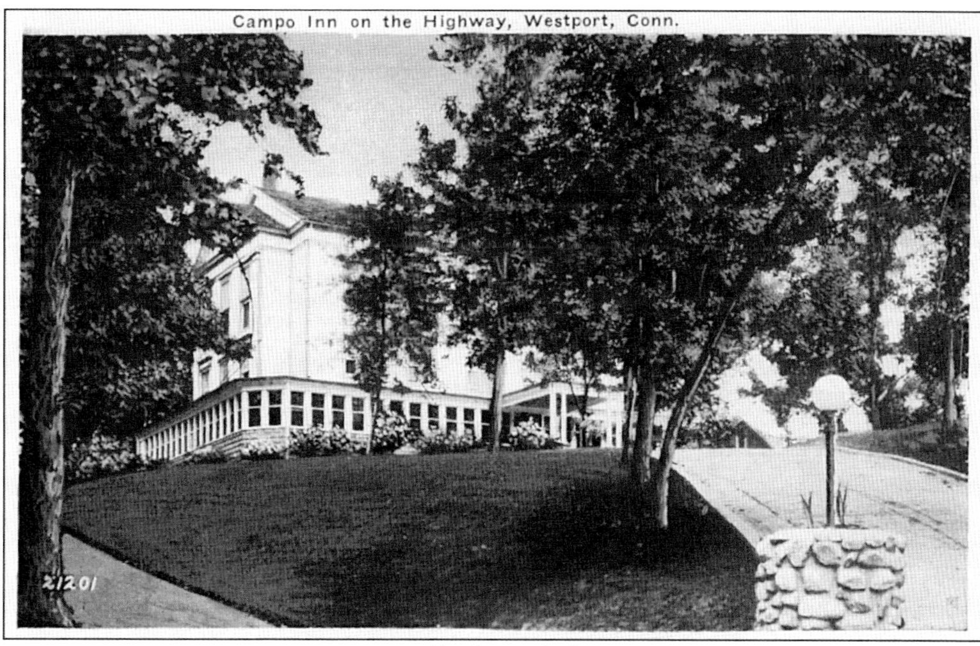

. . . and had a justly famous restaurant called "Tony's" inside.

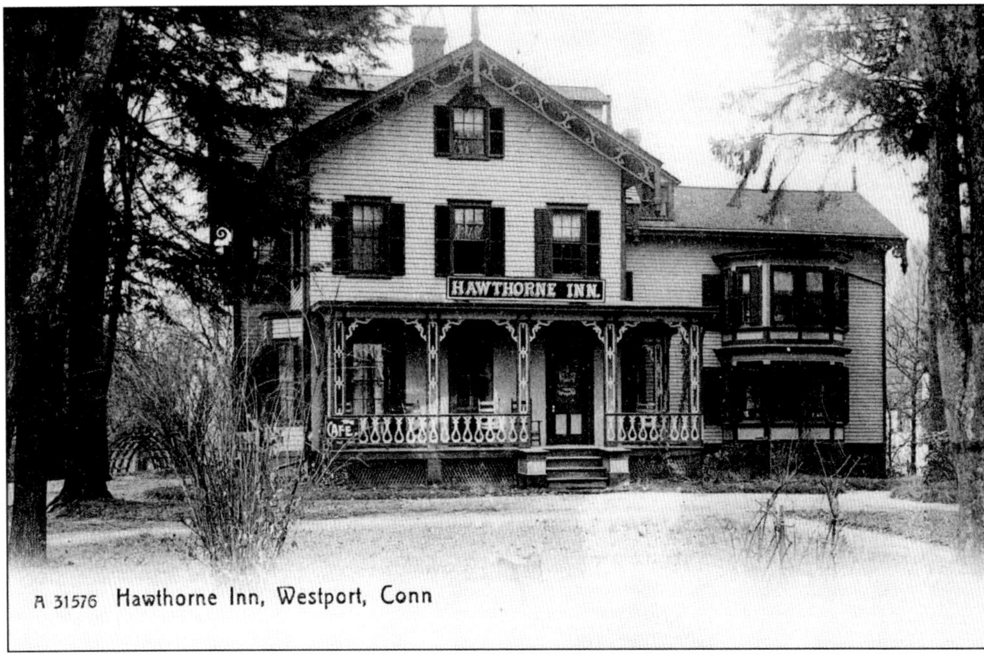

Standing at the southeast corner of Compo Road and the Post Road . . .

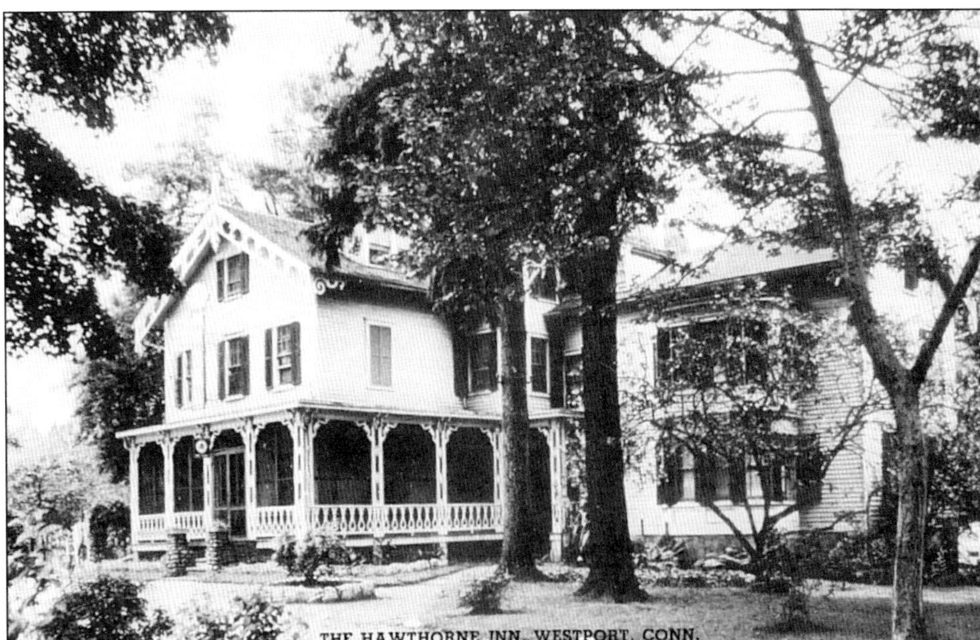

. . . the Hawthorne Inn was demolished to make room for the Compo Acres Shopping Center.

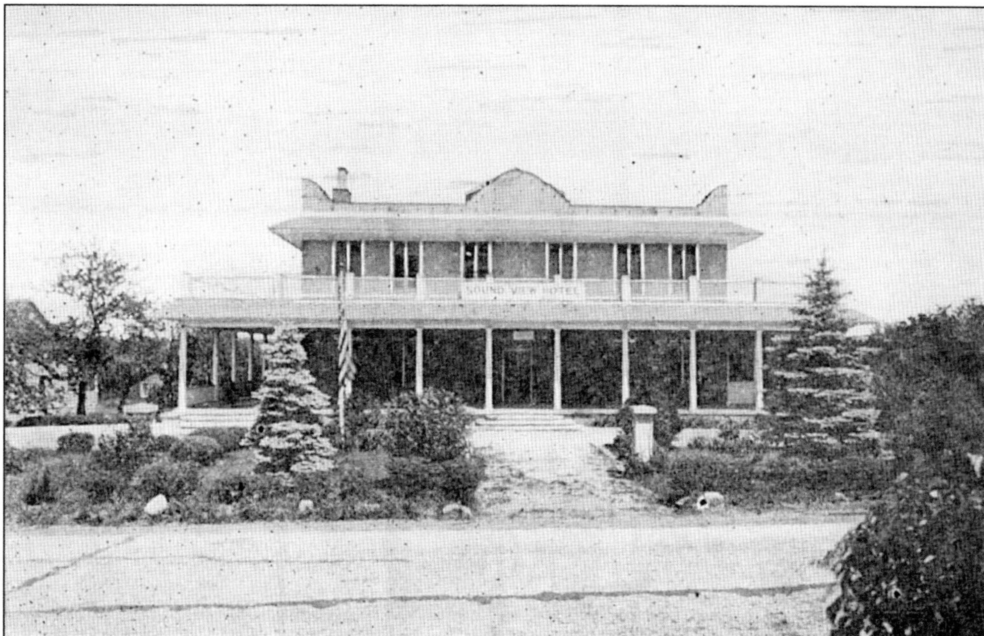

SOUND VIEW HOTEL WESTPORT, CONN.

Also called "The Miramar" and "The Penguin" (which operated from 1919 as a black tie night club), this building was demolished in the early 1980s to make way for Edgewater Condominiums on Hills Point Road.

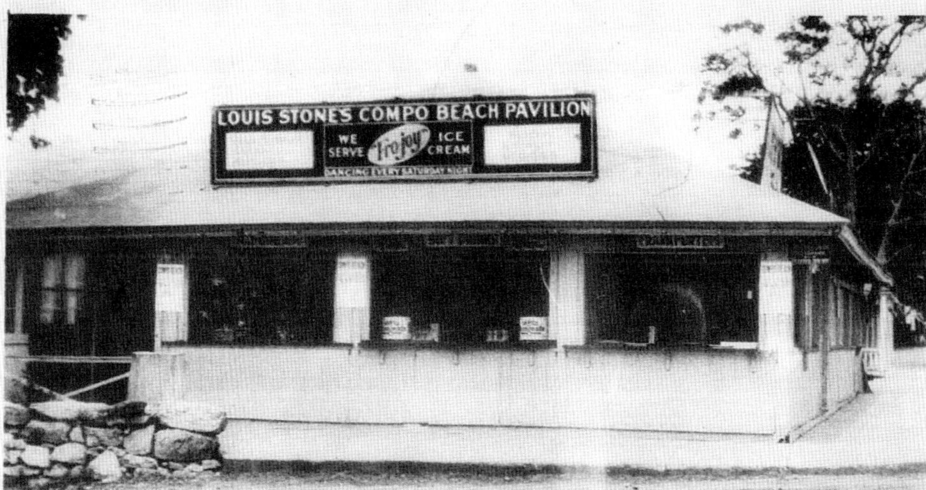

Stone's Pavilion, Compo Beach, Westport, Conn.

In the 1920s and 1930s, this pavilion was used for dining and dancing at the beach. The card was sent on July 26, 1933.

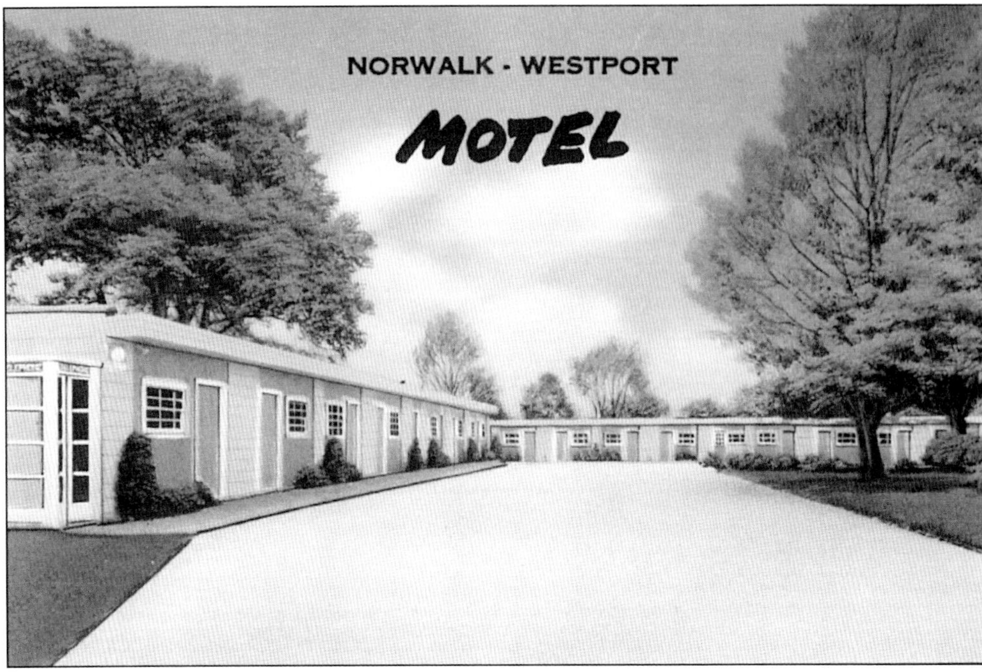

This motel, on the Westport/Norwalk line, built in 1955 . . .

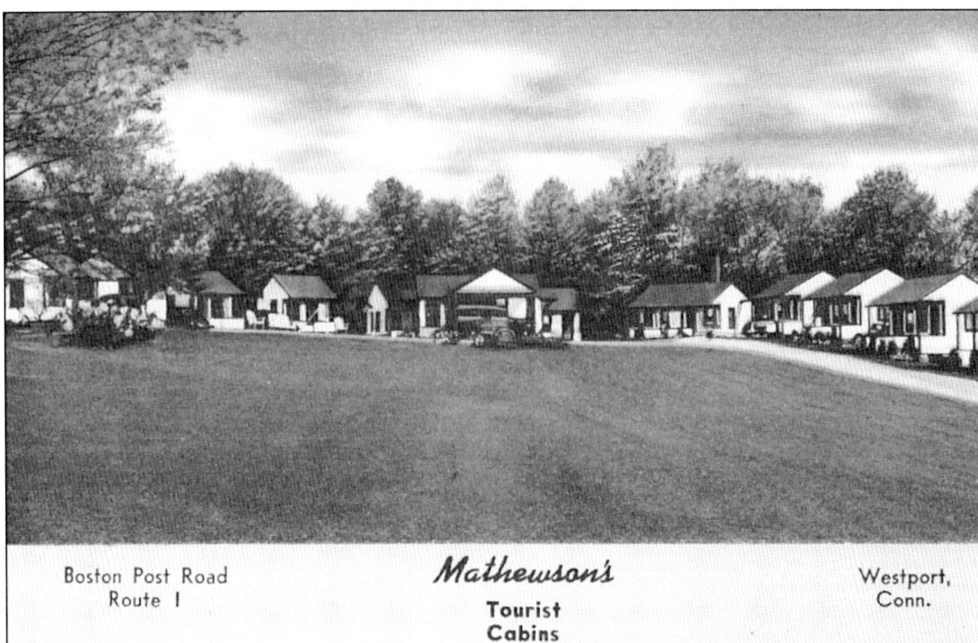

. . . and this motel (seen here on a card dated March 2, 1953) provided accommodations near town.

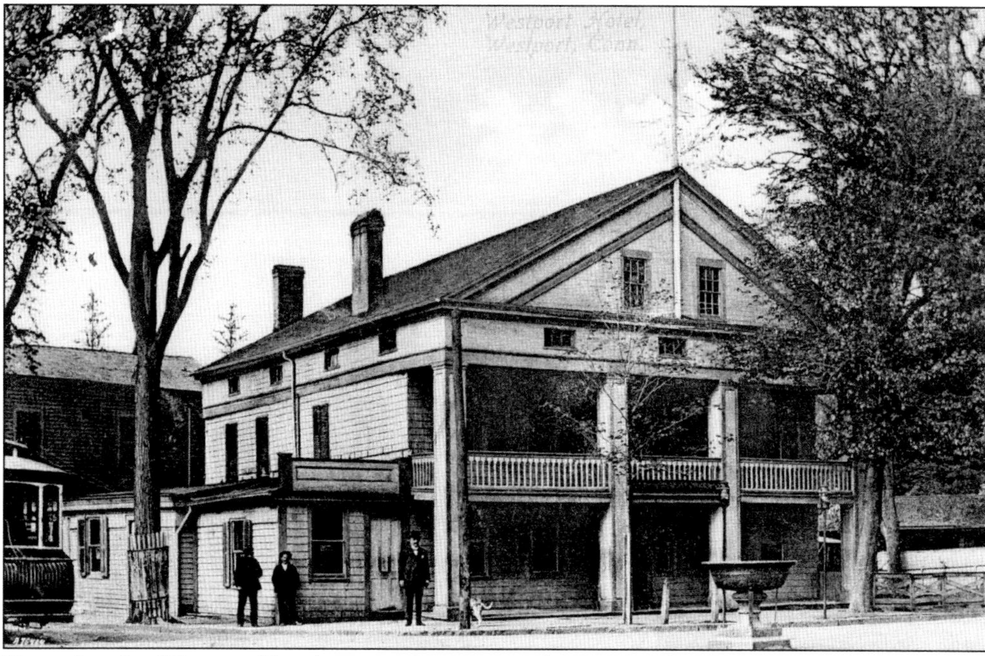

Yesterday, the Westport Hotel attracted visitors to the center of town . . .

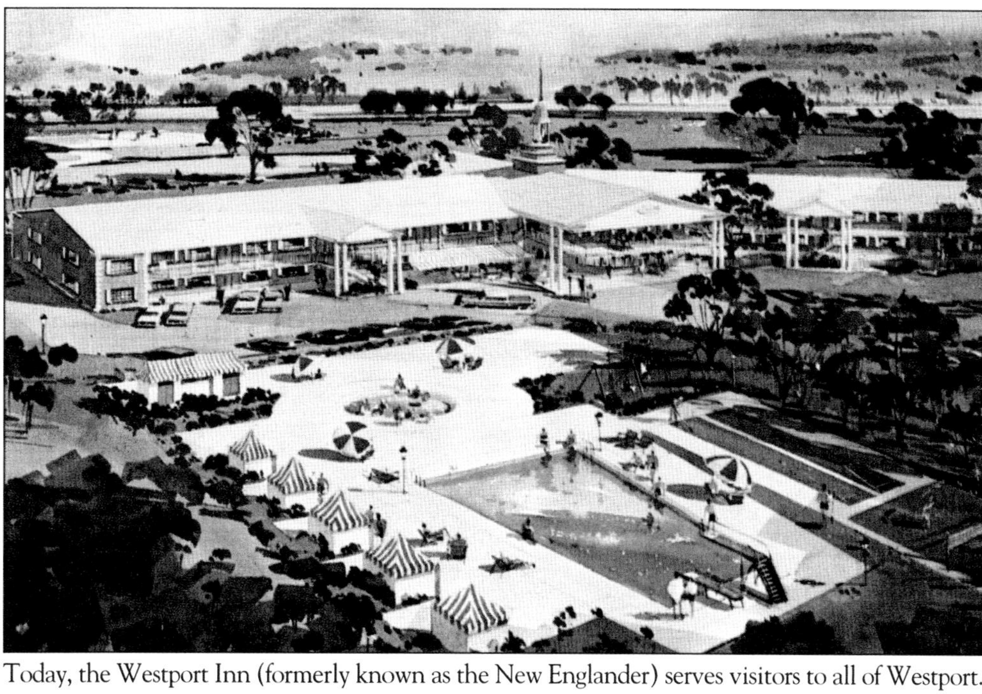
Today, the Westport Inn (formerly known as the New Englander) serves visitors to all of Westport.

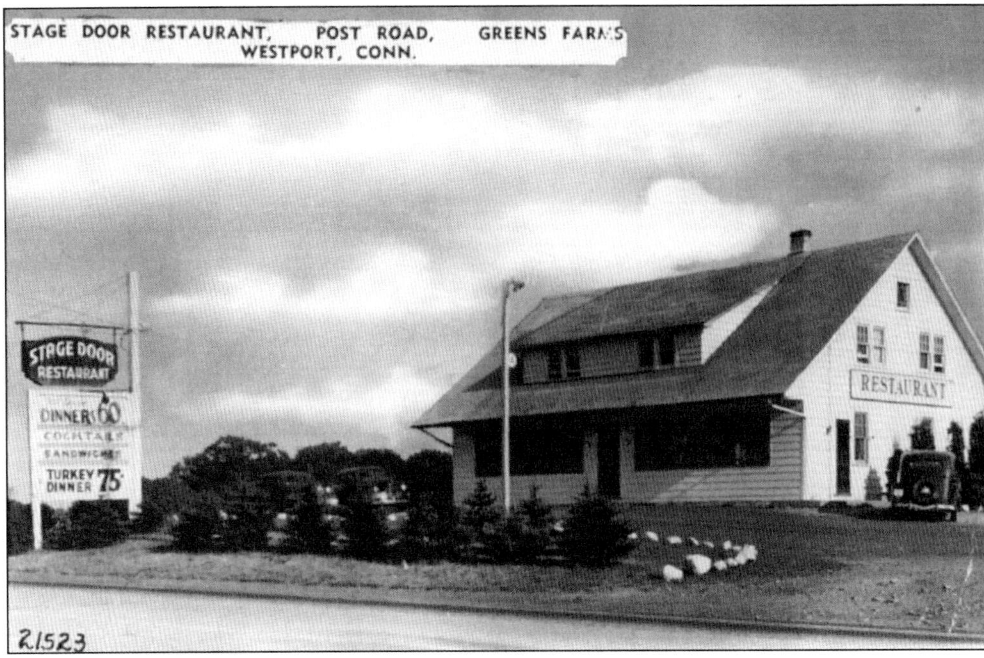

The Stage Door restaurant is long gone, but . . .

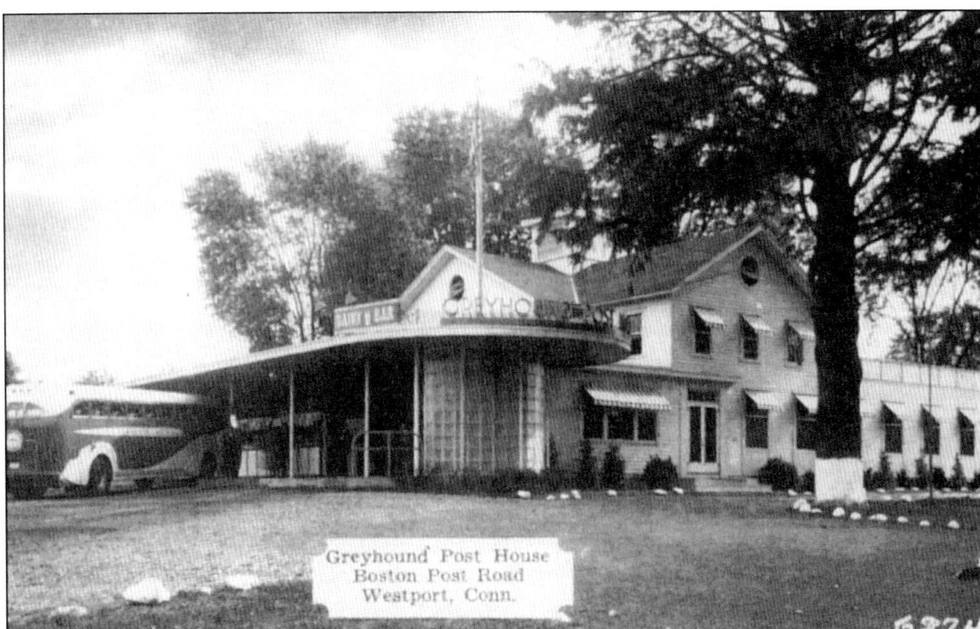

. . . the greyhound bus station is now the Peppermill Restaurant, at 1700 Post Road East.

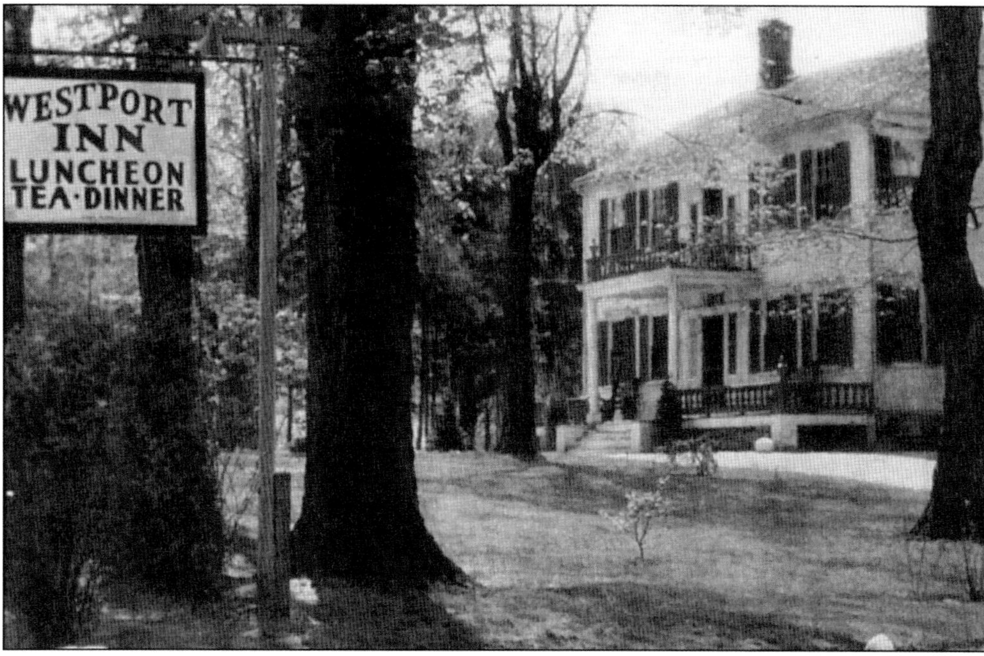

This building is currently the rear building of Colonial Green Shopping Center, having been moved from its original location at the southeast corner of the Post Road and Imperial Avenue, where it was owned by Charles Jesup. The card was sent on July 13, 1936.

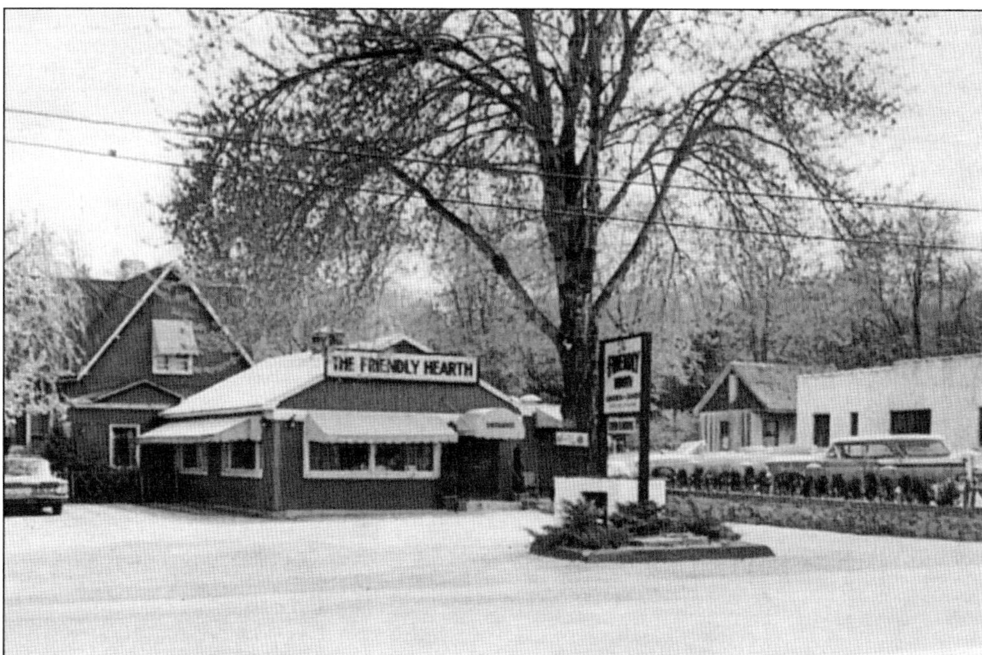

Opened in 1954, the Friendly Hearth was demolished to make room for the Volvo dealership's parking lot at 556 Post Road East.

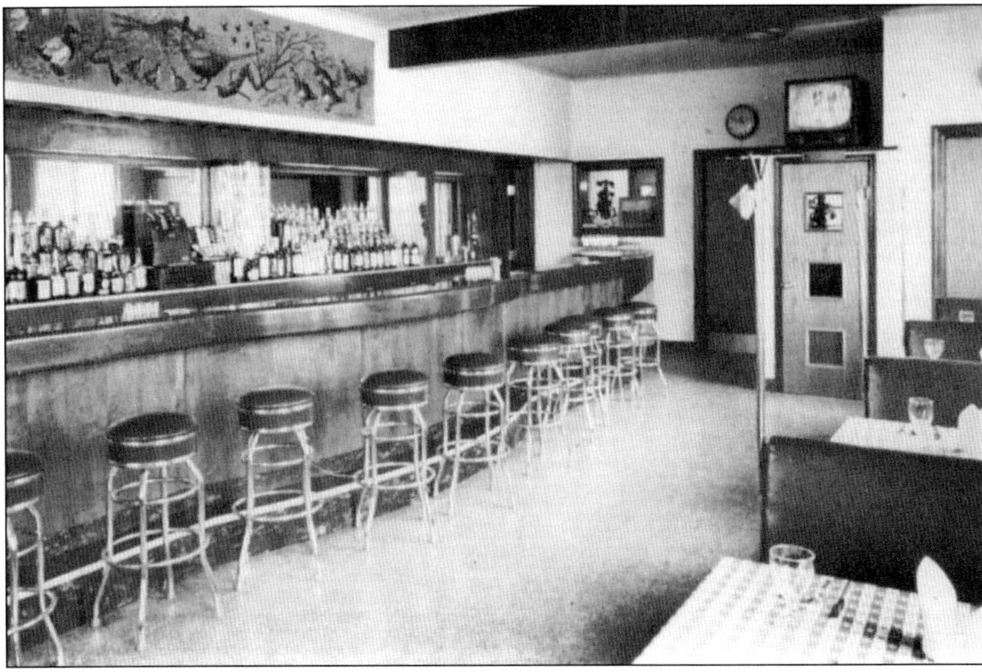

This is the interior of Cafe Barna, where local groups such as the Rotary met in the 1960s.

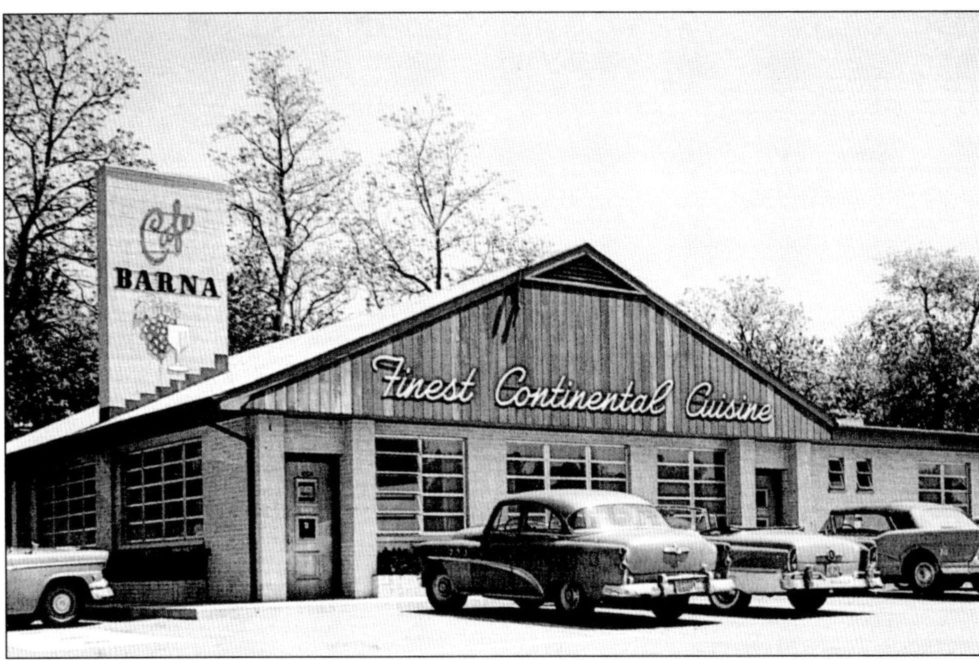

The cafe was demolished to make way for an addition to Mitchell's of Westport, at 670 Post Road East.

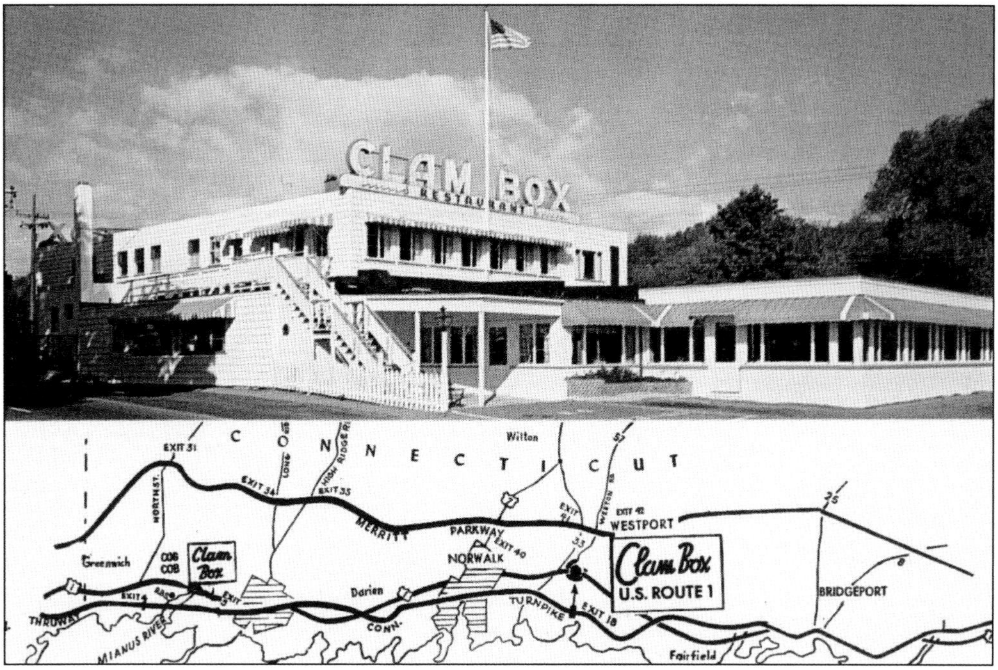

Located at 833 Post Road East in the 1990s, Bertucci's Restaurant . . .

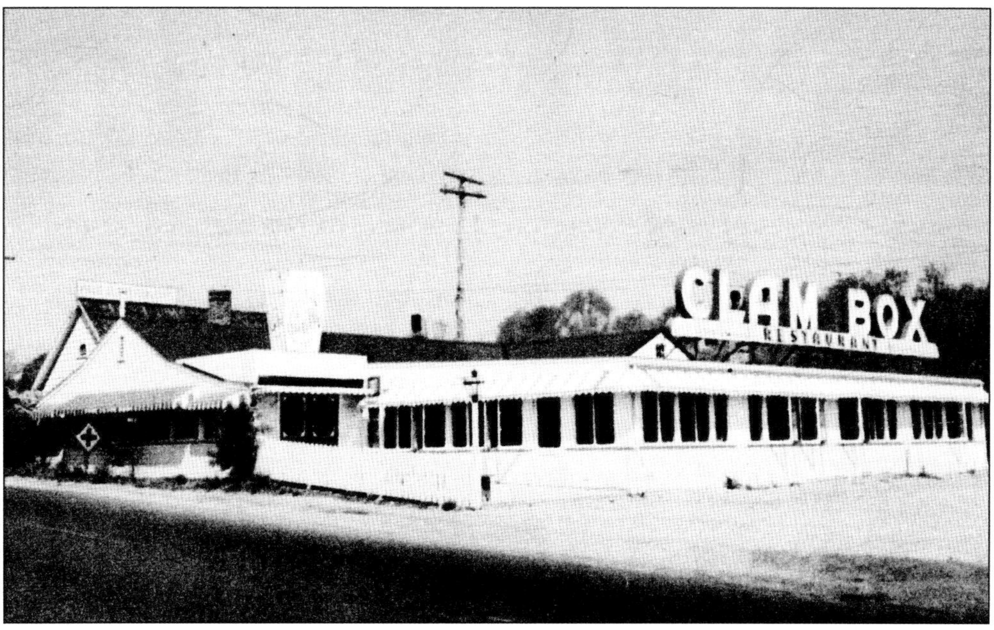

. . . was previously part of a multi-restaurant chain of seafood restaurants called the Clam Box.

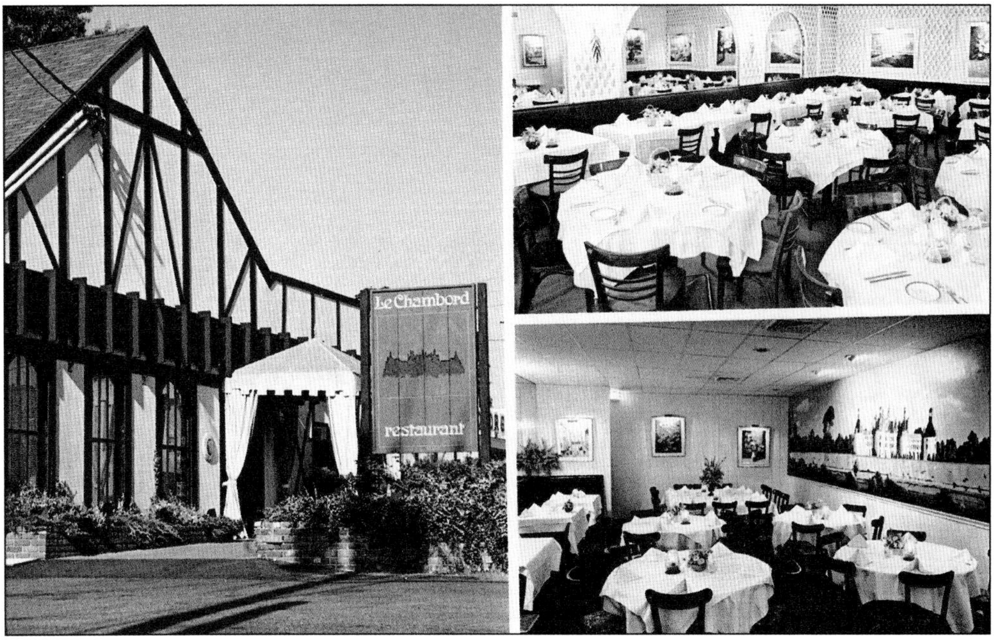

Le Chambord, at 1572 Post Road East, was a "fancy" French restaurant.

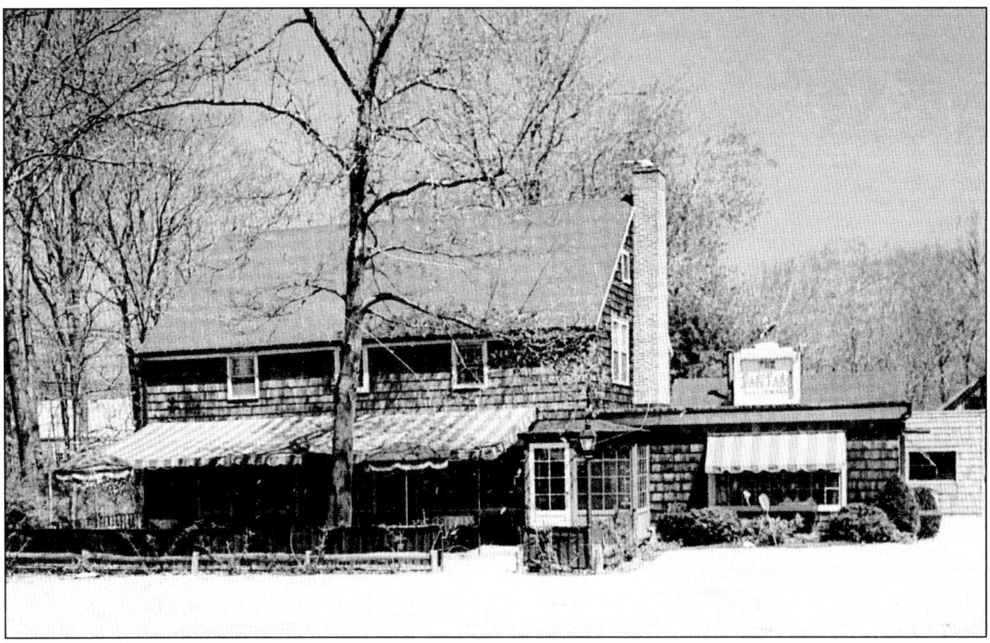

Adjacent to the Westport Inn at 1563 Post Road East (formerly the New Englander Motel), this restaurant has been known as the "Bantam," "Chubby Lane's," and "Promis."

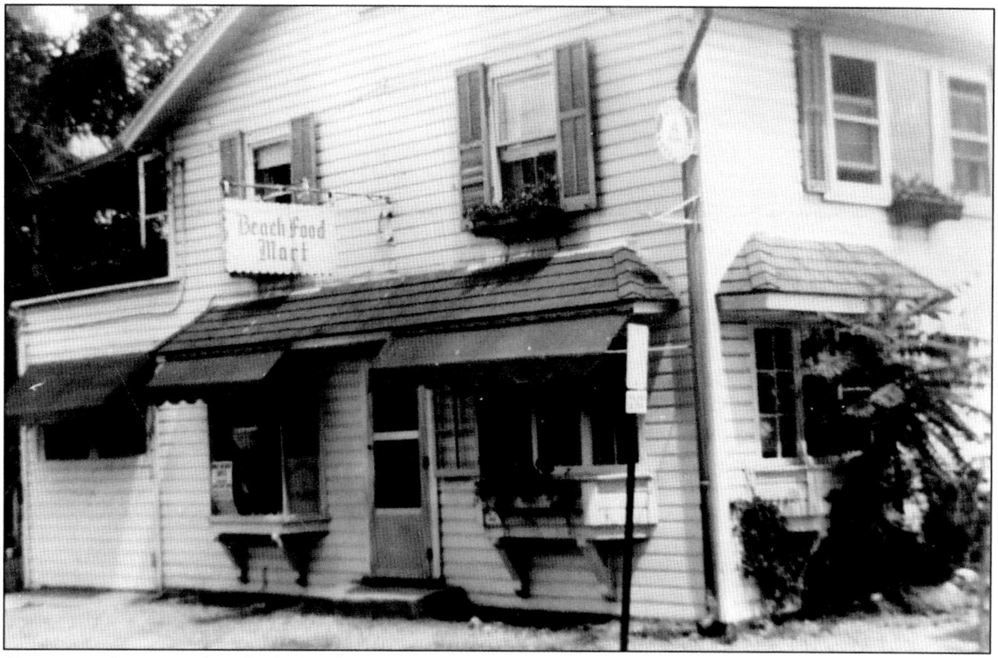

For years the site of Café de la Plage, this building at 233 Hills Point Road is still, in the 1990s, a restaurant.

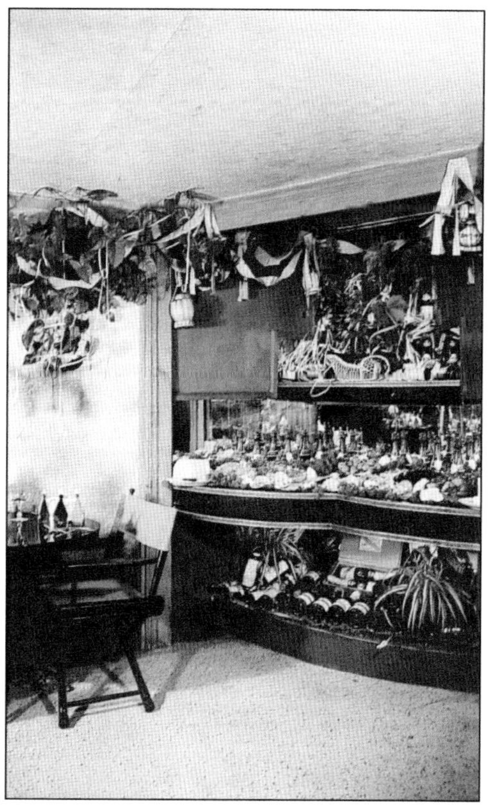

This is the interior of Café de la Plage as it appeared about 1960.

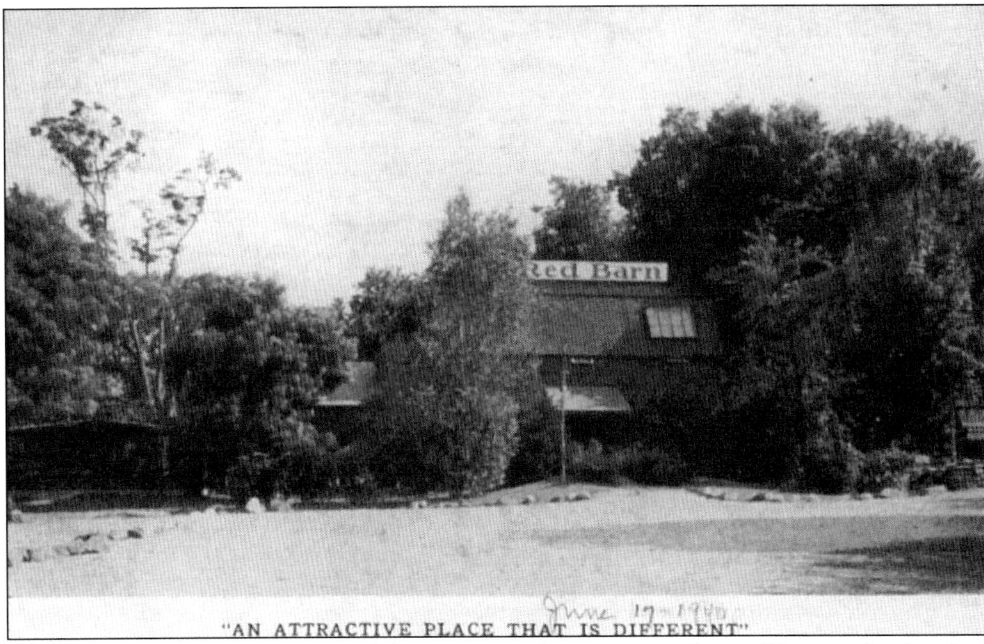

The Red Barn, located at Exit 41 of the Merritt Parkway, is an enduring Westport landmark.

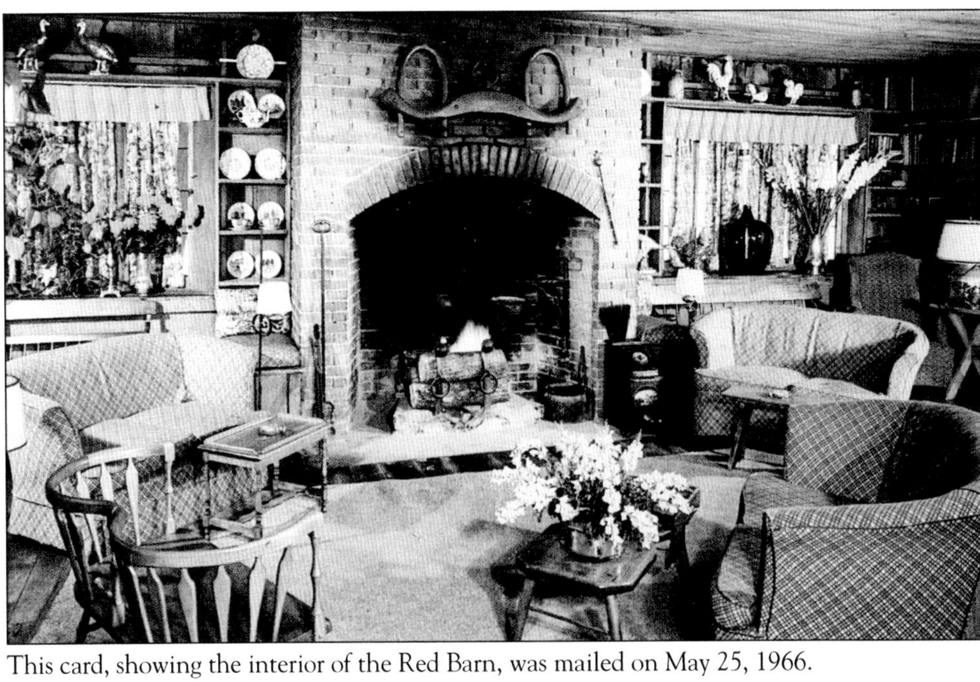
This card, showing the interior of the Red Barn, was mailed on May 25, 1966.

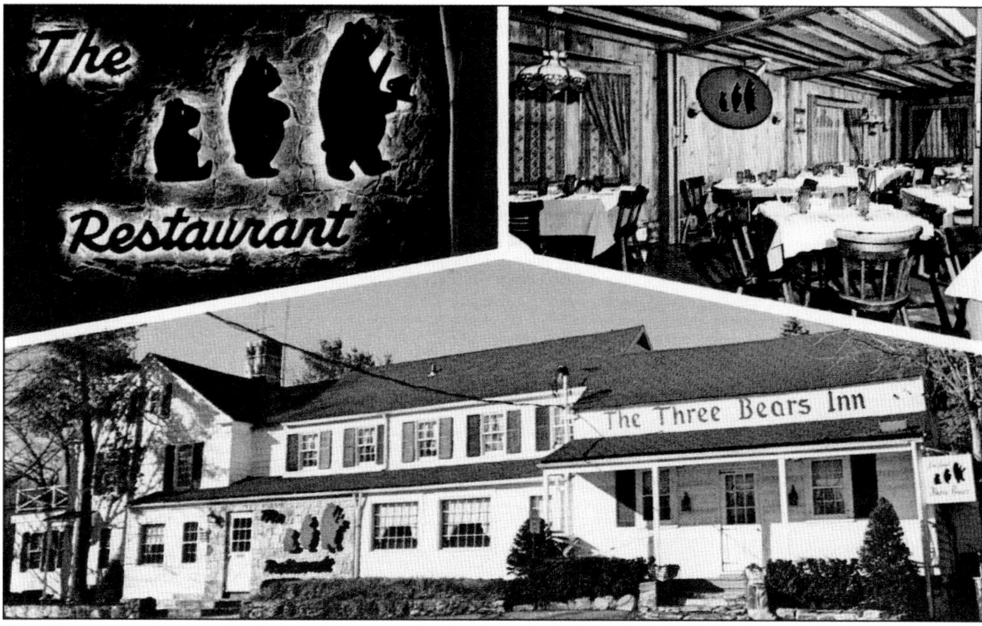

Another restaurant which has hardly changed since this card was mailed in 1982 . . .

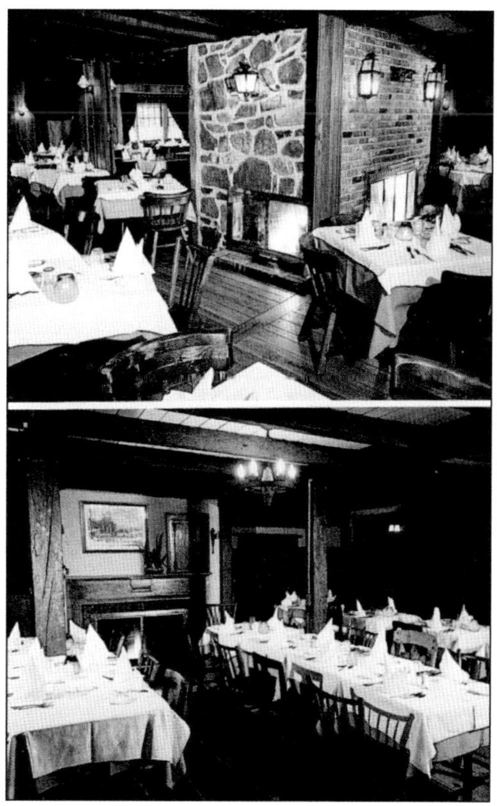

. . . "The Three Bears" stands on Newtown Turnpike near Route 33/Wilton Road.

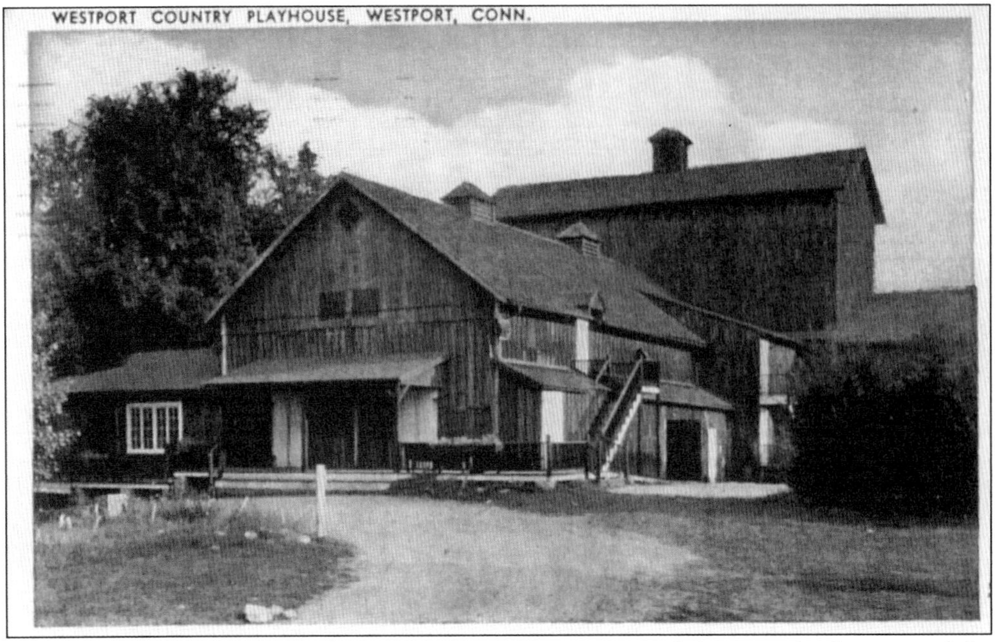

In 1931, this site, where Charles Kemper's tannery once stood, became the location of the Westport Country Playhouse.

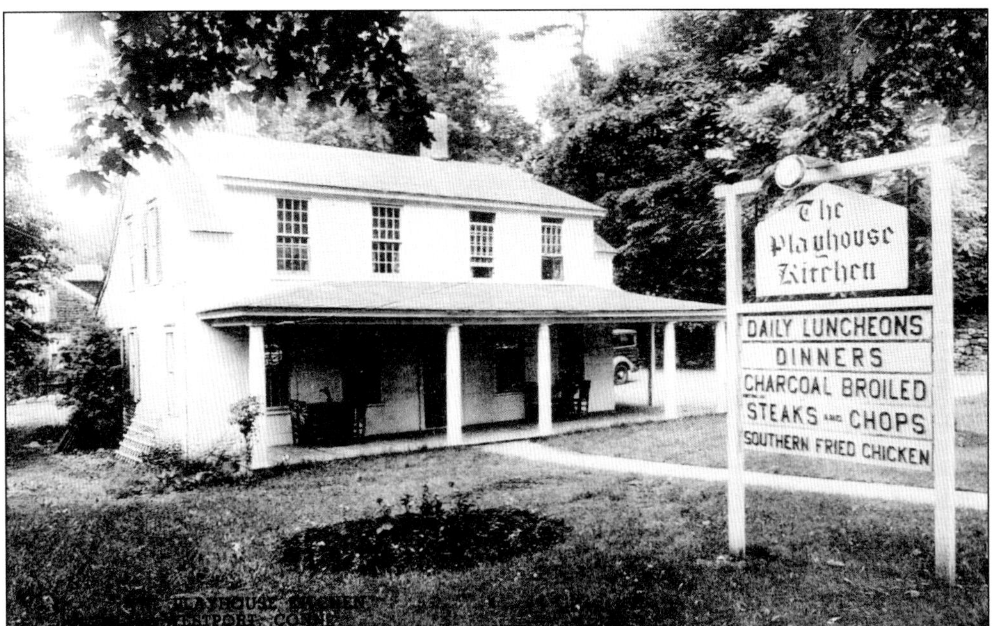

Built as housing for employees of the tannery, this house, still standing at the entrance to the playhouse, also saw service as a restaurant.

Six

The Beach: Compo, Old Mill, and Sherwood Island

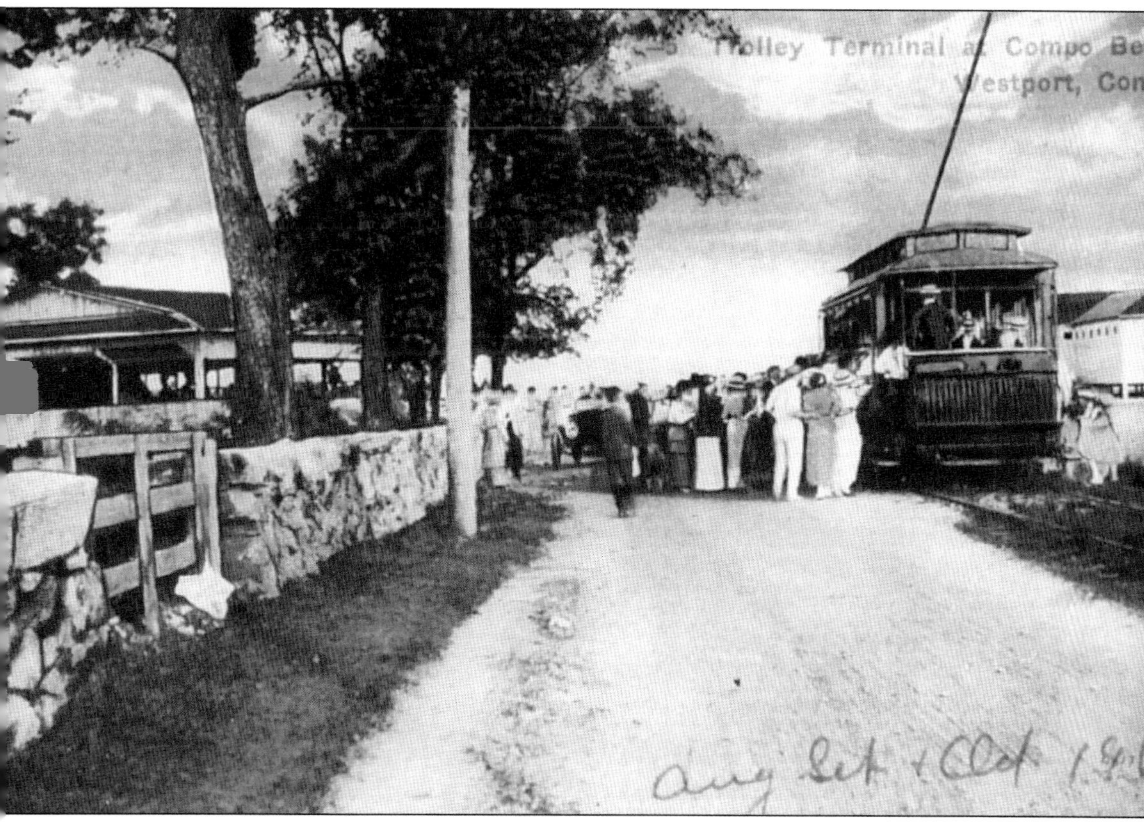

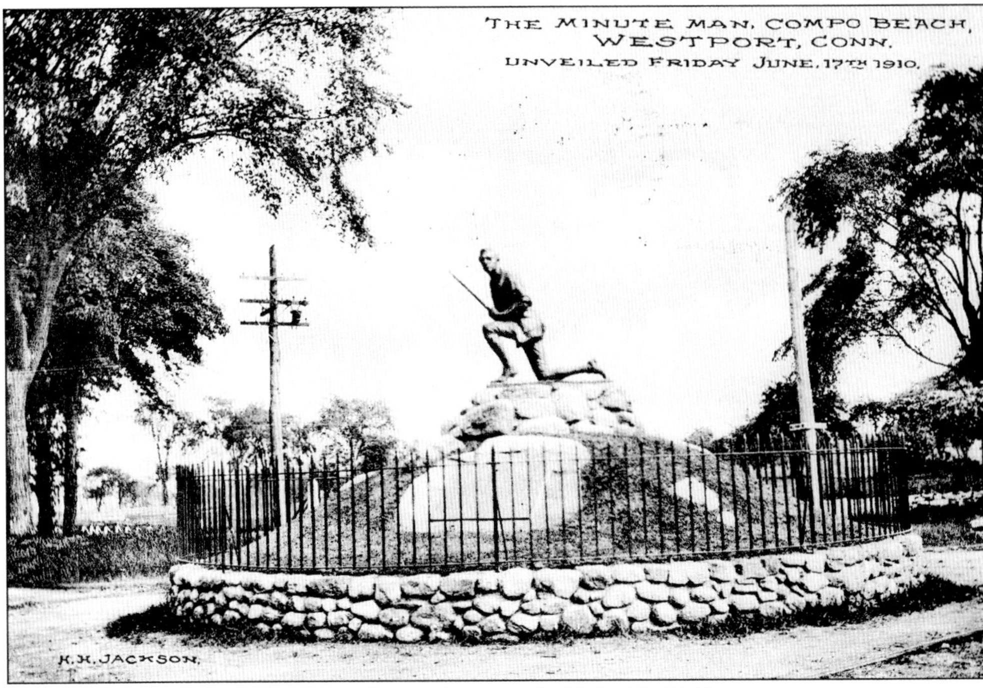

Showing the symbol of Westport, this card was mailed July 16, 1940.

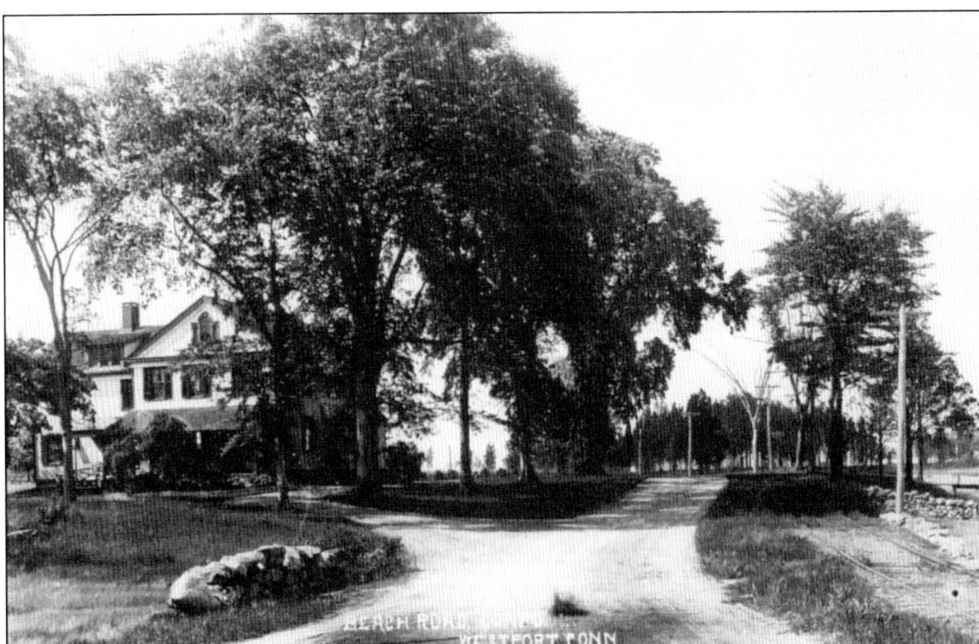

This is the view from the Minuteman statue, looking toward Owenoke. The house on the left still stands.

This is a pre-1907 view of the pavilions at Compo Beach.

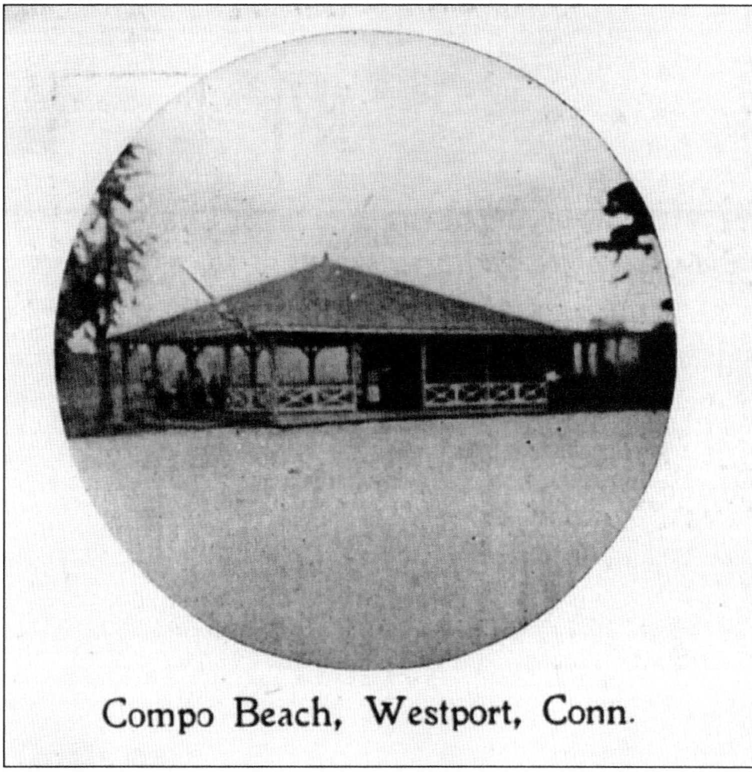

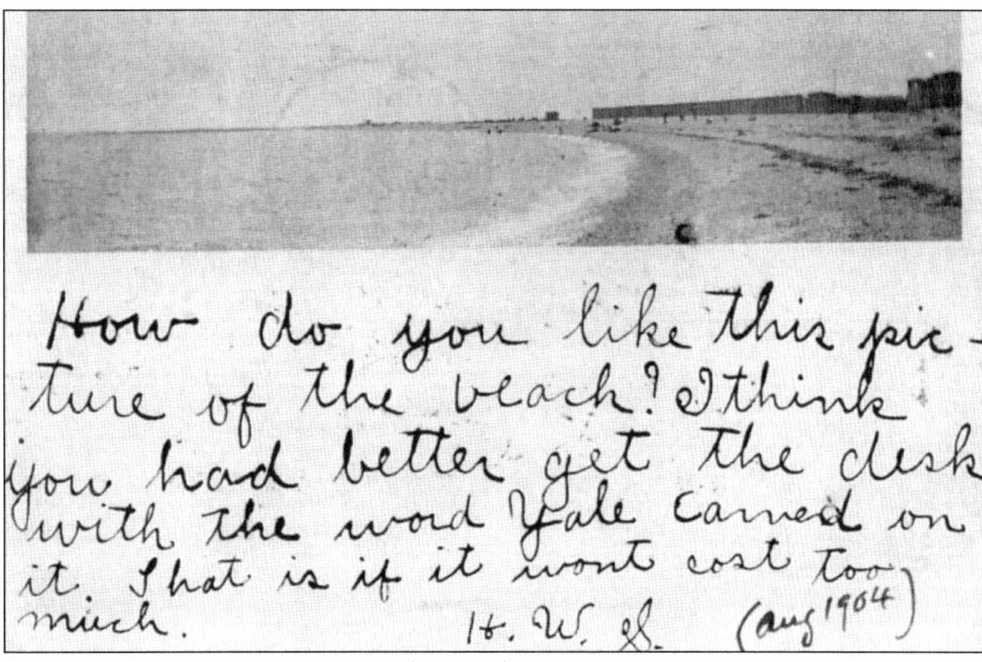

This card was sent to Rev. James E. Coley on July 30, 1904.

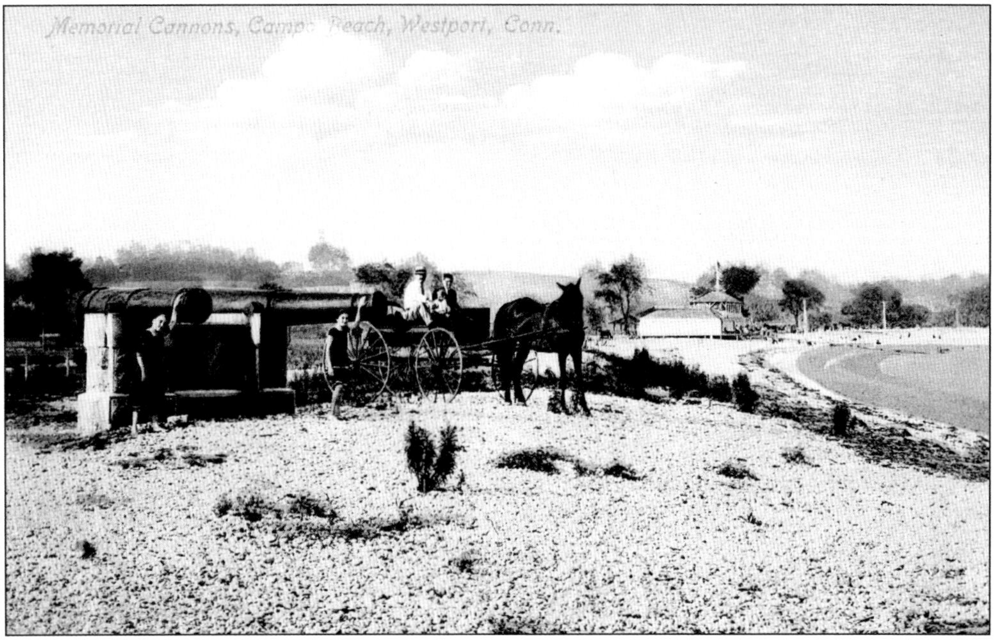

Two early views of the Compo Beach Memorial Cannons . . .

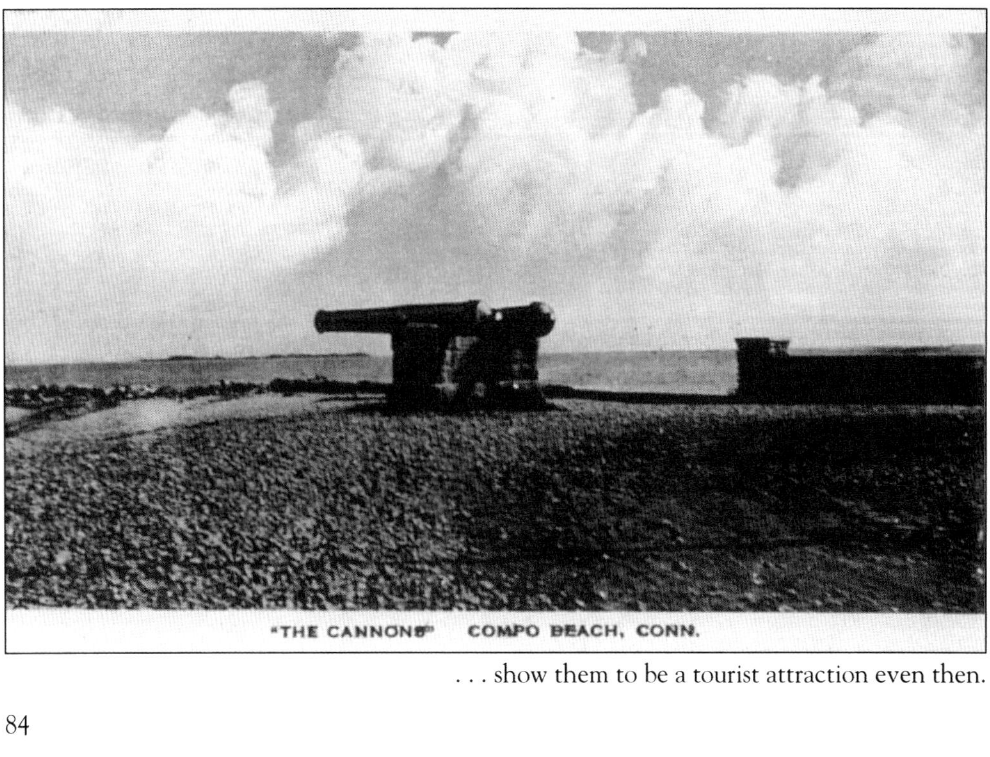

"THE CANNONS" COMPO BEACH, CONN.

. . . show them to be a tourist attraction even then.

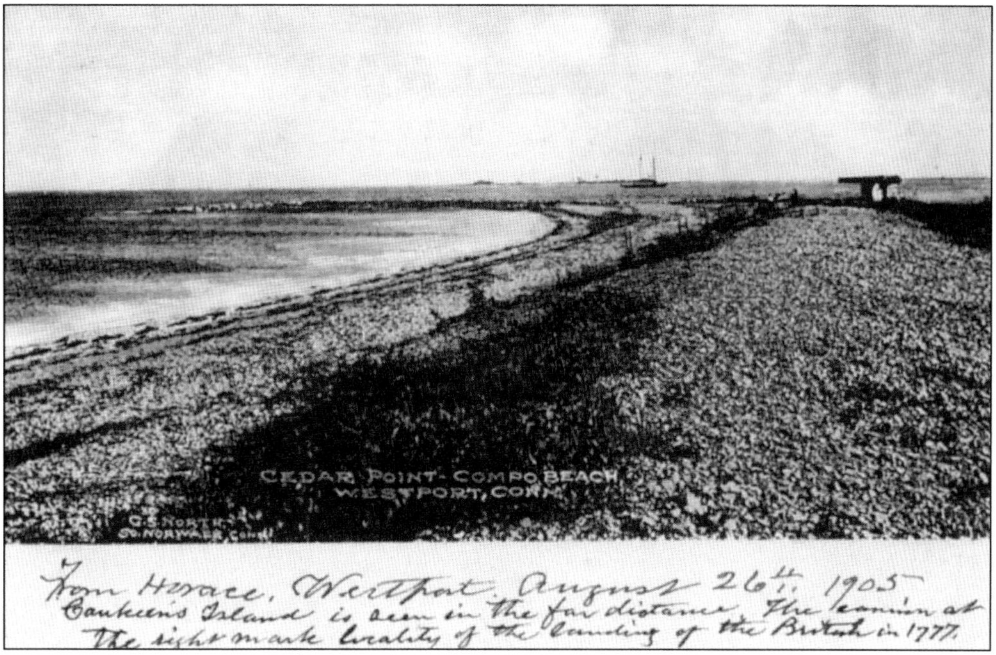

In 1905, the cannons were already a fixture on the beach.

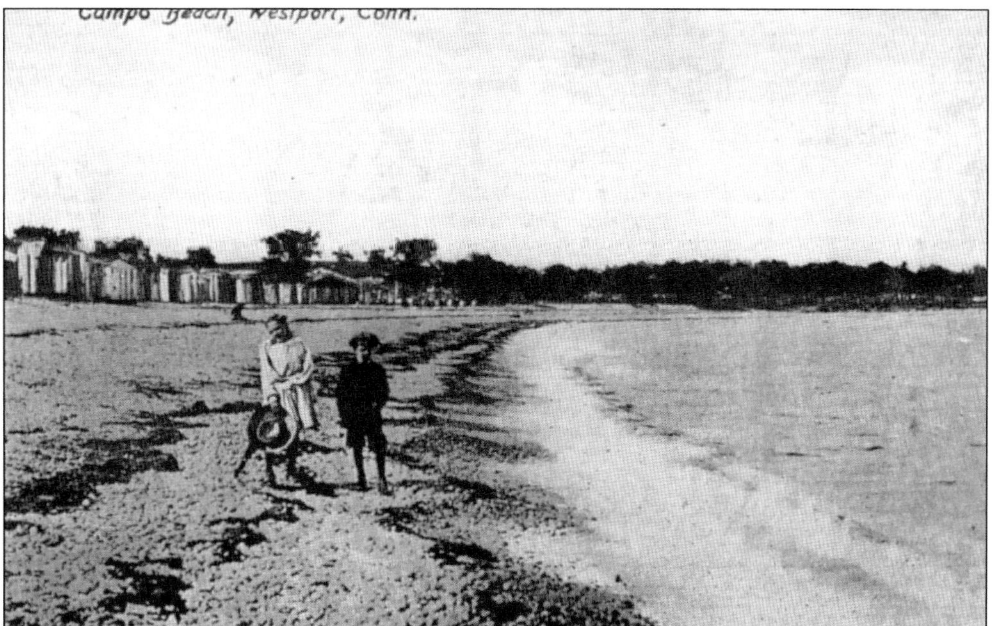

This view looks east from the cannons on the beach, and was mailed March 3, 1914, to East Norwalk.

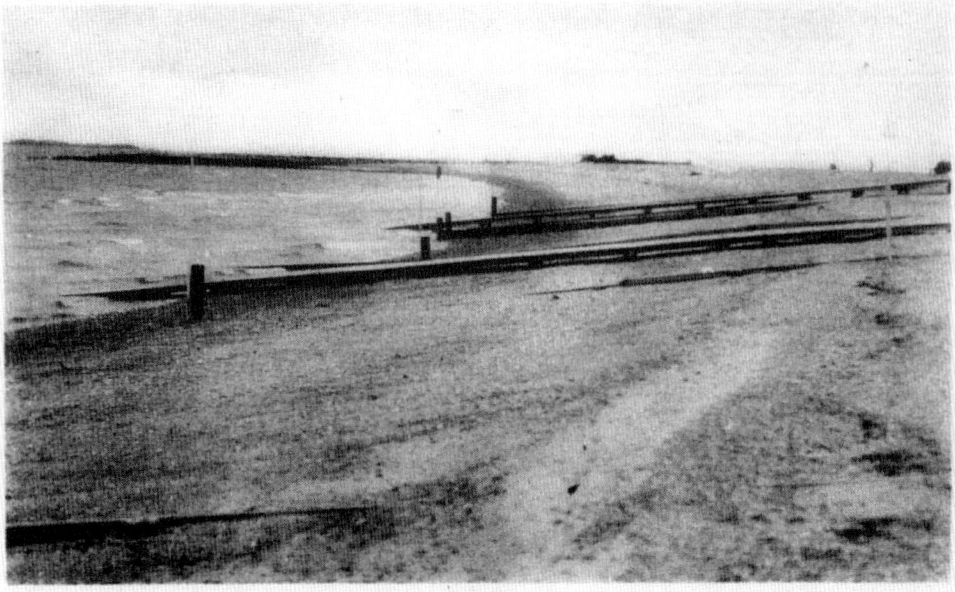

Compo Beach, showing Cockenoe Island, Westport, Conn.

On this card of Compo Beach, published after 1907, note the wooden walkways to the water.

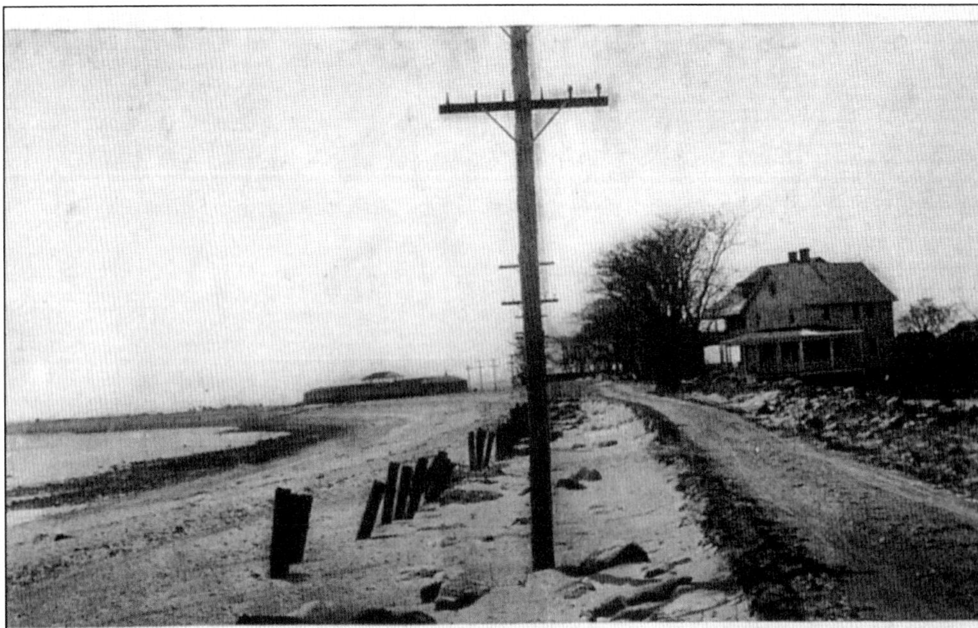

COMPO BEACH, Westport, Conn.

Located on Soundview Avenue (shown here about 1919, in a view looking west), this house still stands, flanked by many others today.

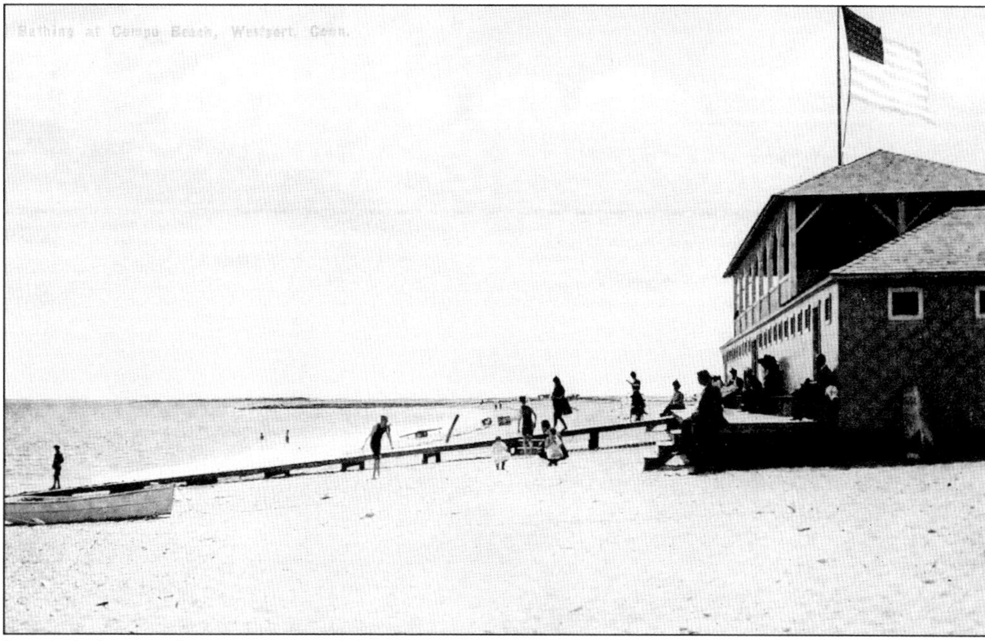

In 1919 the pavilion was opened. By 1927 . . .

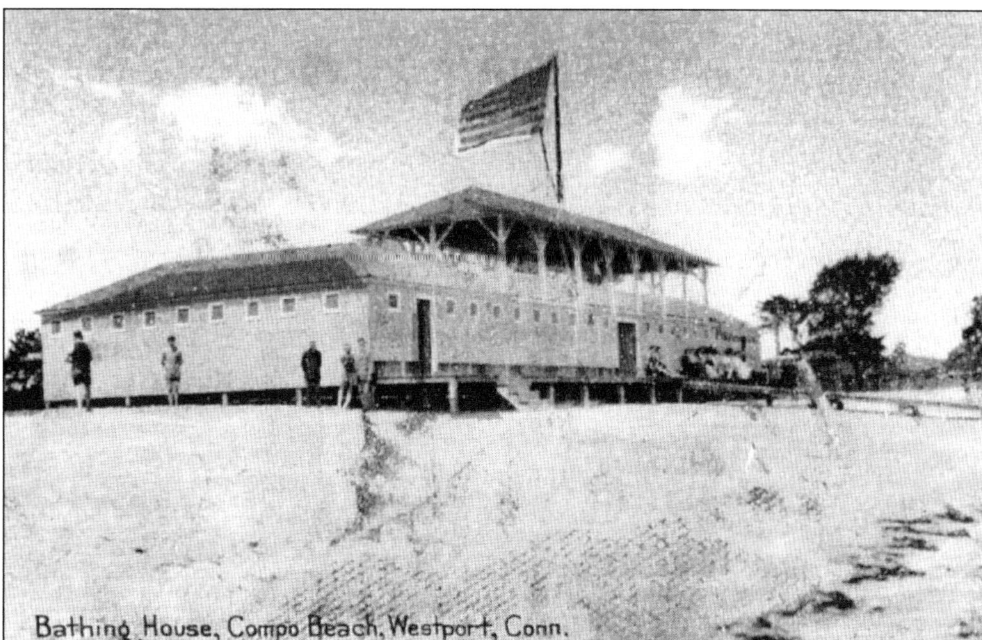

. . . the beach had 750 bathhouses as well as dining and dancing areas.

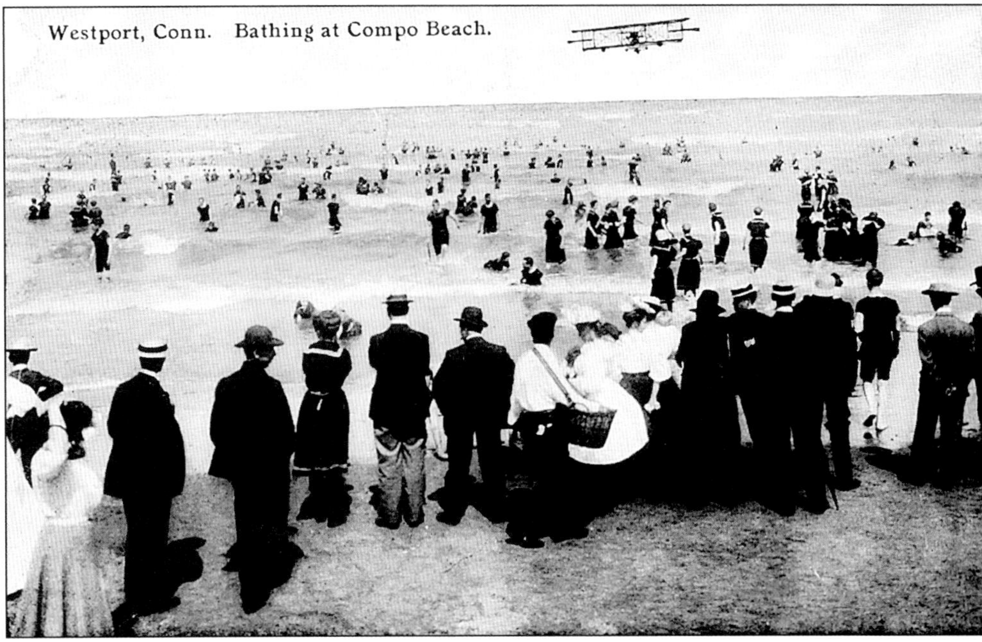

This card was mailed October 18, 1911, to Mt. Kisco, New York. (The airplane was probably added by the publisher.)

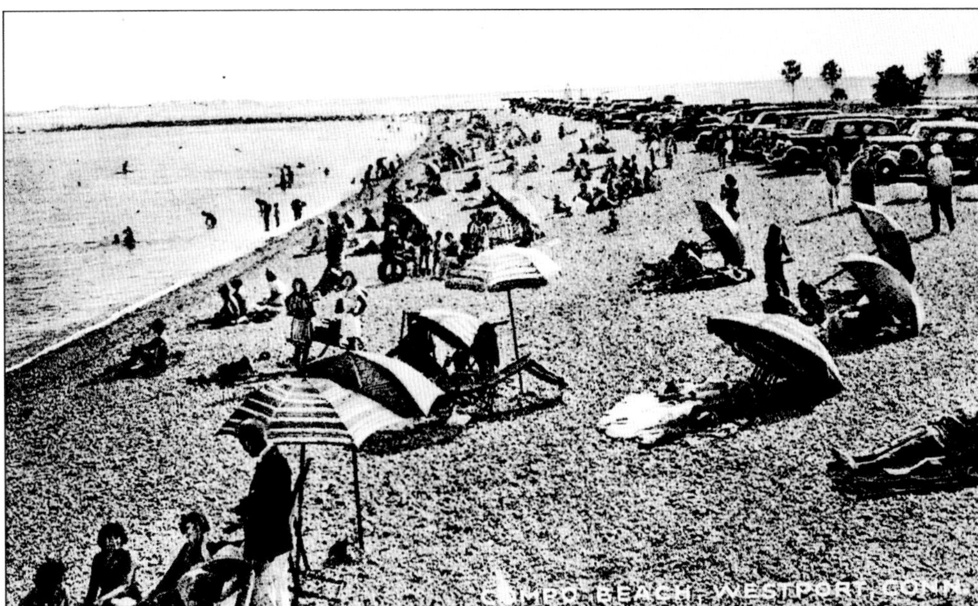

The beach has always drawn crowds, as shown here in a view looking toward the cannons.

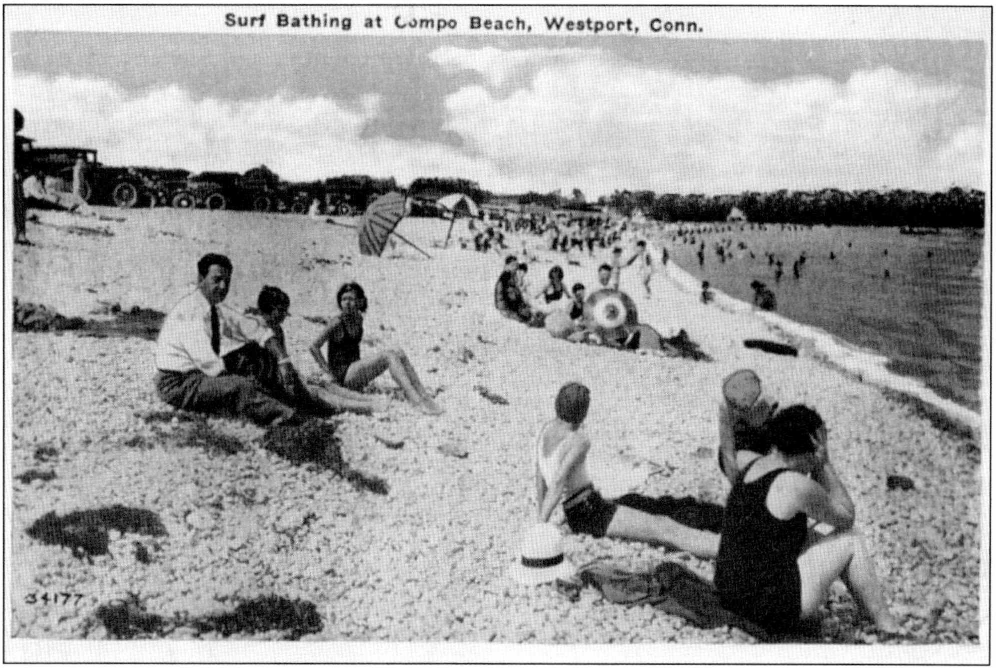

Fashions in beachwear changed over the years . . .

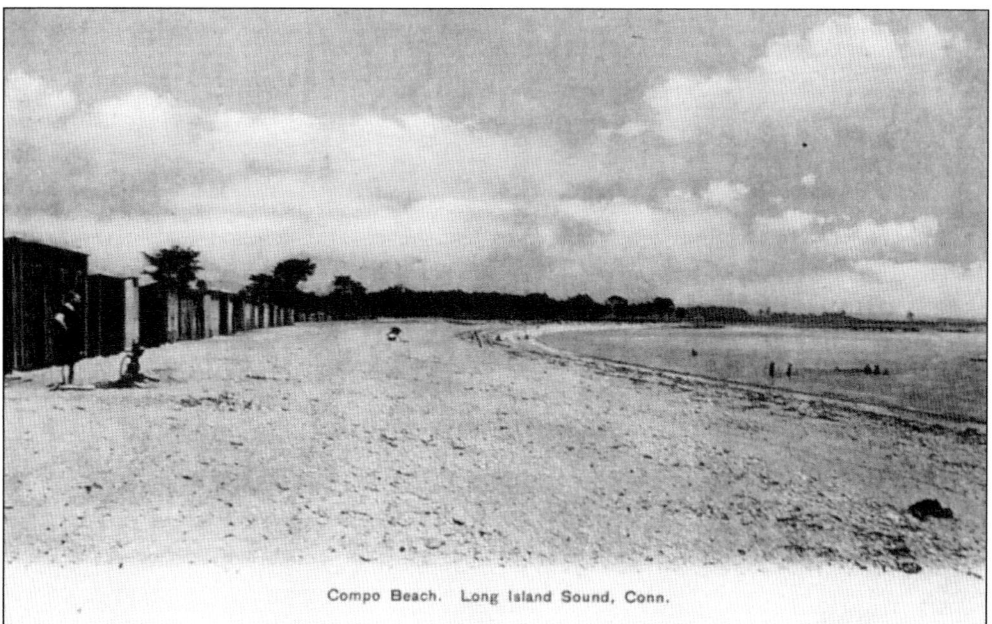

. . . and the line of bathhouses seen here no longer exists.

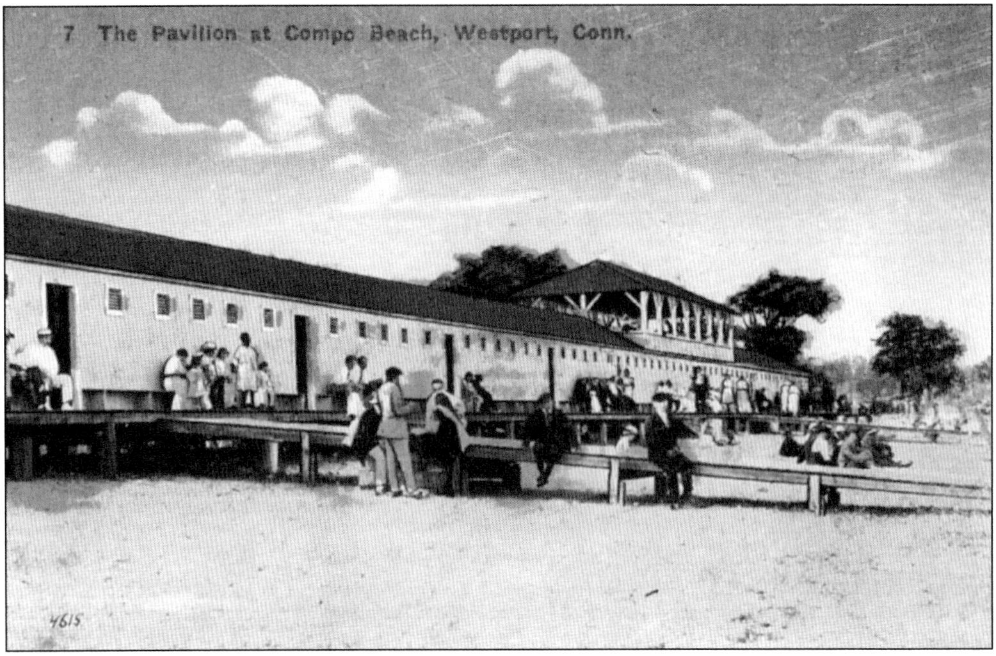

Sections of these pavilions remain at Compo . . .

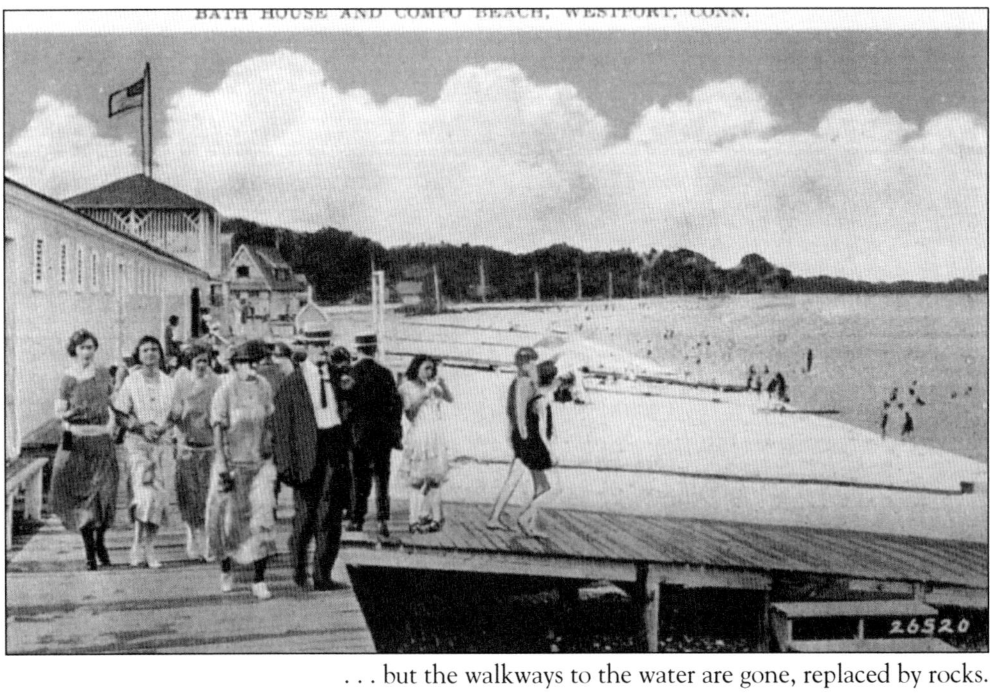

. . . but the walkways to the water are gone, replaced by rocks.

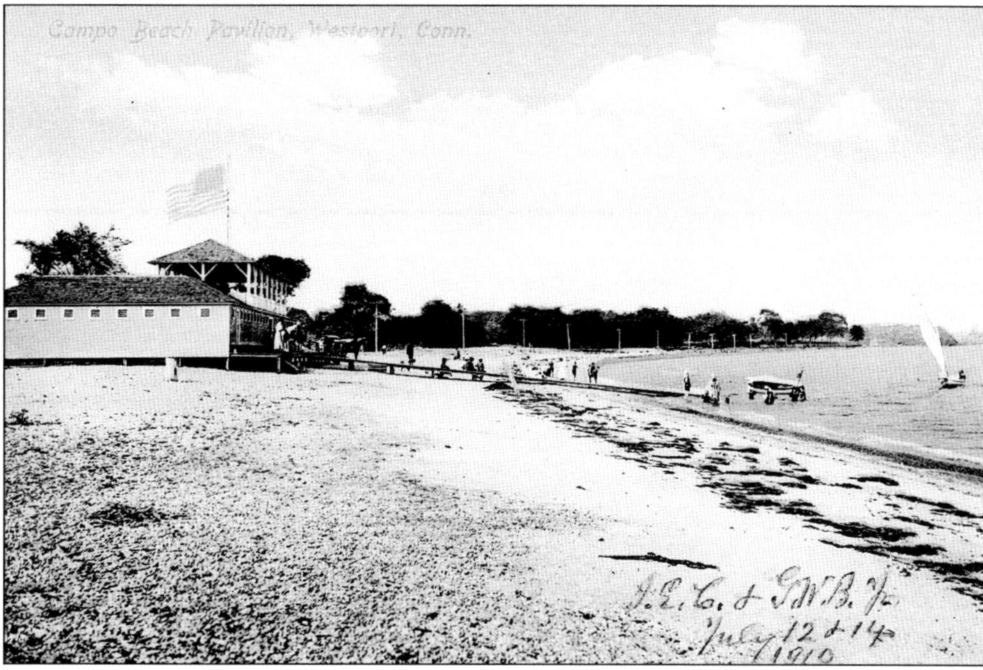

This early pavilion was new in 1900.

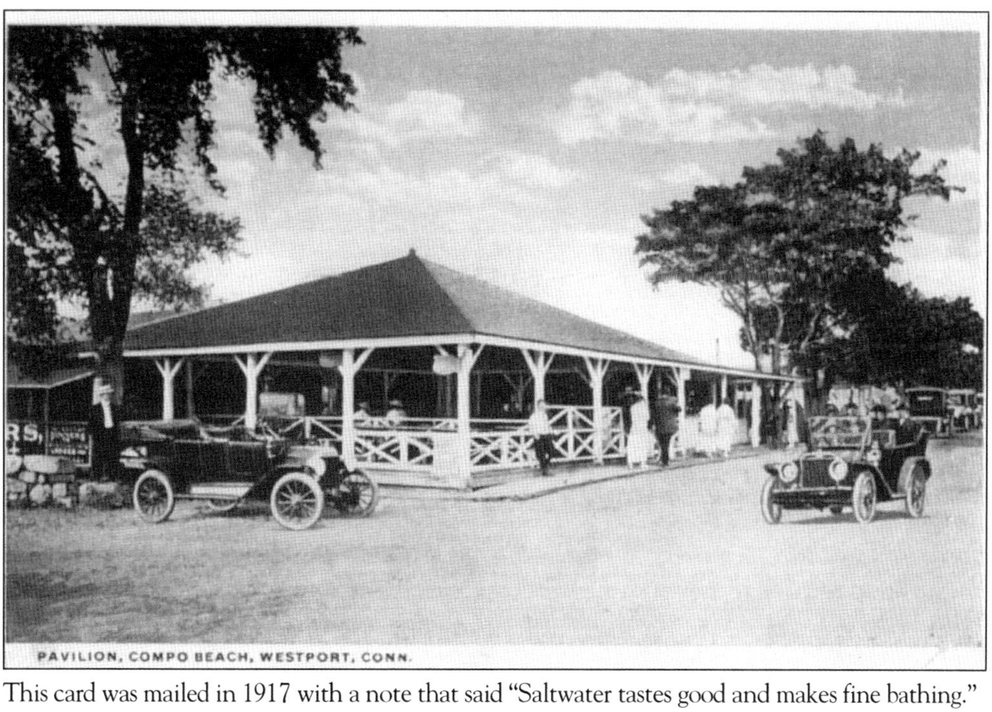

This card was mailed in 1917 with a note that said "Saltwater tastes good and makes fine bathing."

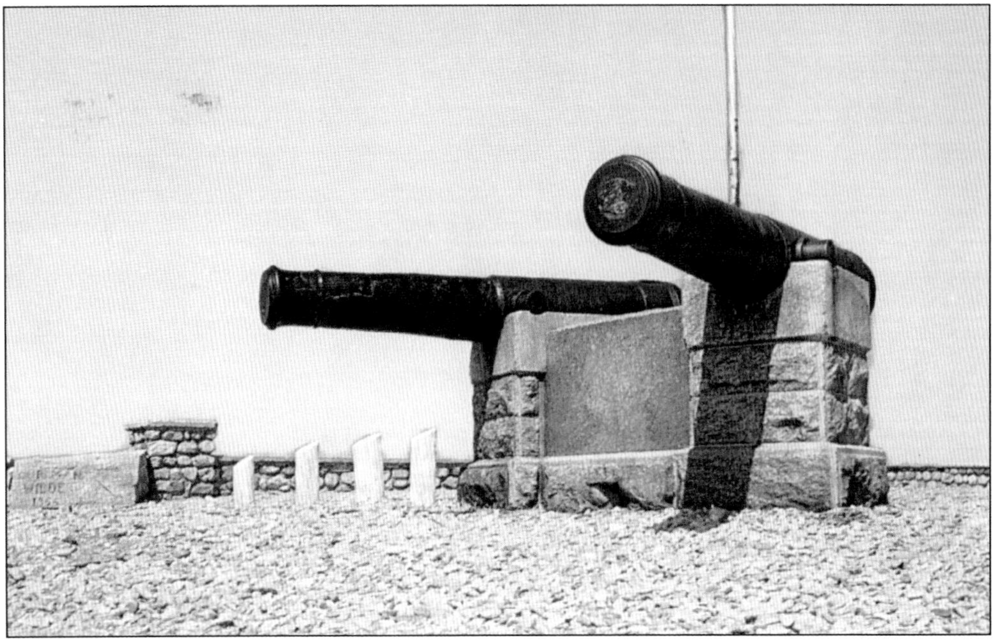

This card, mailed June 2, 1971, shows the cannons as they look in the 1990s . . .

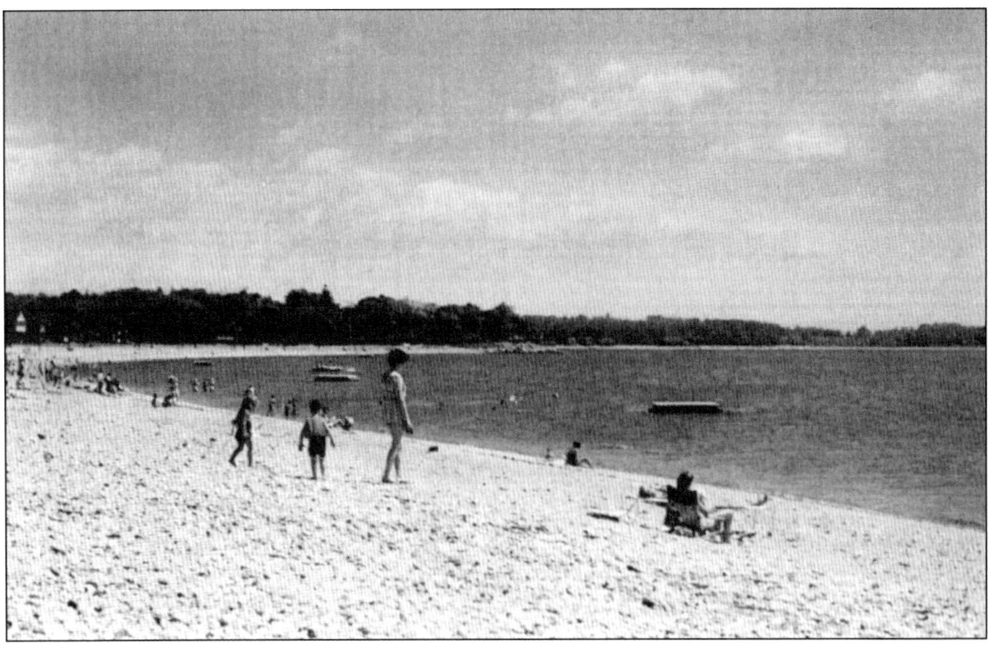

. . . but, by the 1990s, the floats were no longer in the water.

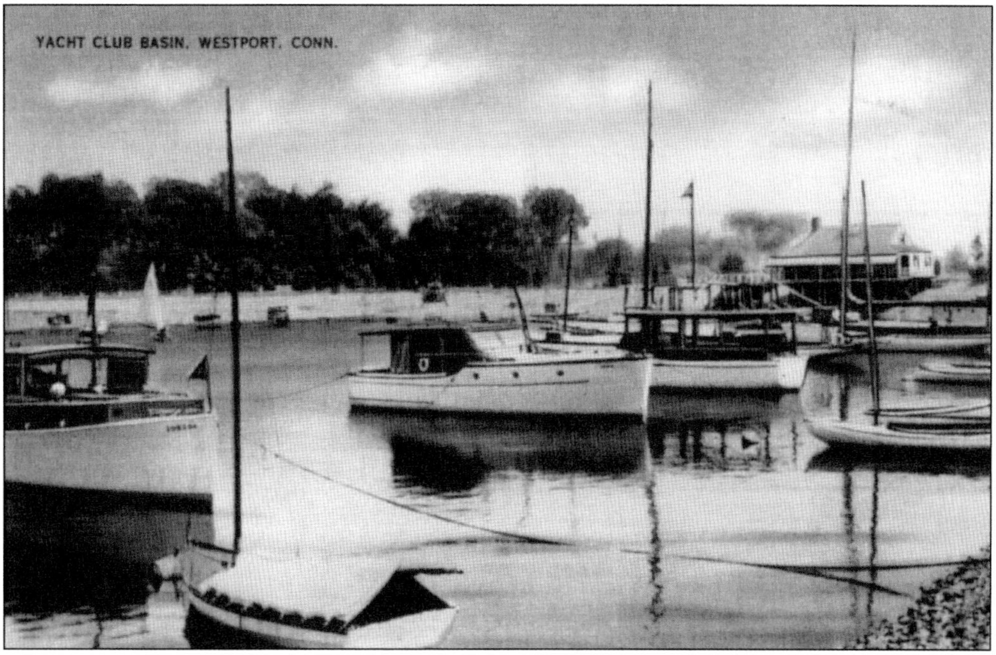

This card was mailed July 22, 1951, to Miss Bessie Jennings at the National Audubon Camp in Maine.

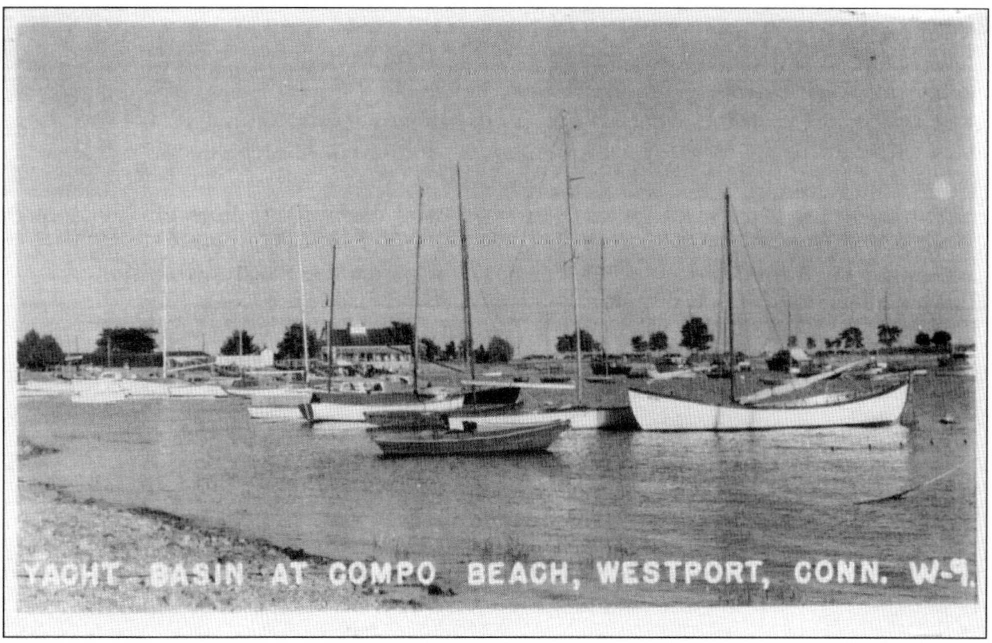

Fifty years ago, just as in the 1990s, many boats moored off Compo's shores.

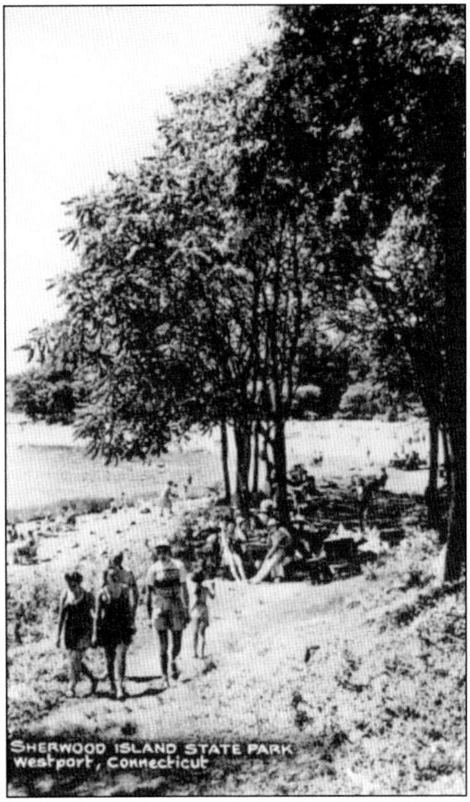

The following six cards are from a series showing Sherwood Island, Westport's state beach.

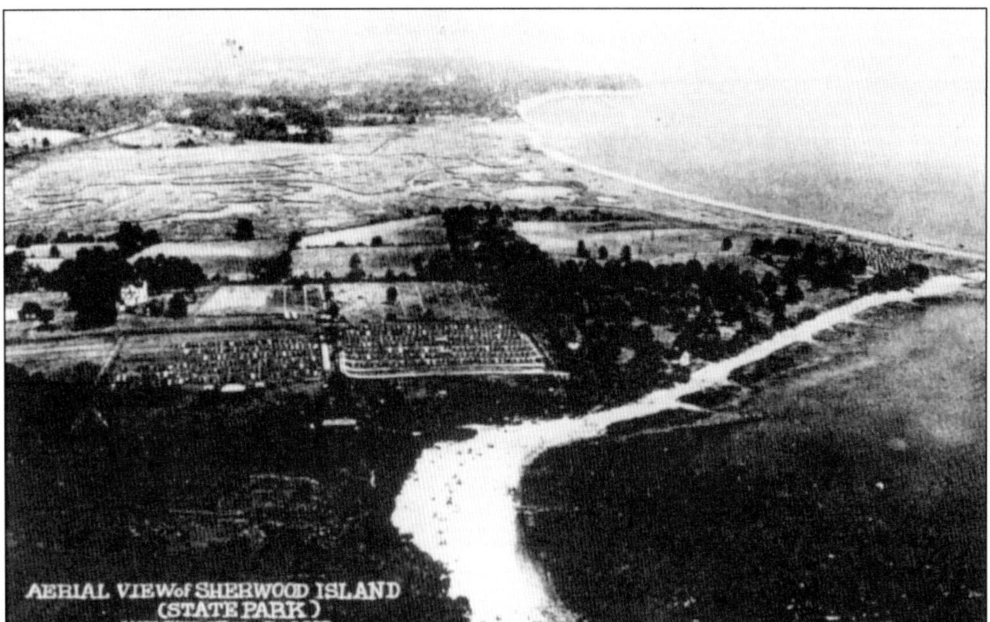

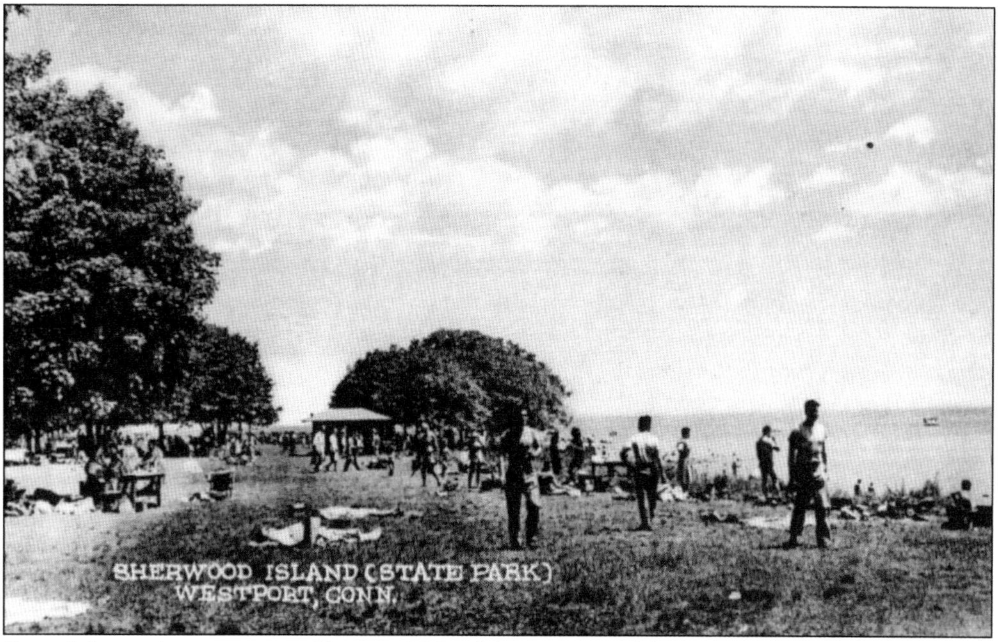

Crowds have always come to Sherwood Island from near and far . . .

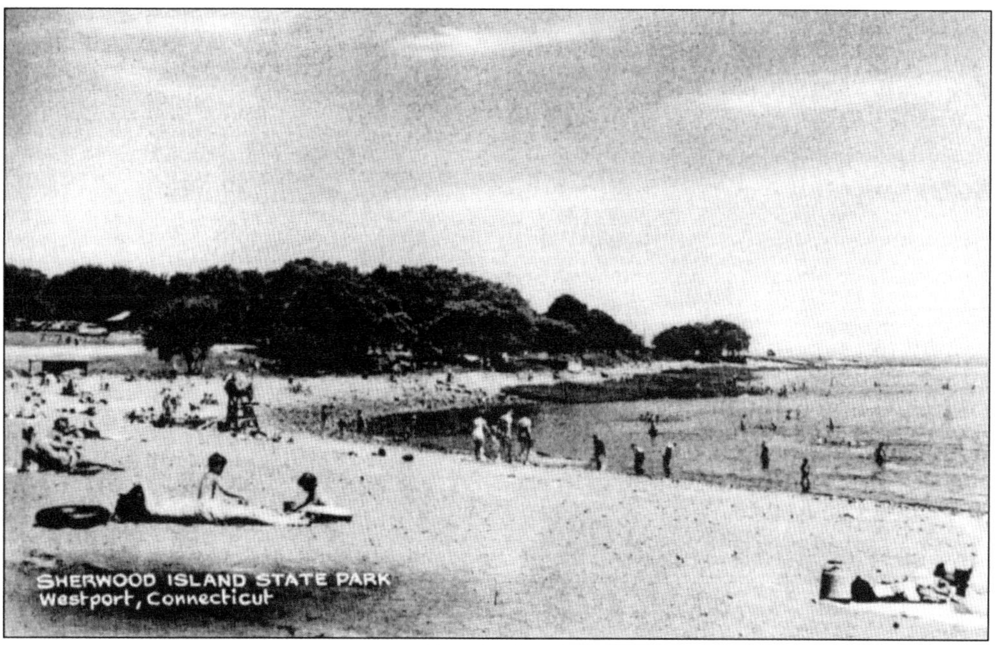

. . . to enjoy picnic areas as well as the beach at the first State-owned shoreline park.

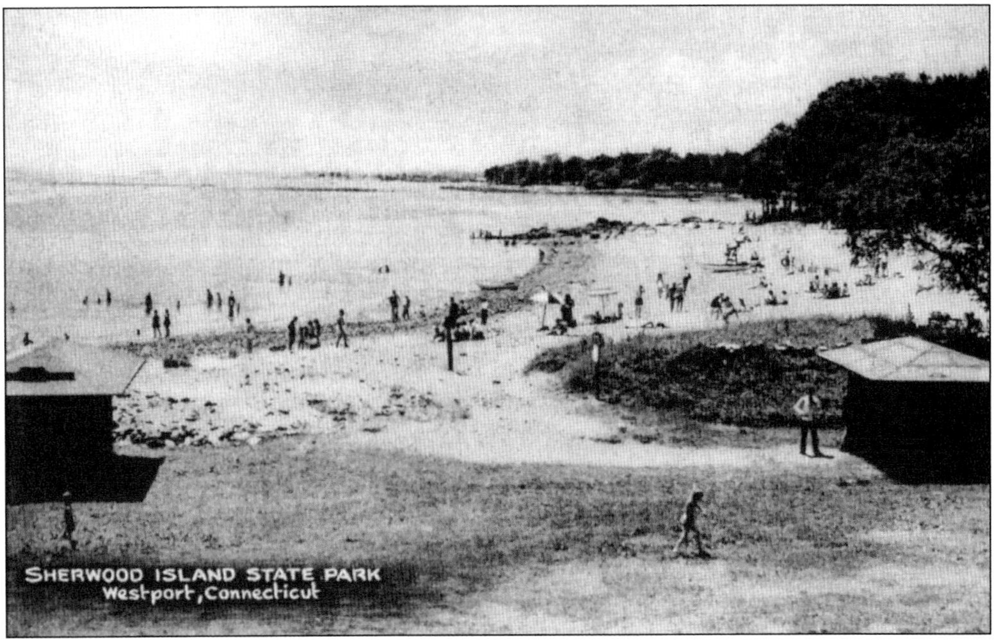

These are more views of the beach at Sherwood Island . . .

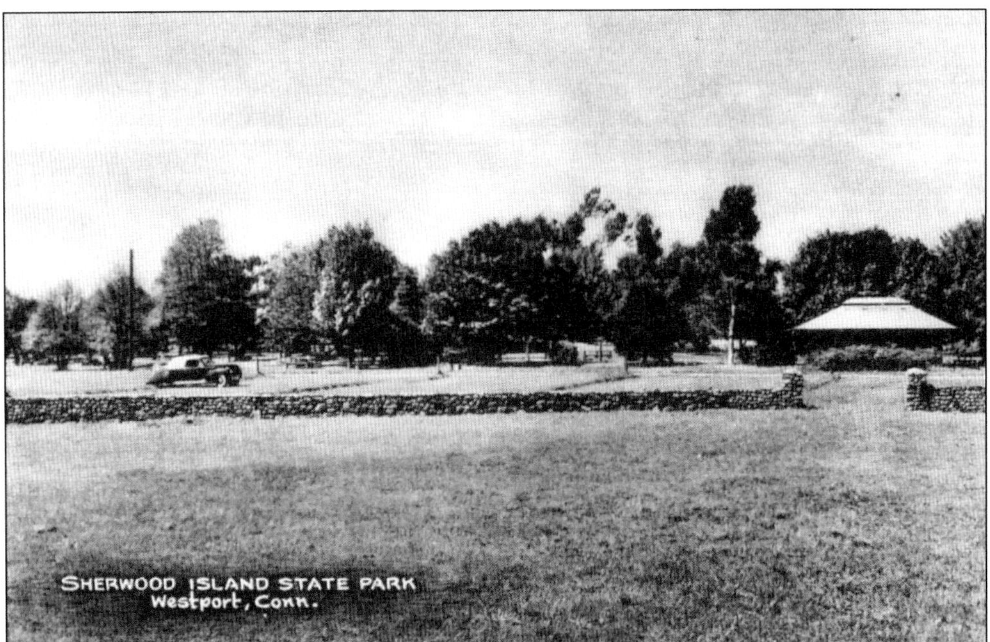

. . . and the acres of park land.

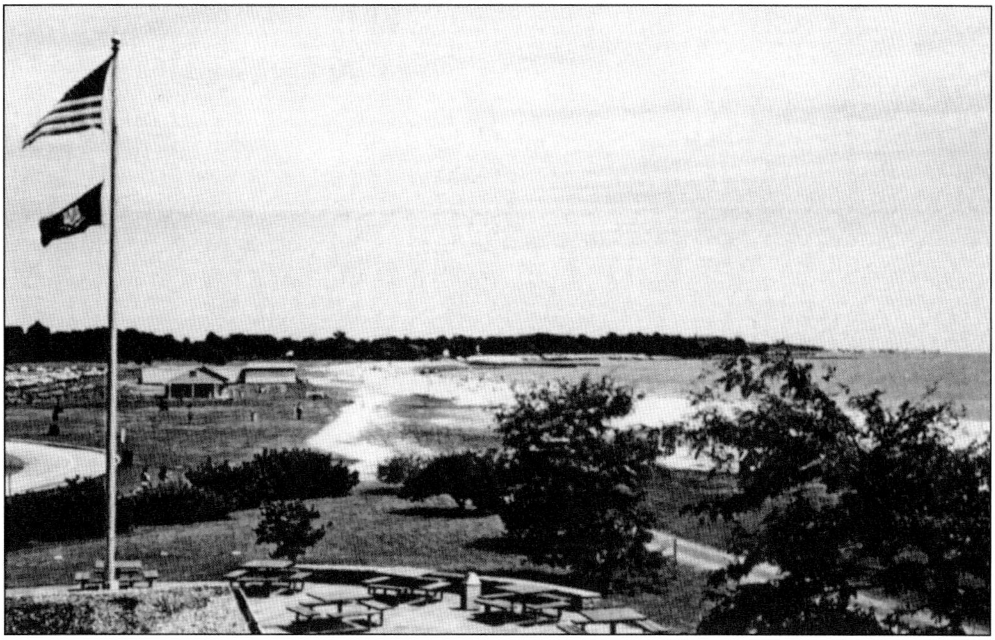

Mailed in 1975, this card, which cost 8¢ to mail, shows a Sherwood Island much like that seen in the 1990s.

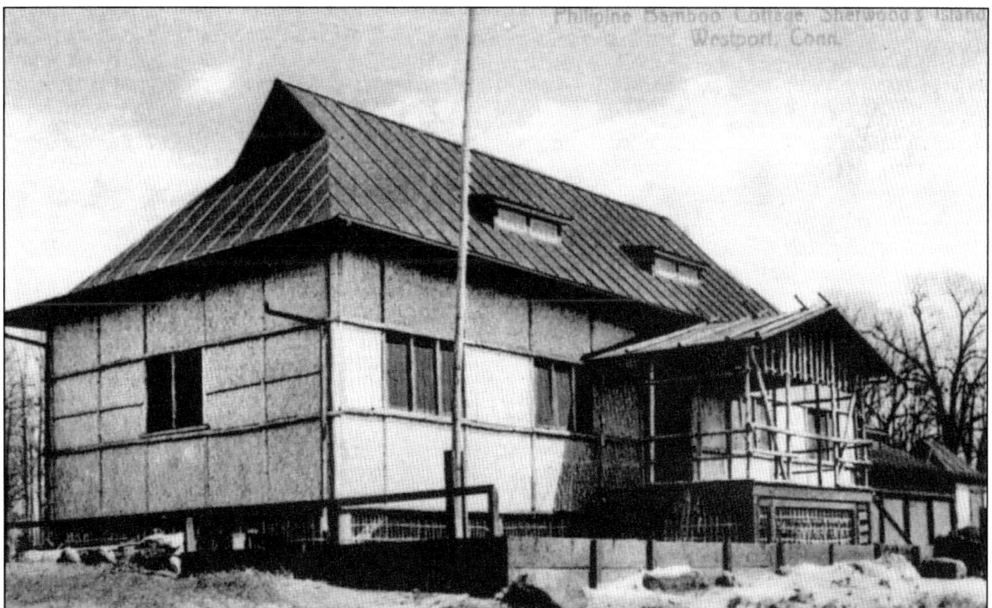

This card, mailed September 2, 1909, shows a bamboo cottage brought from the Philippines by President Bumpus of the Smithsonian. The structural outline, though none of the original bamboo, can be seen at Campo Cove next to Sherwood Island.

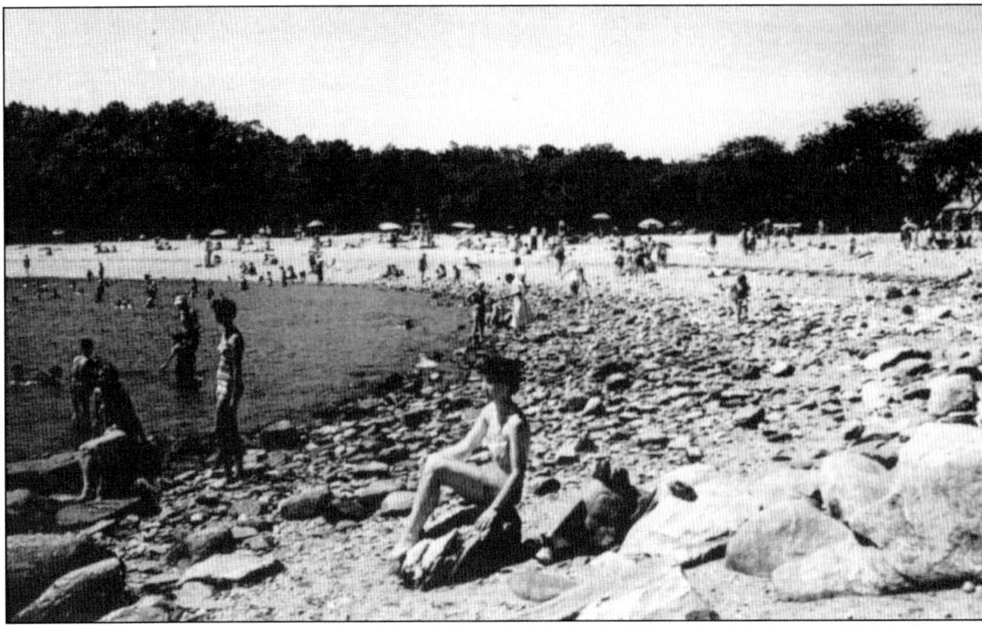

In 1956, "May" wrote that there was a band here but that she never goes in the water "because it's *dirty!*" . . .

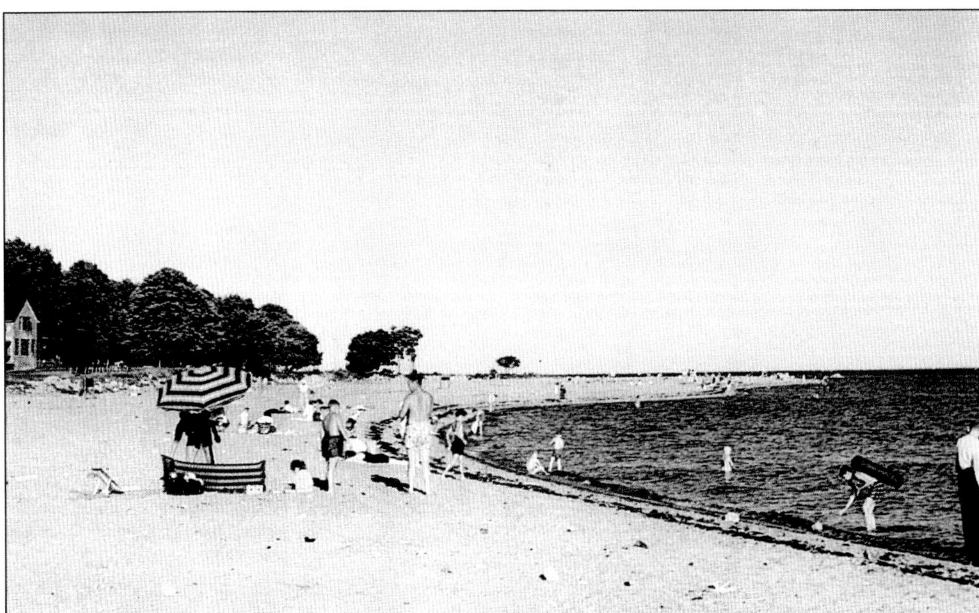

. . . but most cards show lots of people enjoying the water.

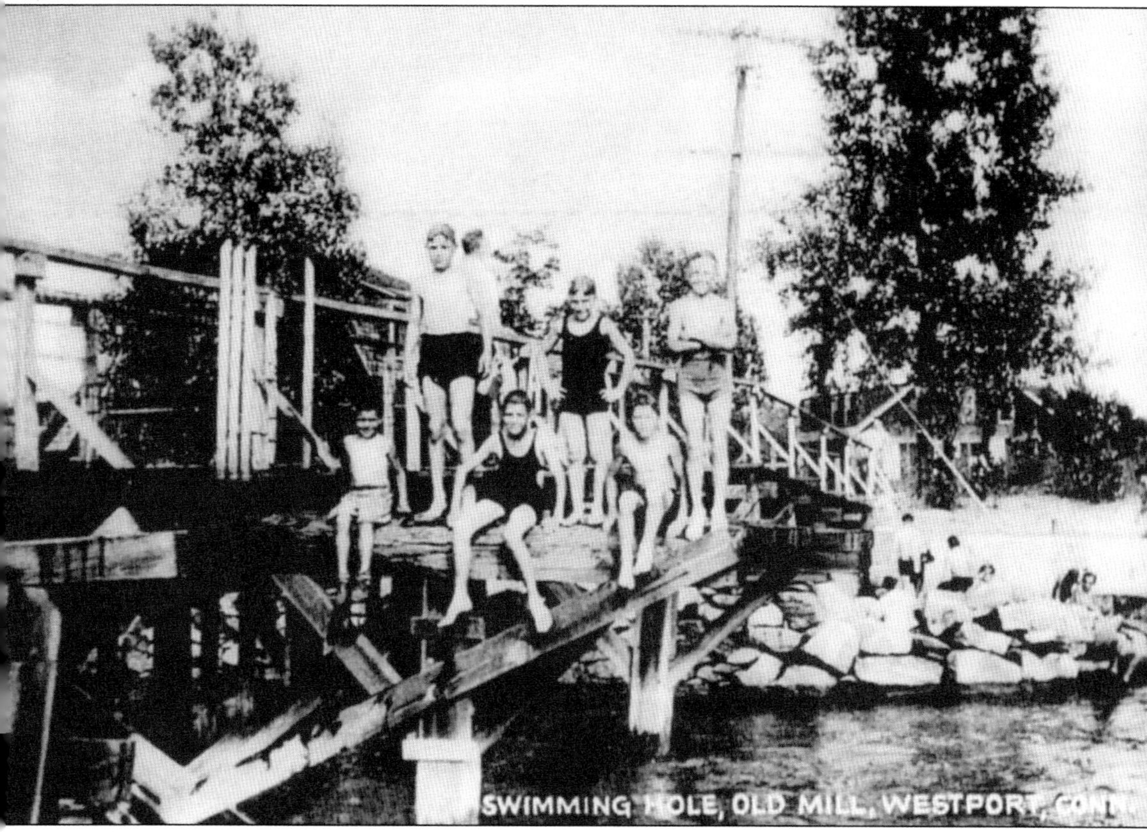

Public access to the waterfront in Westport has always provided summertime fun for young and old alike.

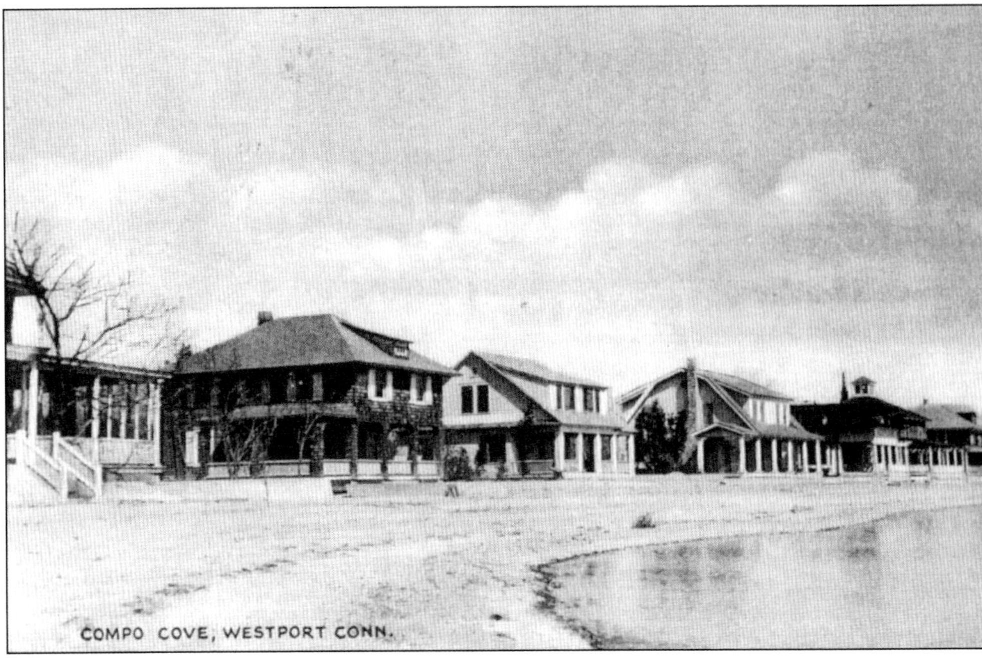

Still accessible only by foot, the summer houses at Compo Cove . . .

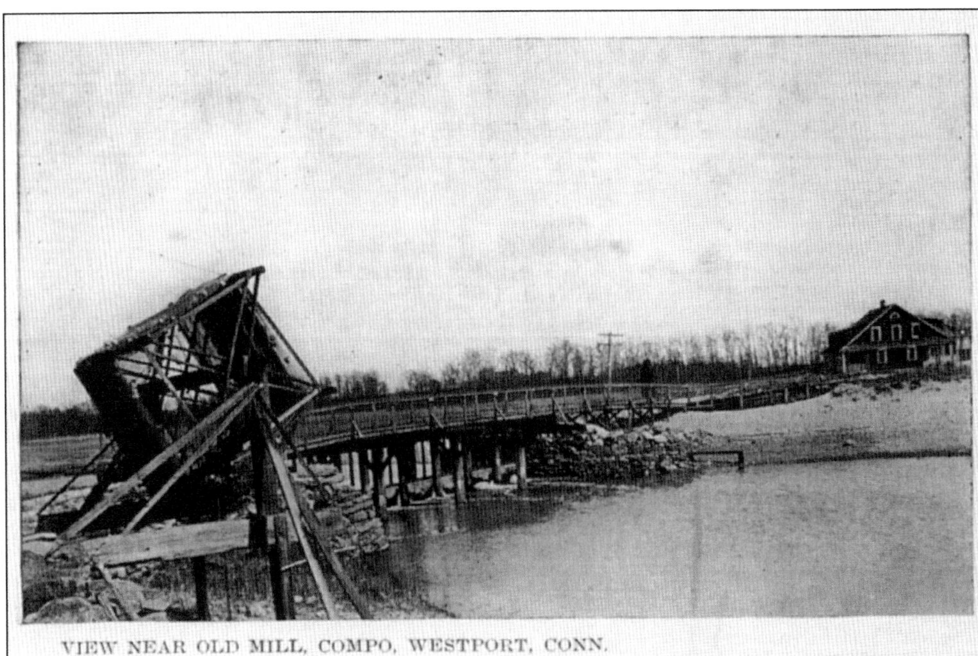

. . . are reached by crossing this bridge.

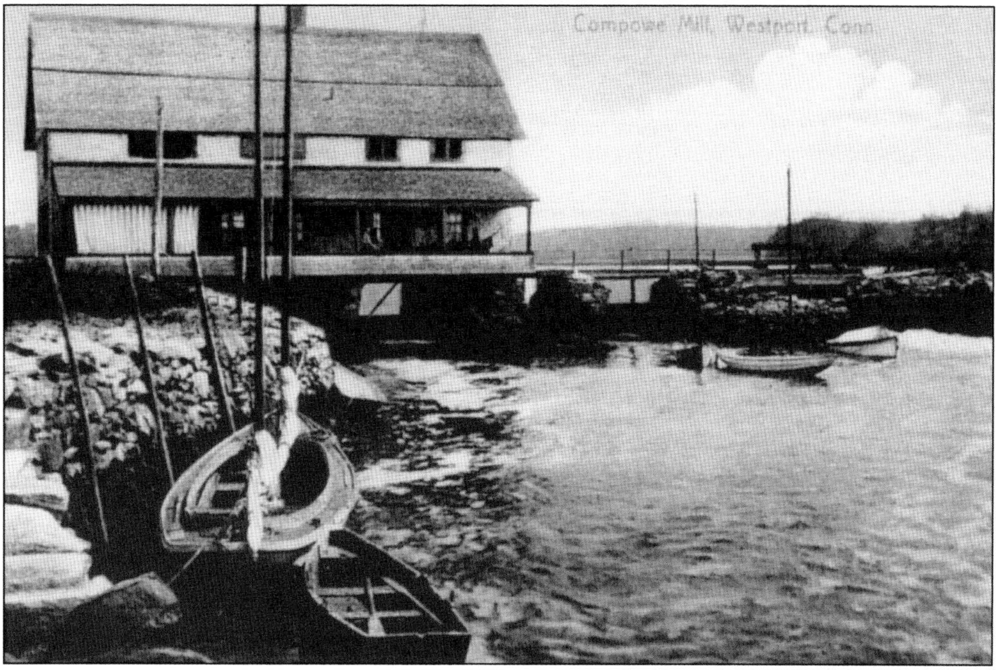

This house, built on the site of the tide mill, was pictured on a card sent on August 26, 1910, to South Norwalk.

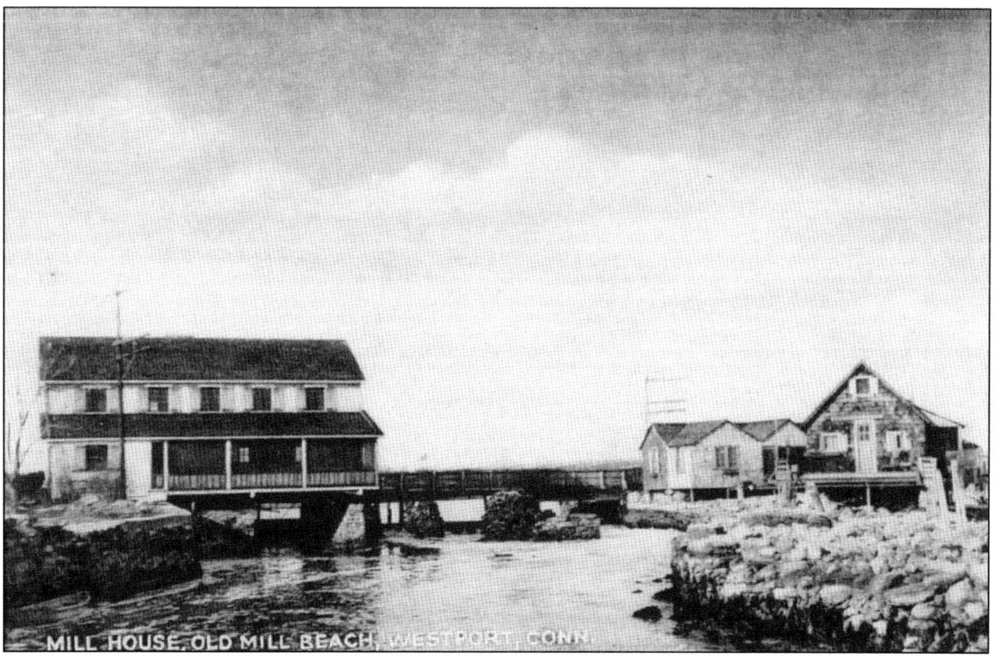

Later, Compo Cove summer houses had begun to be constructed. On the right are the three Hank Harrington cottages.

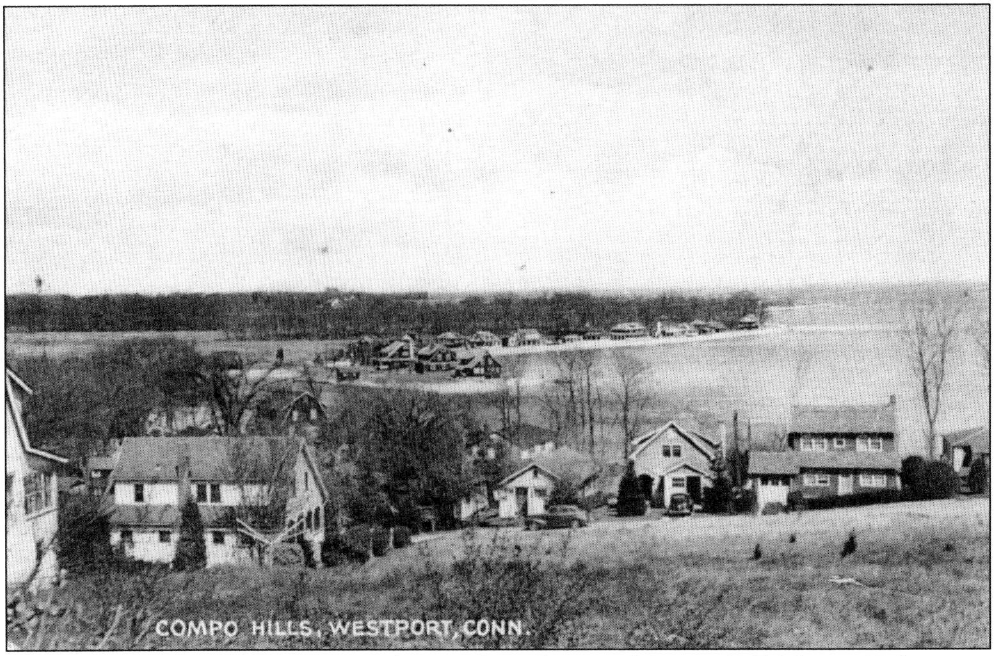

Here are two views of Compo Cove, this one from the top of Compo Hill (about 1936) . . .

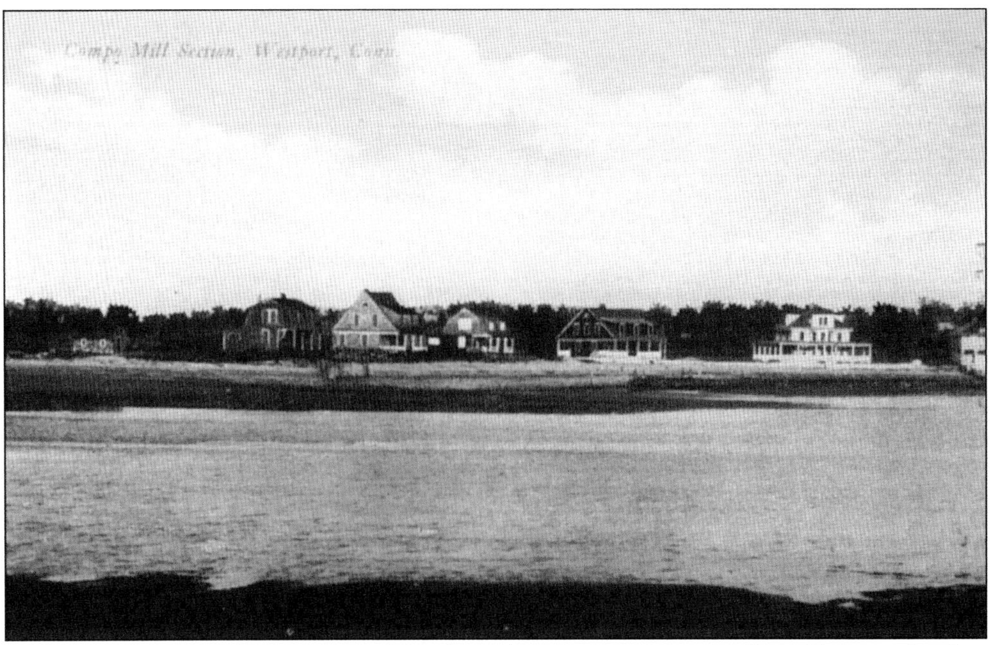

. . . and this from the water. No cars are allowed here to this day.

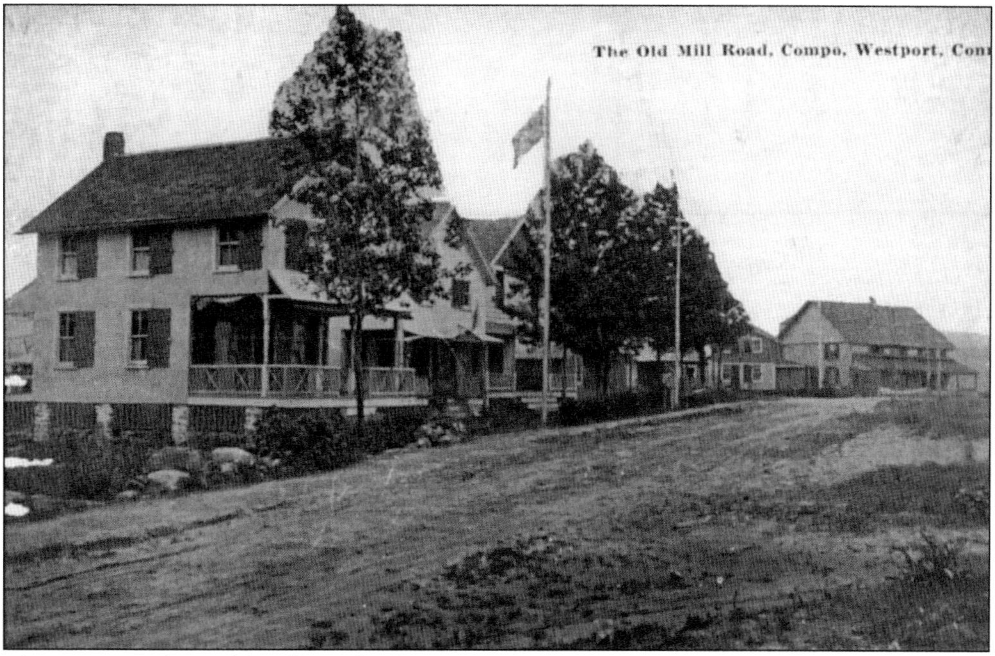

These cottages line Old Mill Road, where . . .

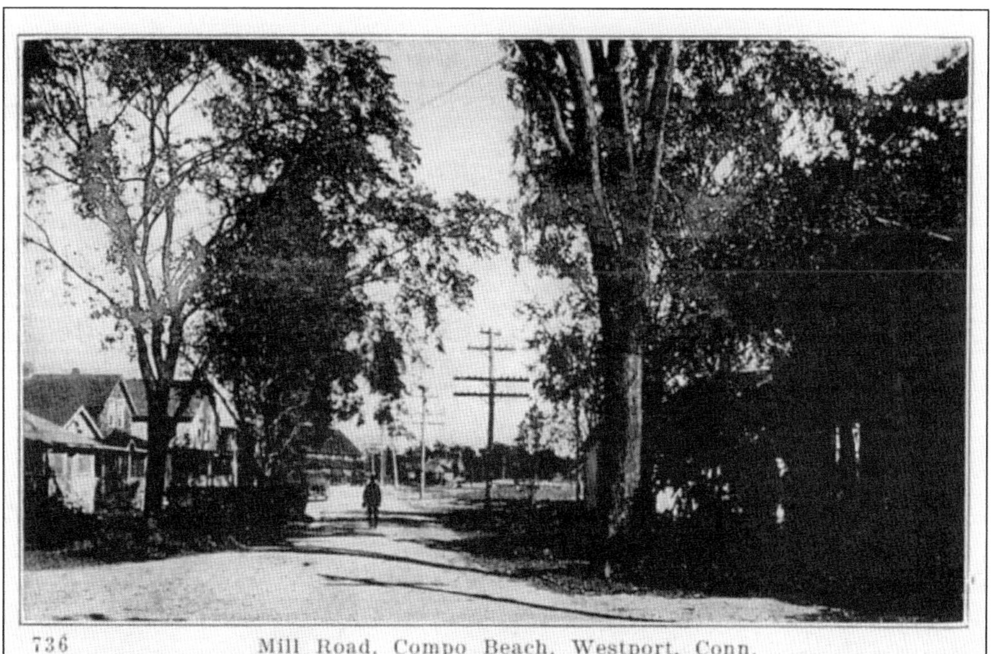

. . . the year-round residences were framed by trees.

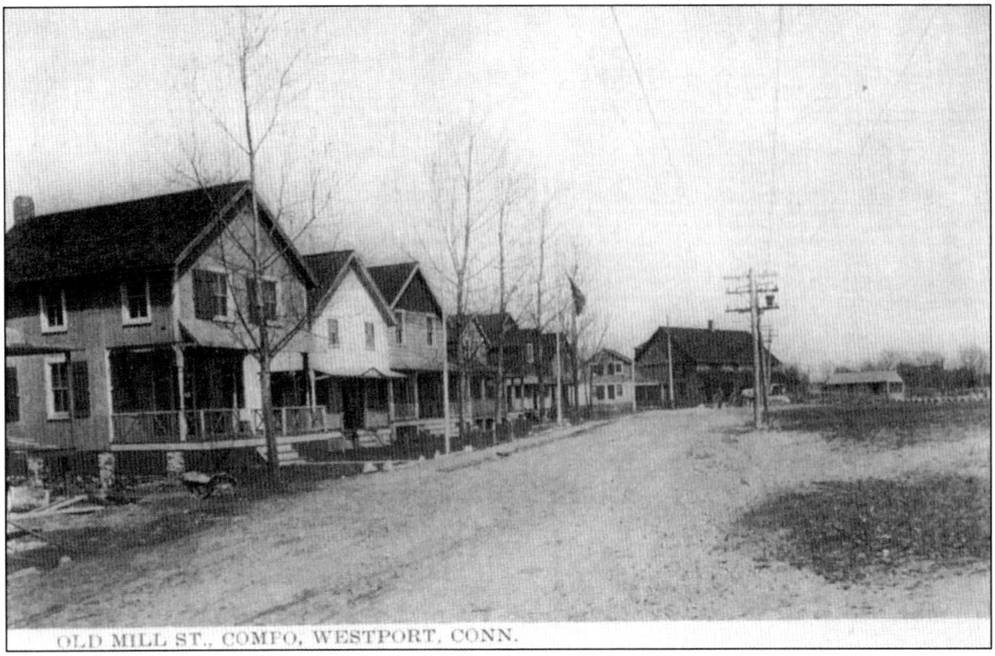

The houses on Old Mill Road enjoyed views of the water . . .

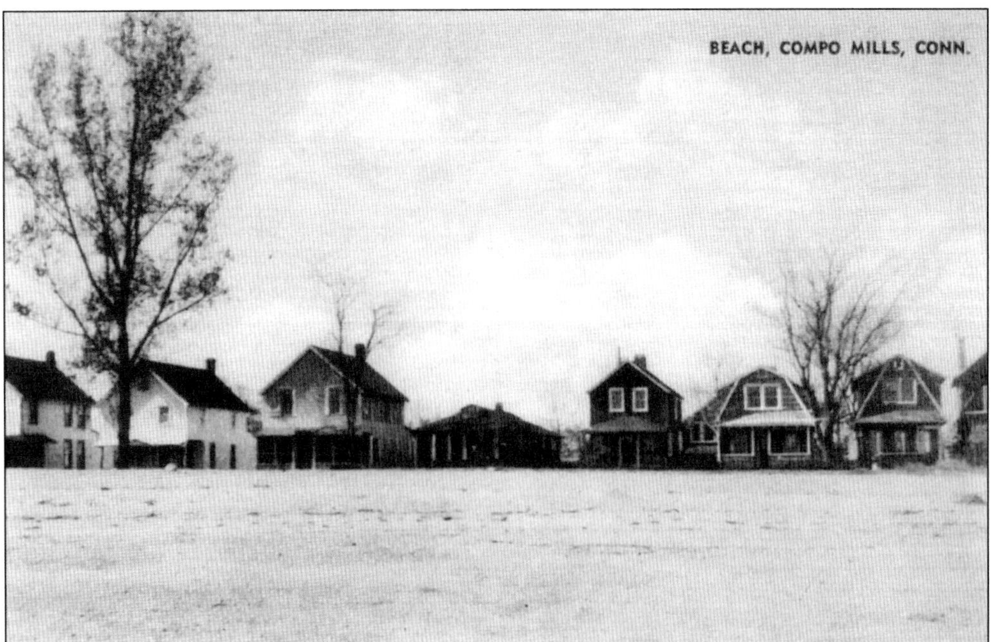

. . . and here are the houses, in turn, viewed from the water.

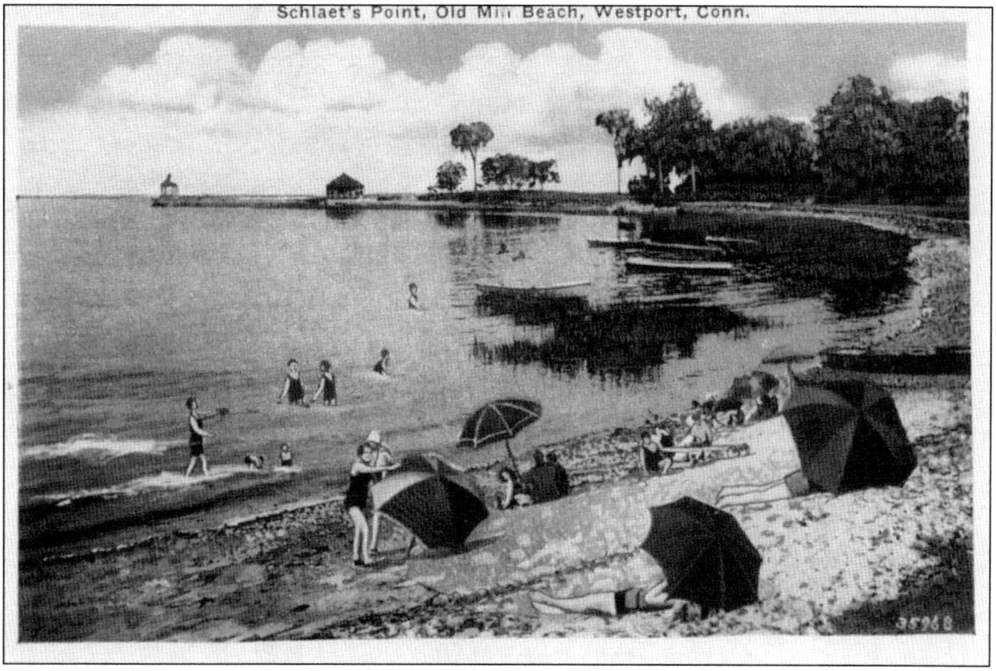

Here are two views of Old Mill beach looking west . . .

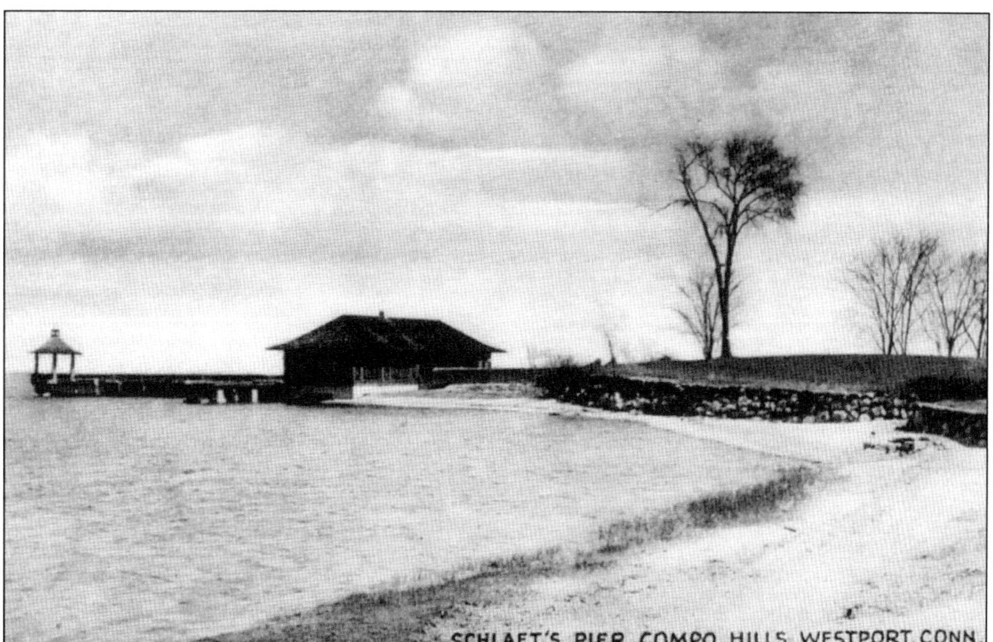

. . . where the stone wall is still holding back Long Island Sound.

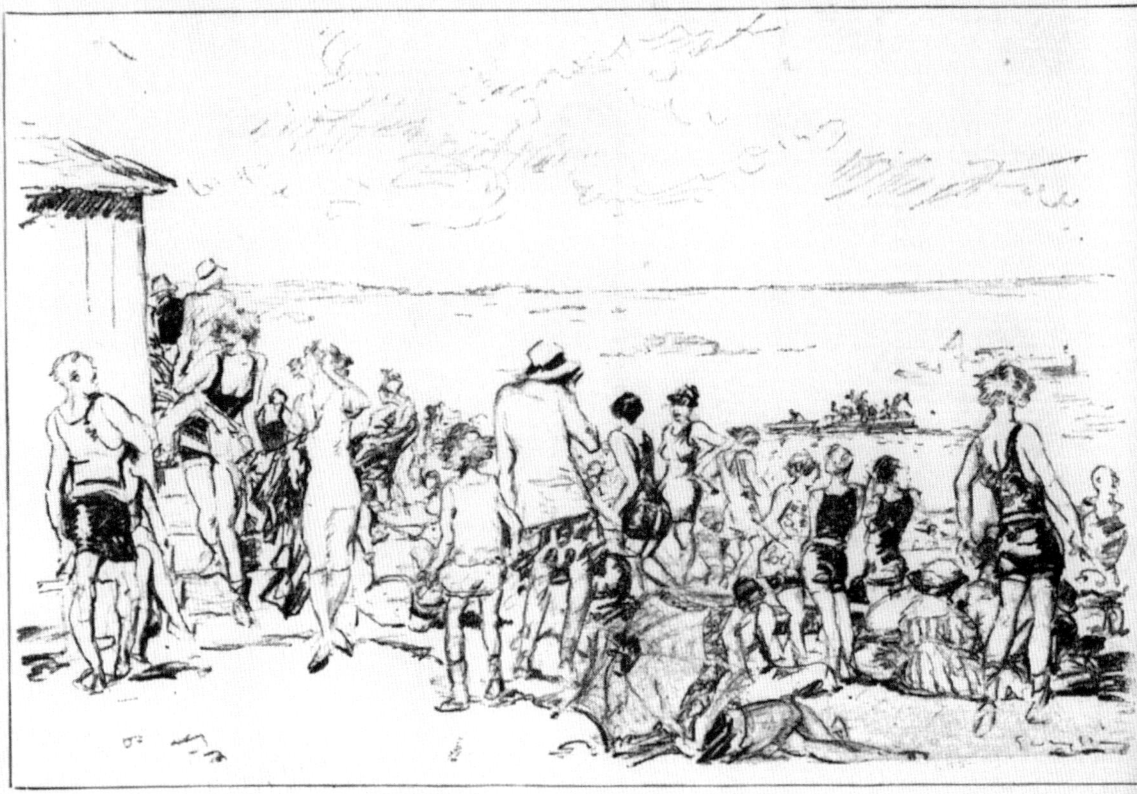

COMPO BEACH, WESTPORT, CONN.

Seven

WESTON:
TOWN AND COUNTRY

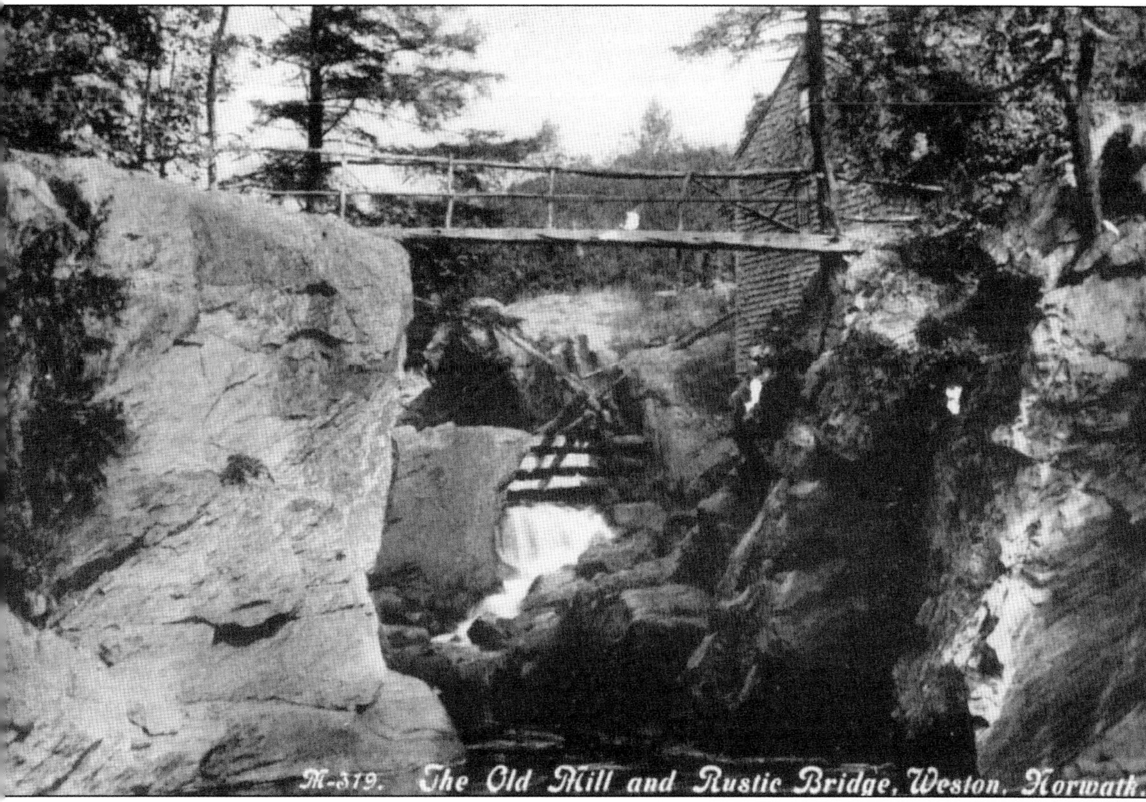

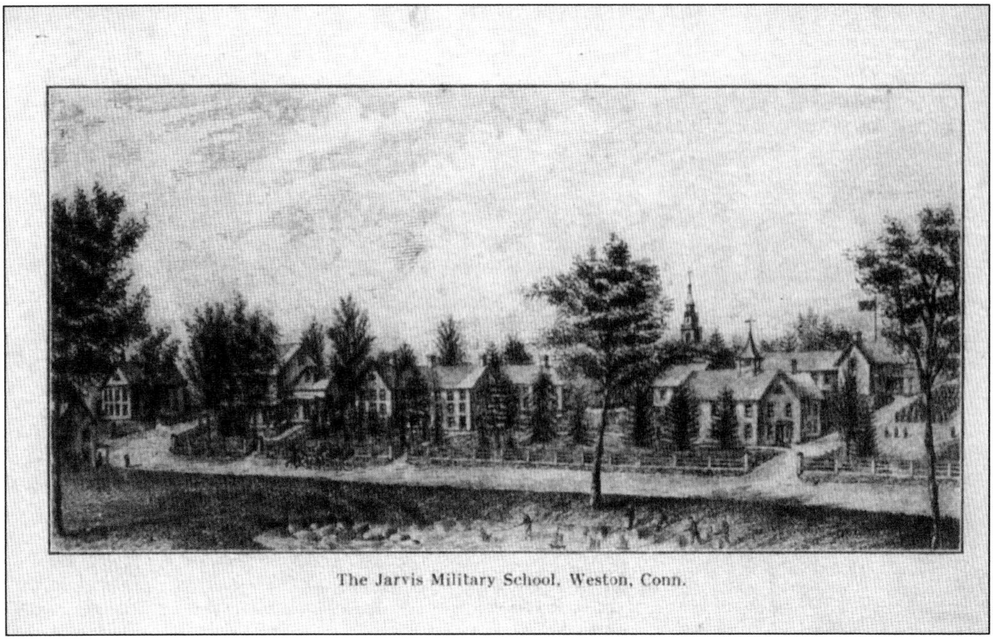

This card shows the Jarvis School, the site of an archeological study in the 1990s . . .

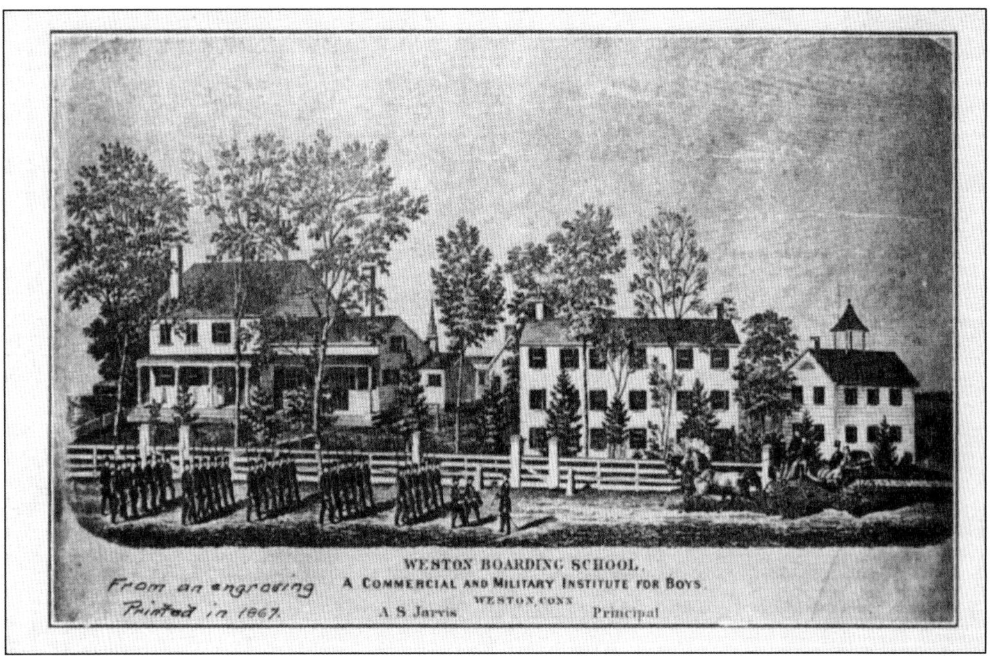

. . . which can still be seen at the southeast corner of Weston Road and Norfield Road.

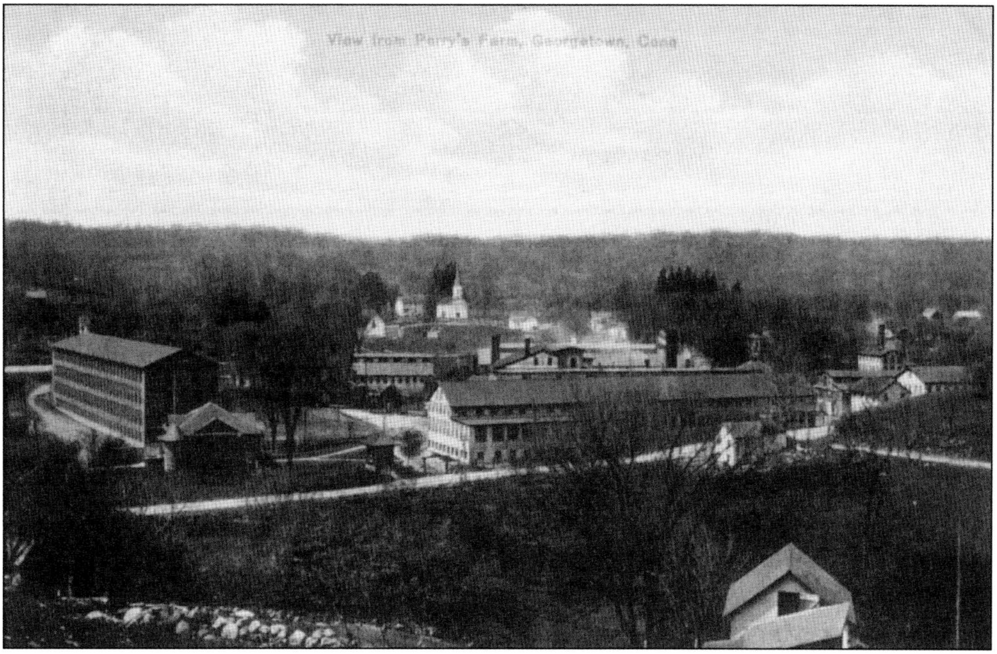

The Perry family had extensive holdings in Weston, from Georgetown Road to north of Valley Forge.

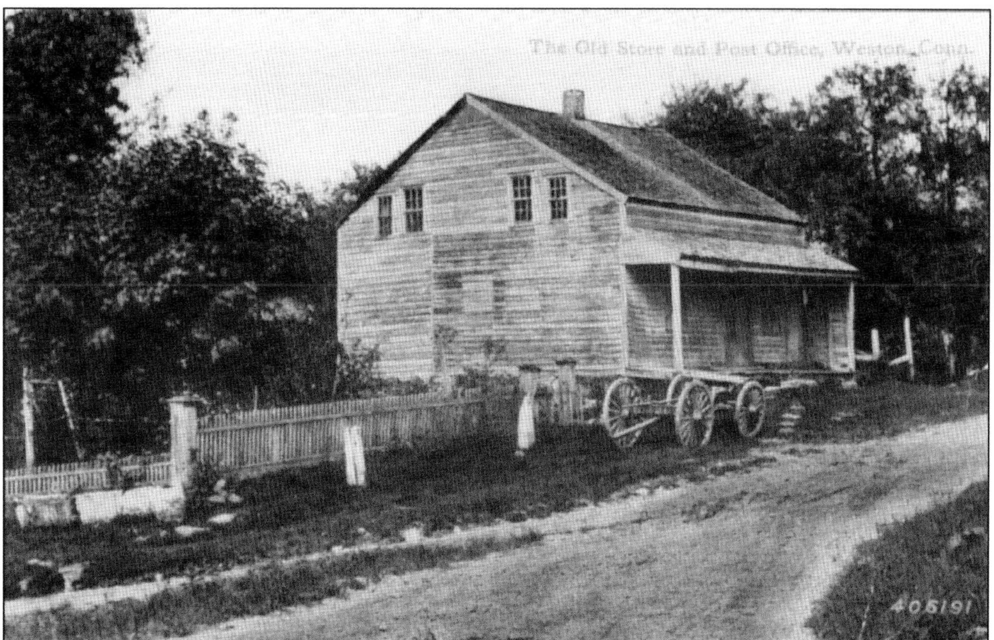

This card, showing the Weston General Store, still present on Weston Road, was mailed December 28, 1915.

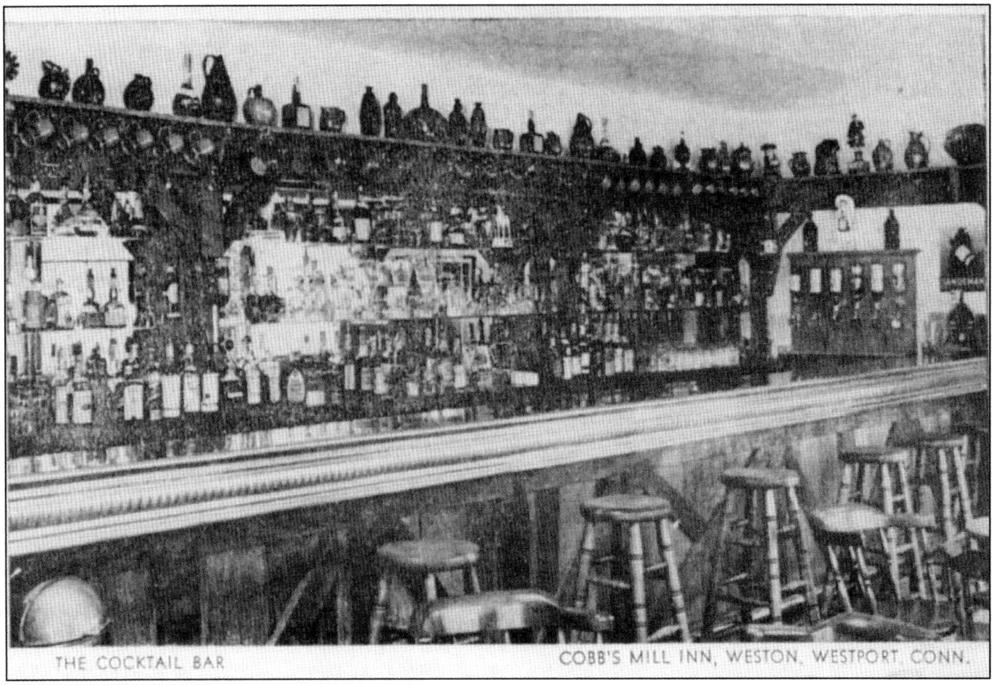

The Cobb's Mill bar was salvaged from the luxury liner *Normandie*, which sank in the 1940s.

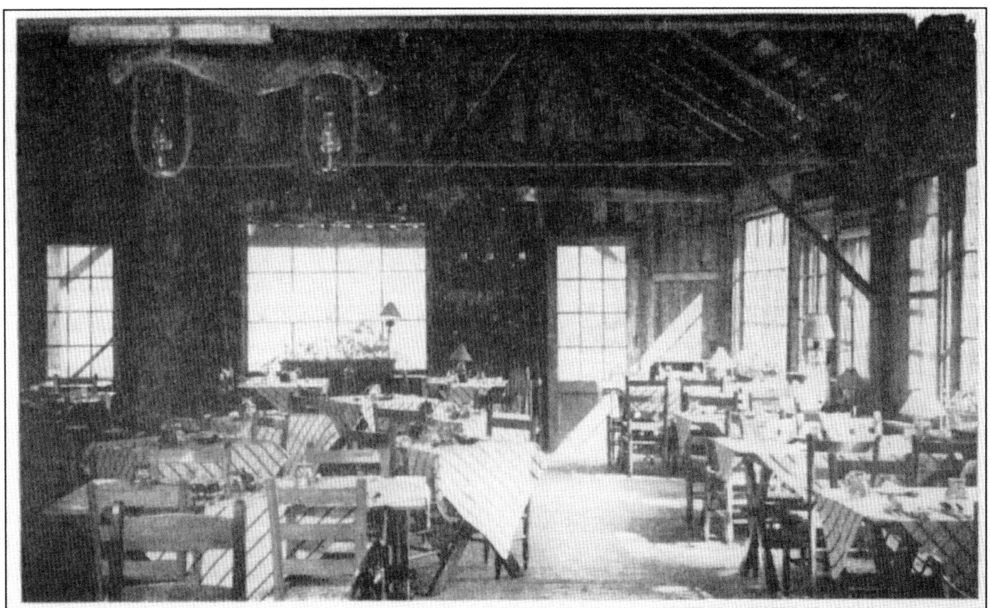

Cobb's Mill had the capacity to seat over 400 people.

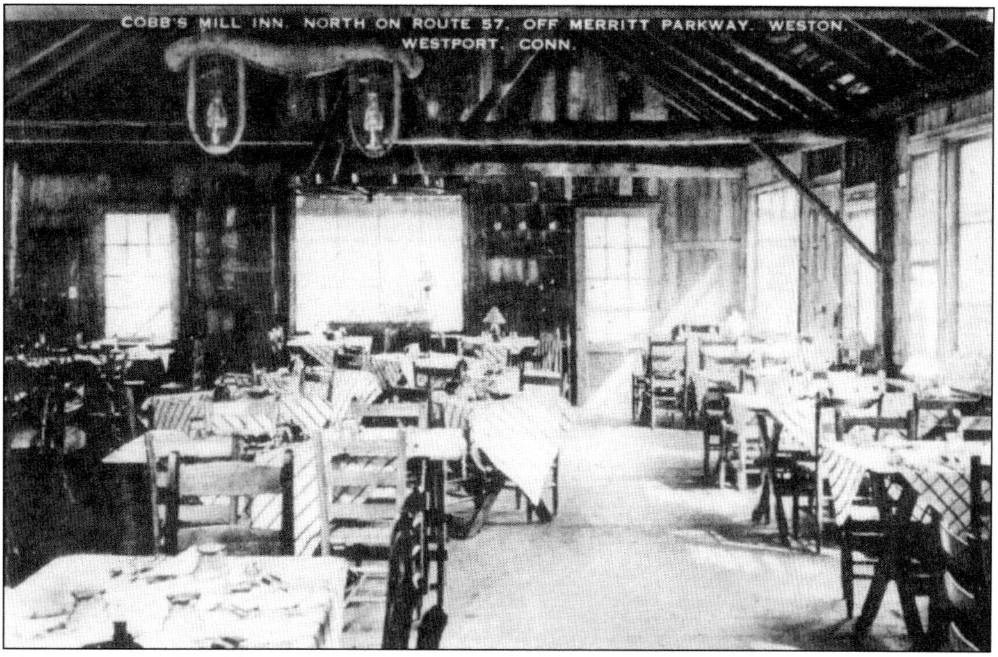

These scenes of Cobb's Mill remained the same from July 7, 1949, when this card was mailed . . .

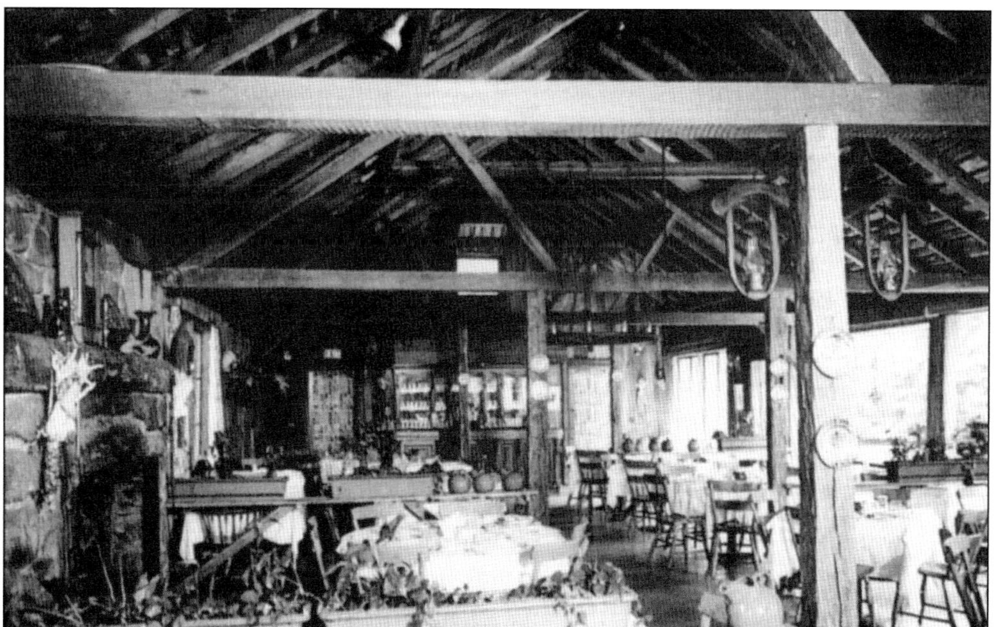

. . . until the early 1950s.

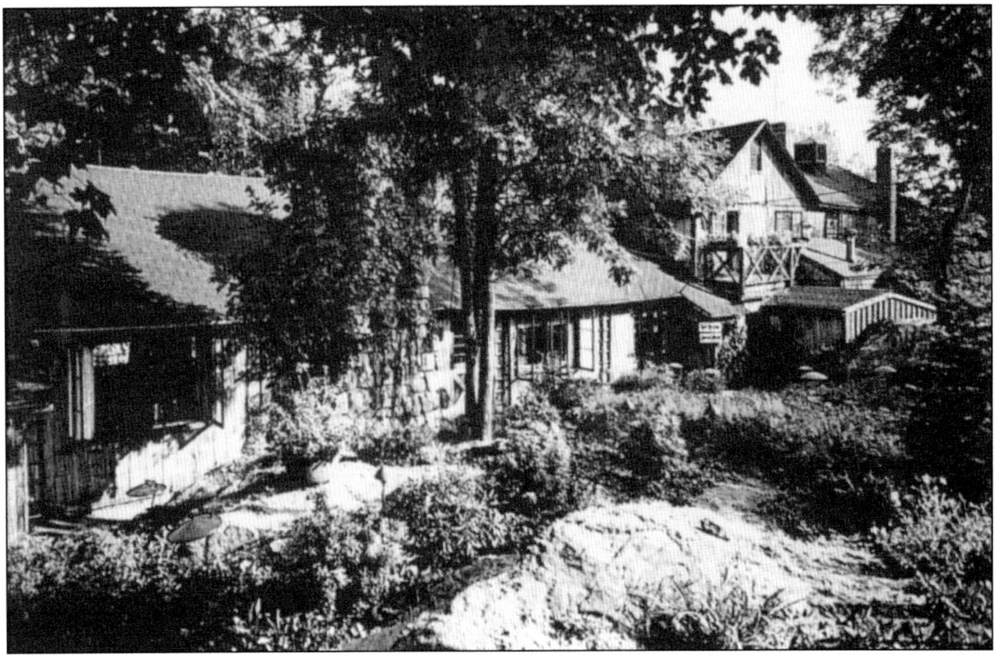

Since June 1952, Cobb's Mill . . .

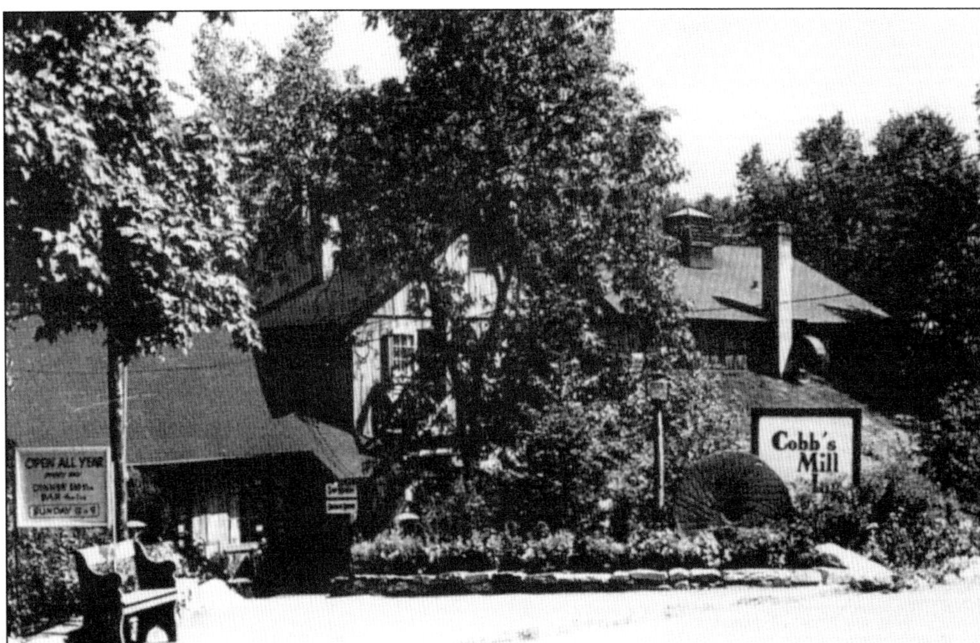

. . . has been a full-service restaurant.

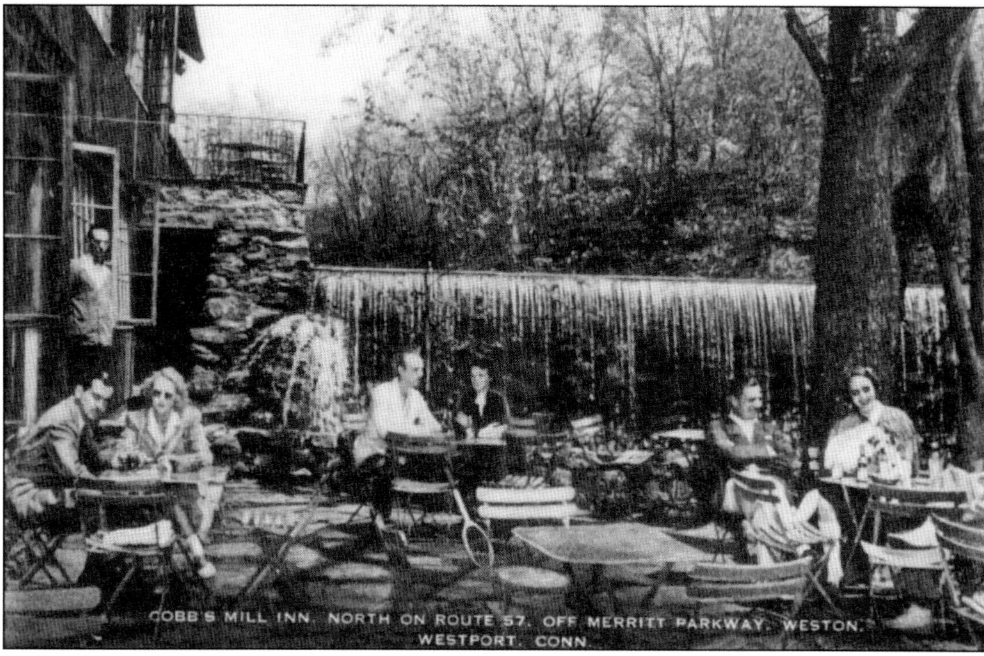

Before that, it was an antique store and tea room . . .

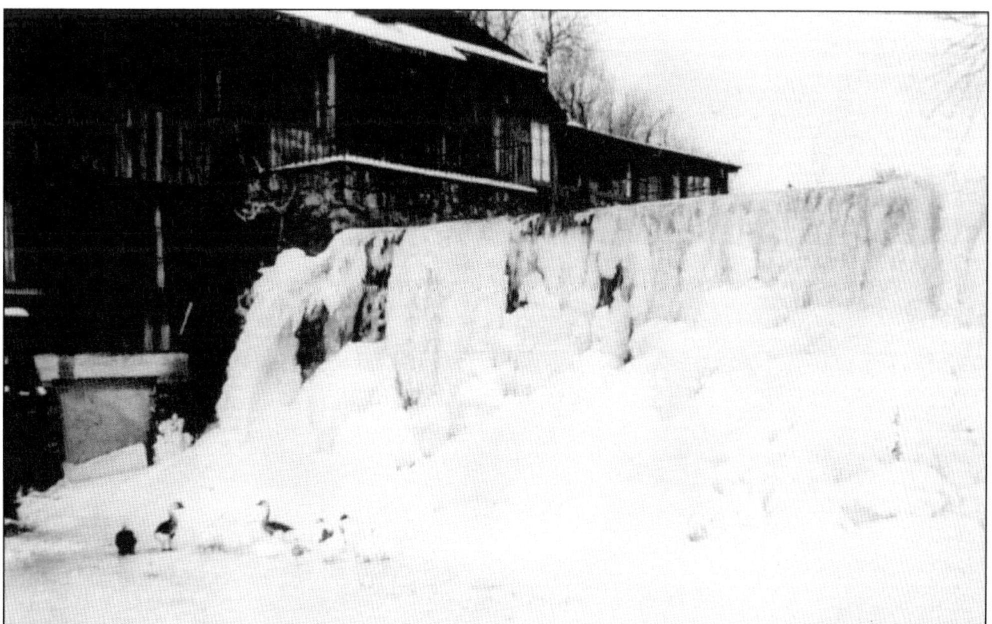
. . . and before that, it was owned by Frank Cobb, editor-in-chief of the *New York World* newspaper.

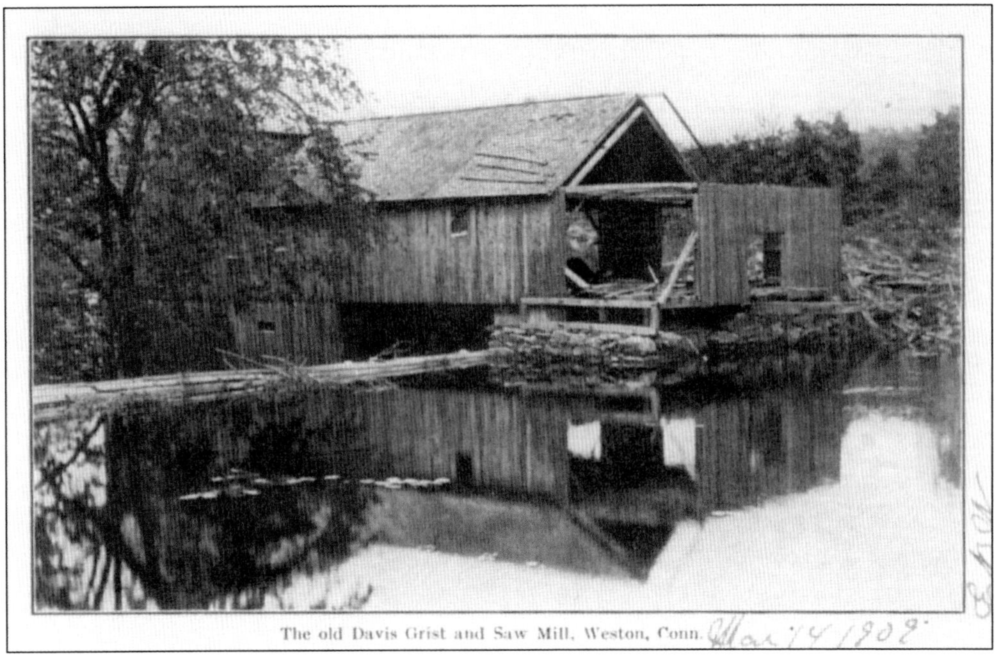

This is what Cobb's Mill looked like in 1909.

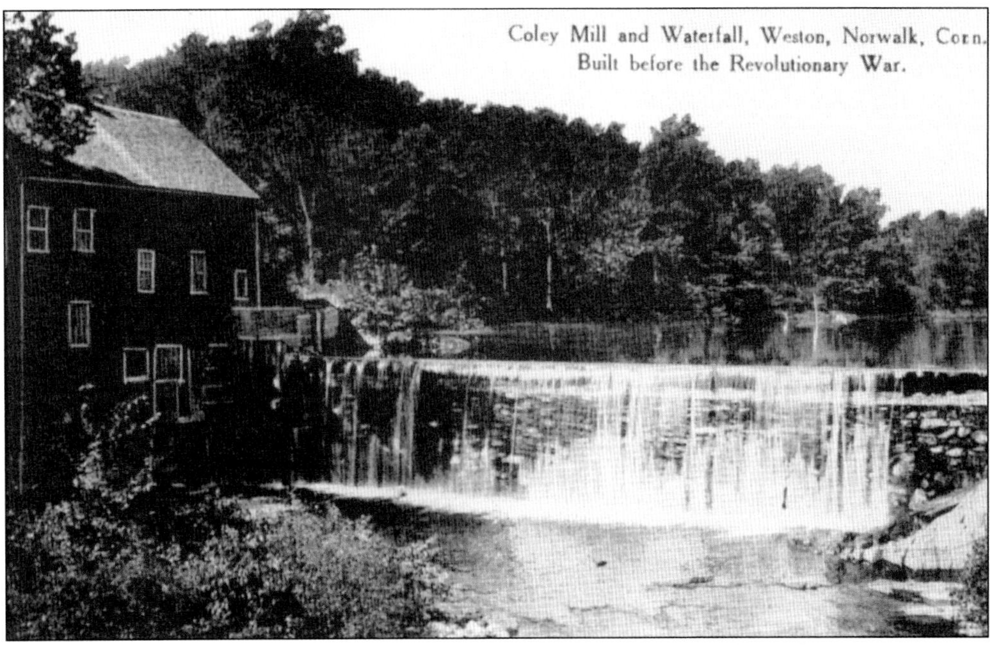

The Coley family, an important name in Weston, owned this mill in the 19th century.

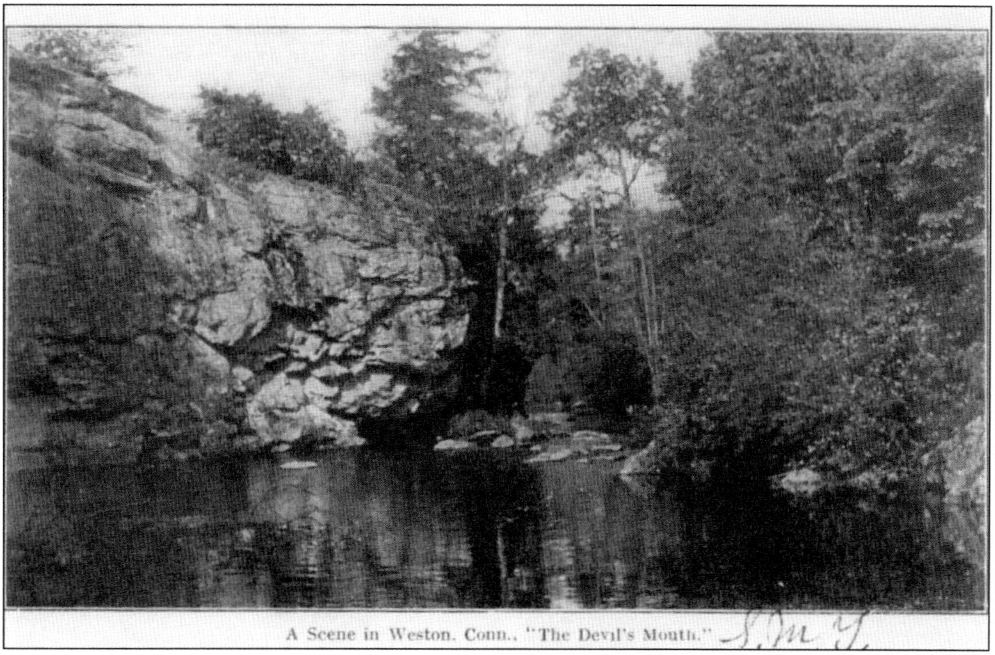

This card, showing what we now know as Devil's Den, was mailed November 6, 1909.

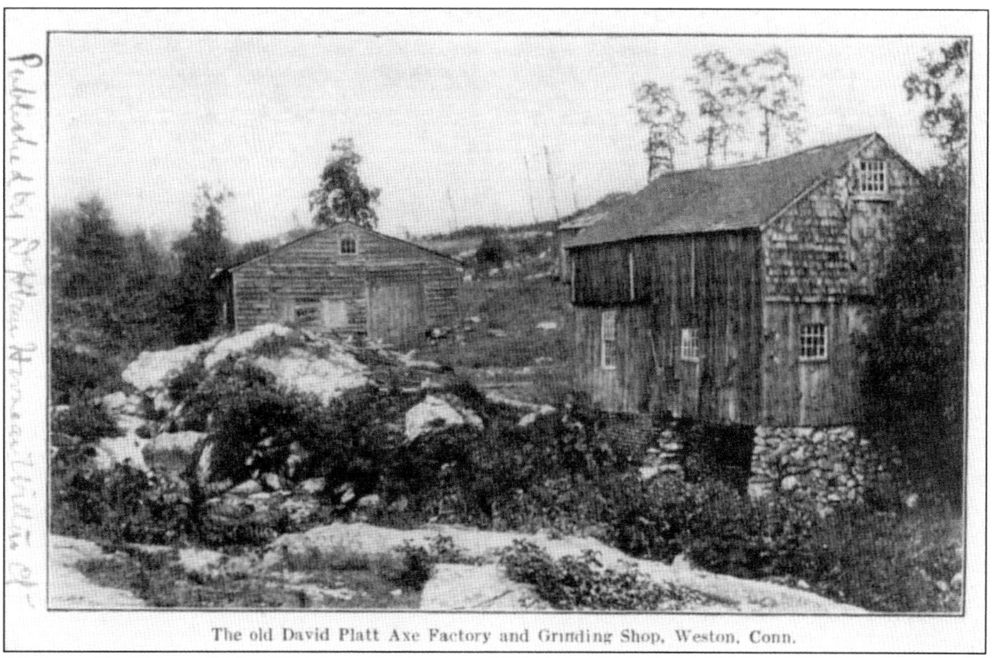

This card was mailed on May 23, 1911. The David Platt ax factory was located near Goodhill Road.

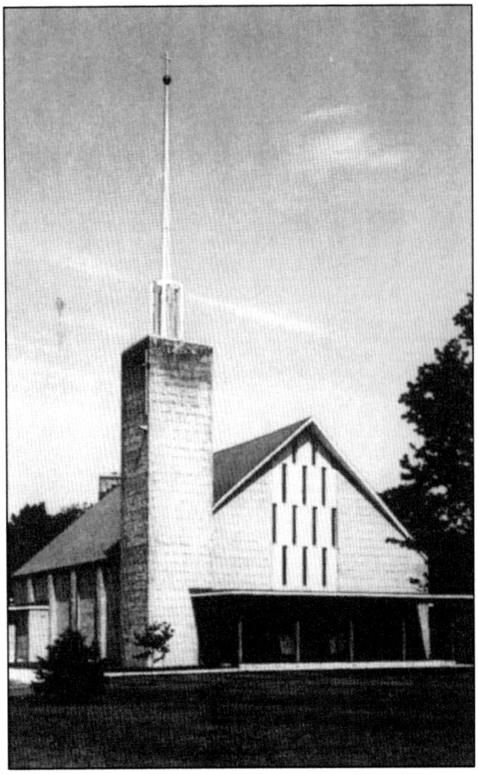

Two very different churches stand on Norfield Road: St. Francis of Assisi Church . . .

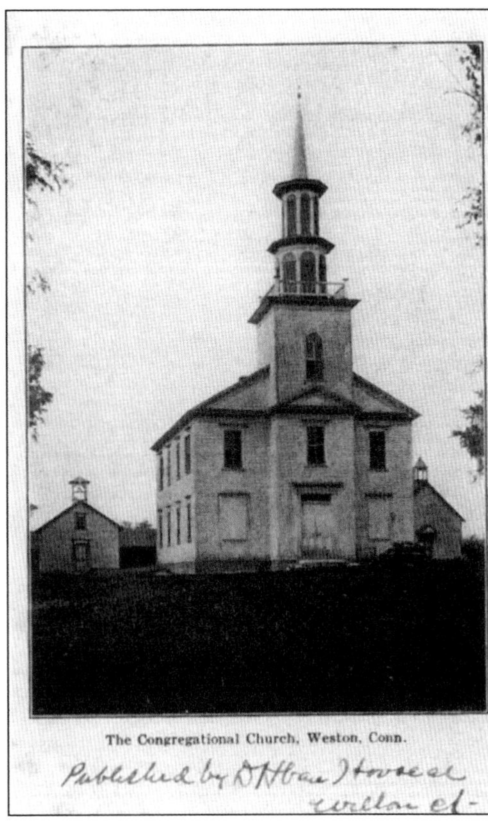

. . . and the Norfield Congregational Church.

Eight

Odd Lots

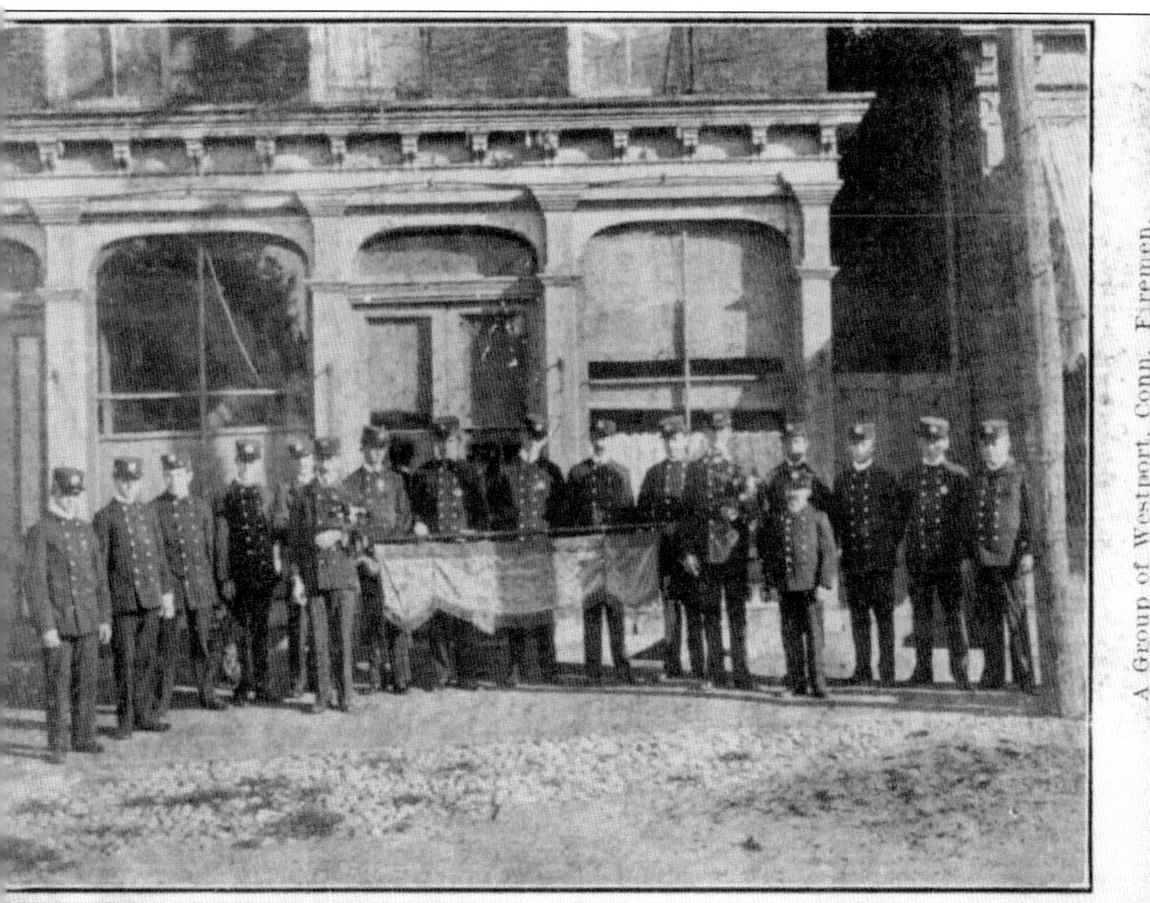

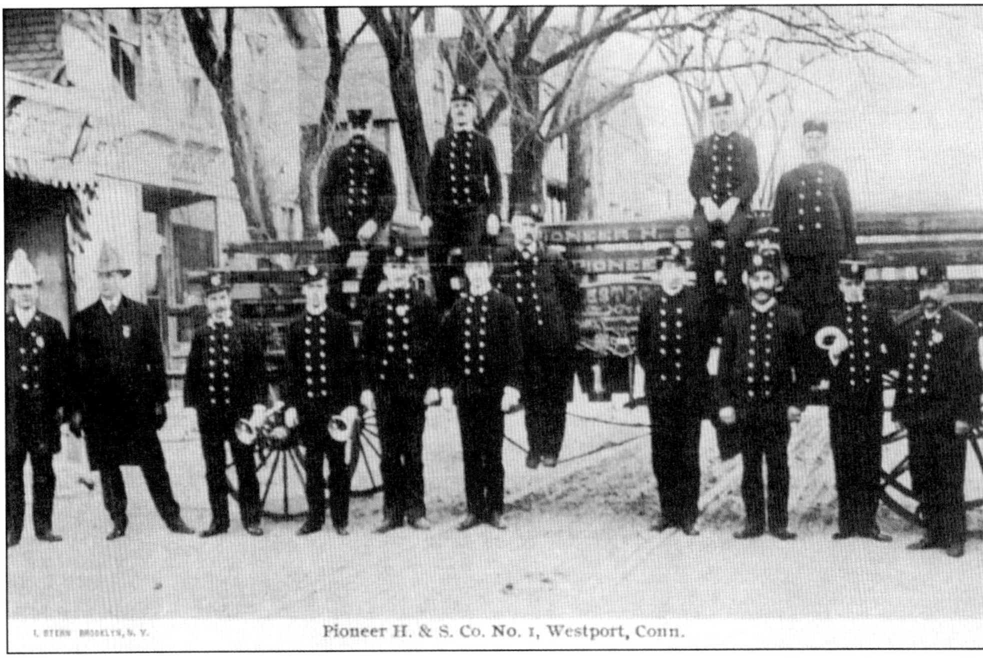

The first hook and ladder company was formed in 1874 by Ambrose Hurlbutt, who owned a nearby block of stores.

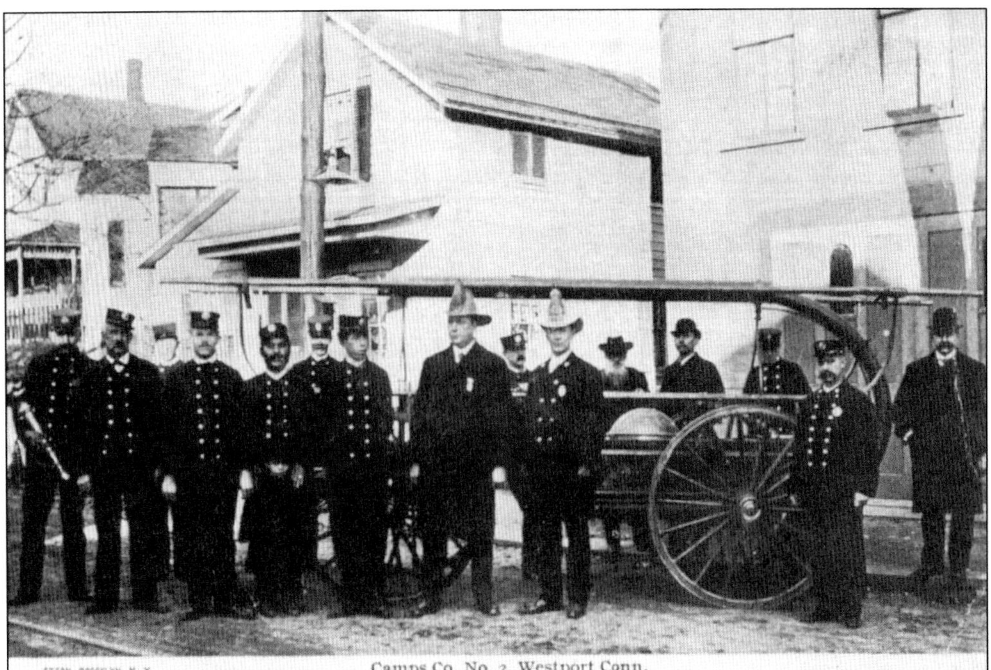

Compo (not "Camps") Engine Co. No. 2 (chartered in 1859), currently on the Post Road, was previously housed in the center part of the current YMCA.

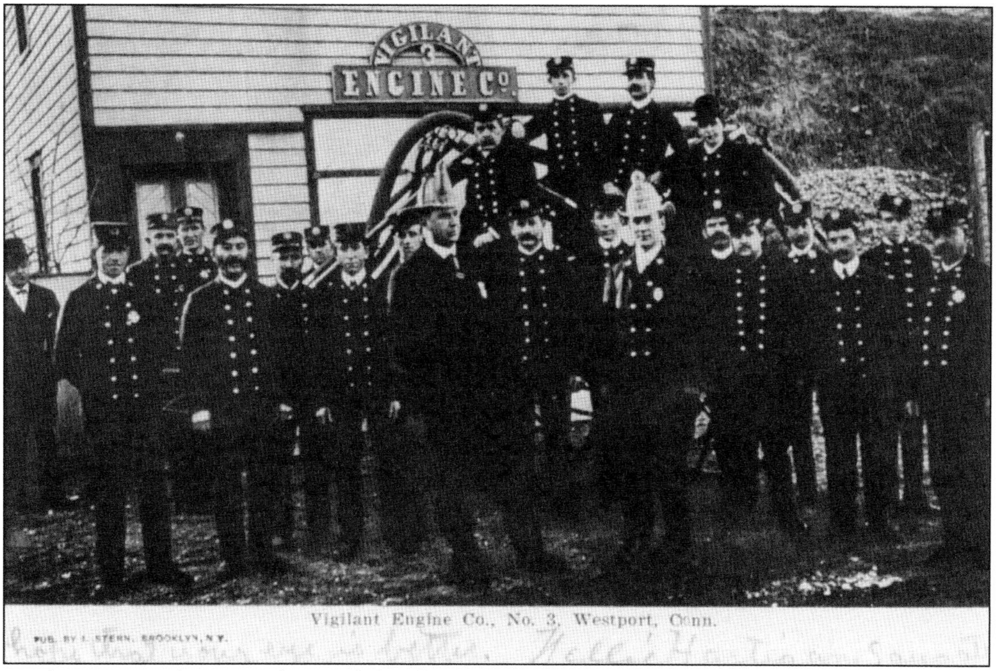

Vigilant No. 3, shown in this card dated October 20, 1906, was housed on Wilton Road. They later moved across the street to the building which, in the 1990s, now houses a pizza restaurant.

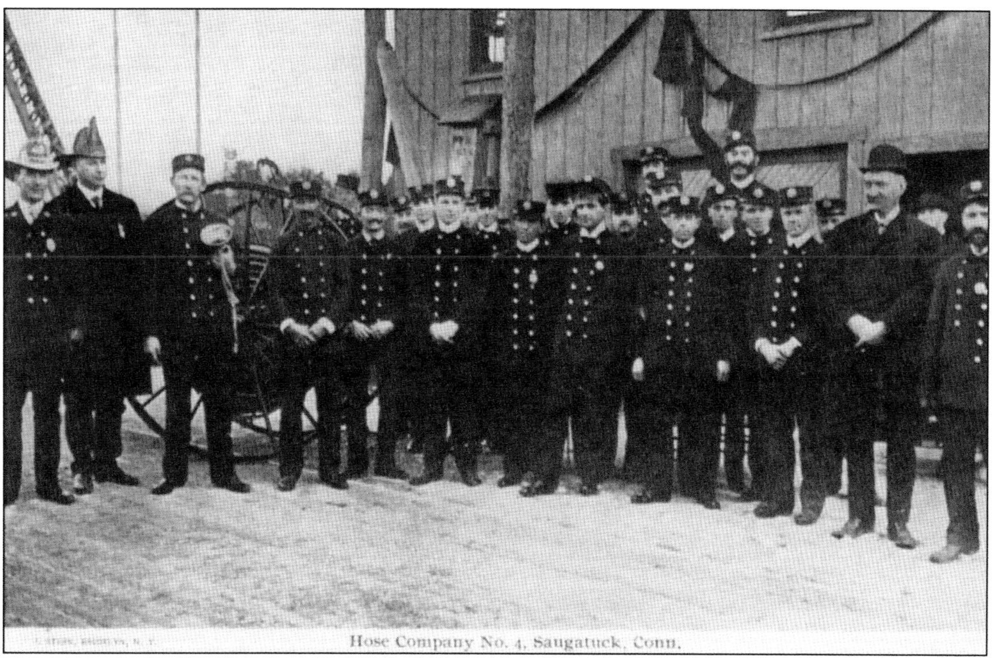

Founded in 1880, Saugatuck No. 4 was located on Bridge Street.

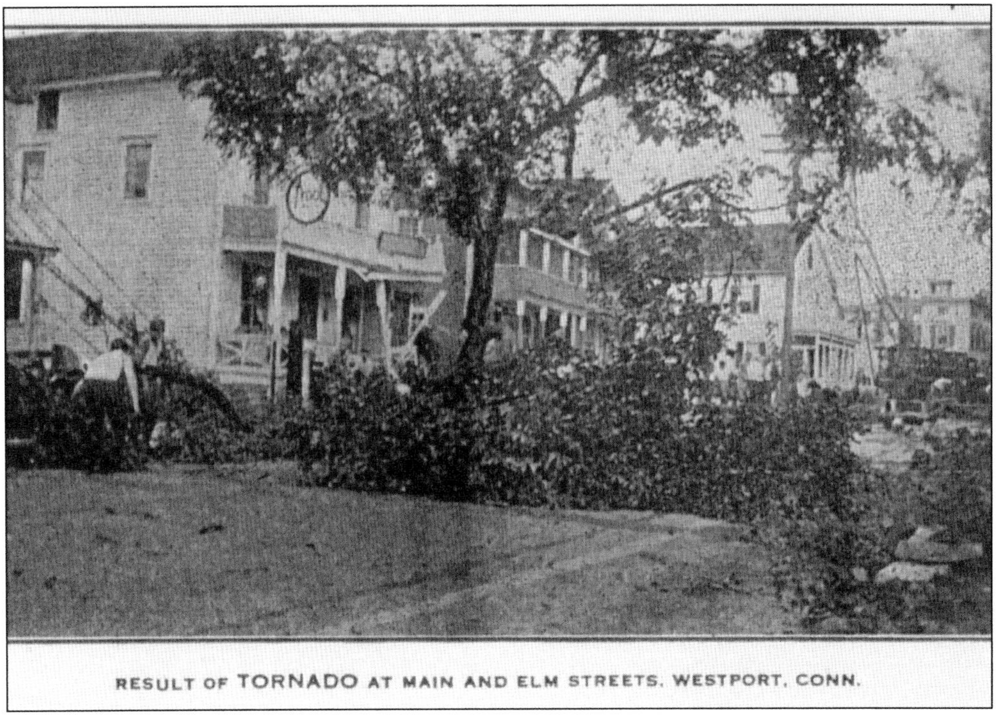

RESULT OF TORNADO AT MAIN AND ELM STREETS, WESTPORT, CONN.

One of Westport's true disasters . . .

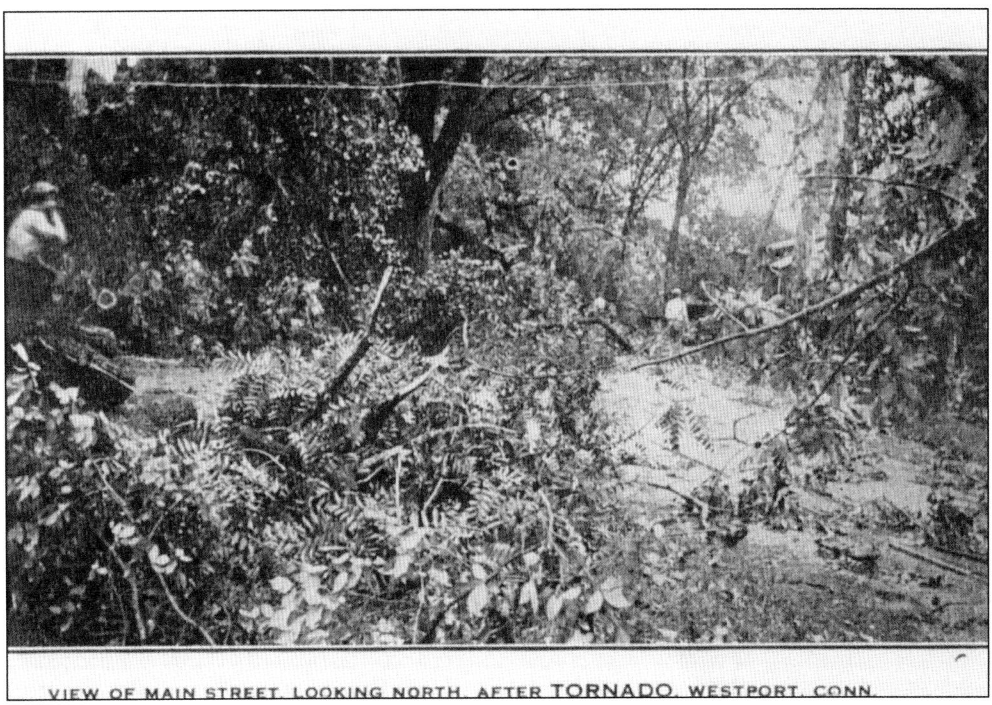

VIEW OF MAIN STREET, LOOKING NORTH, AFTER TORNADO, WESTPORT, CONN.

. . . merited several postcards.

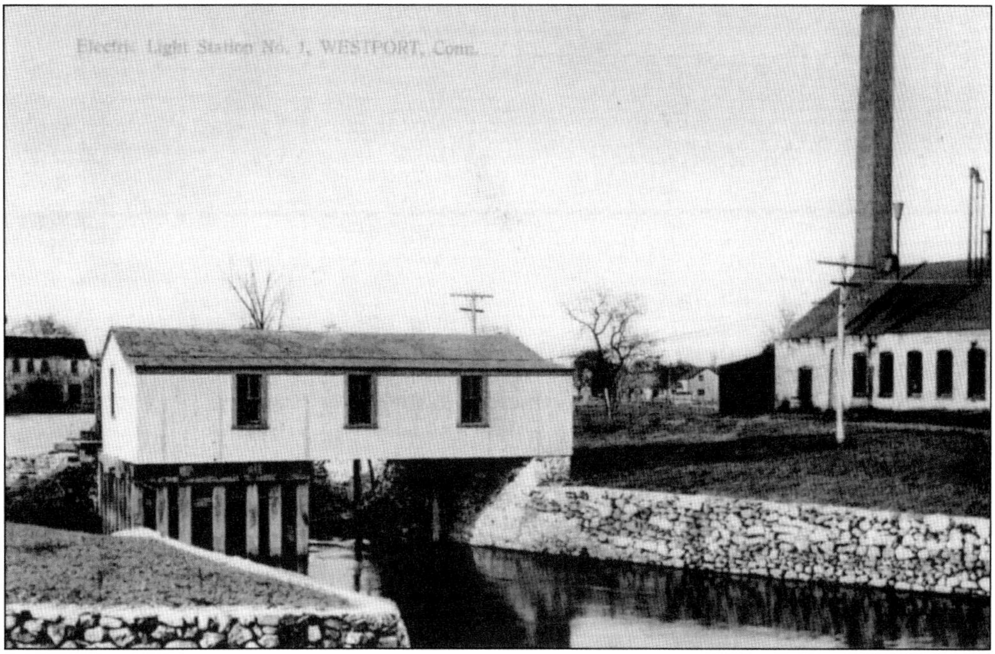

Electric light stations seem an odd subject for a postcard . . .

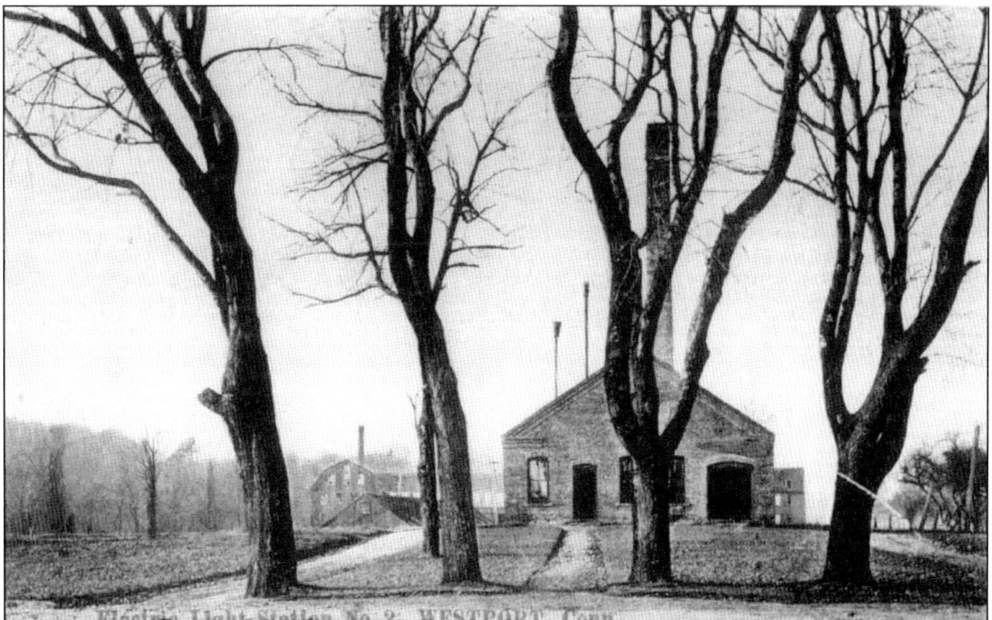

. . . but they have a certain elegance and simplicity. This card was mailed November 24, 1908, to Georgetown.

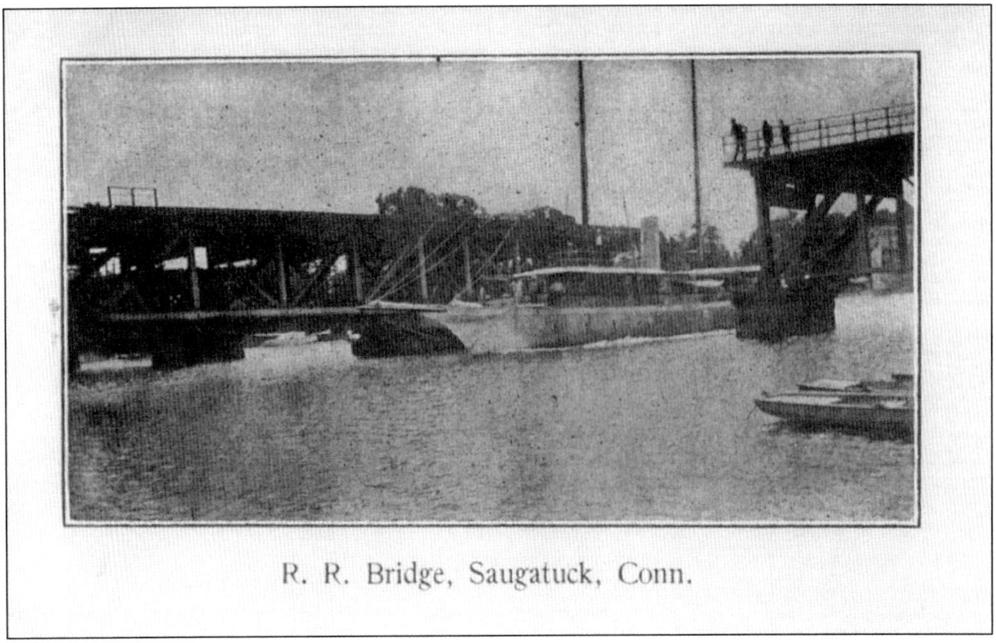

Once the railroad bridge was open, barges like this could go upriver to deliver oil and other cargo.

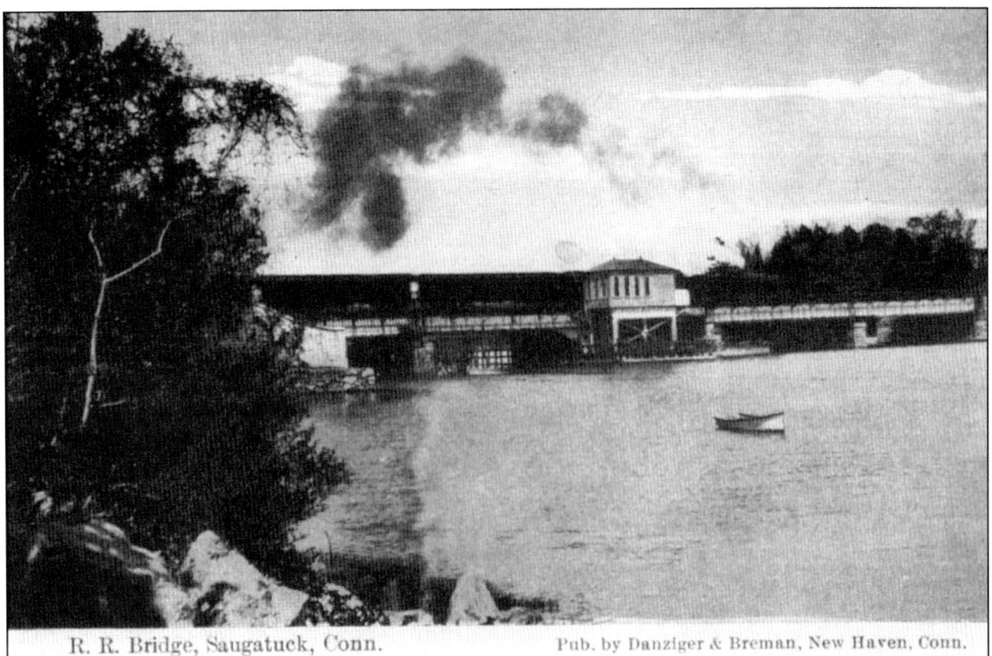

This view up the river shows smaller craft enjoying the river as well.

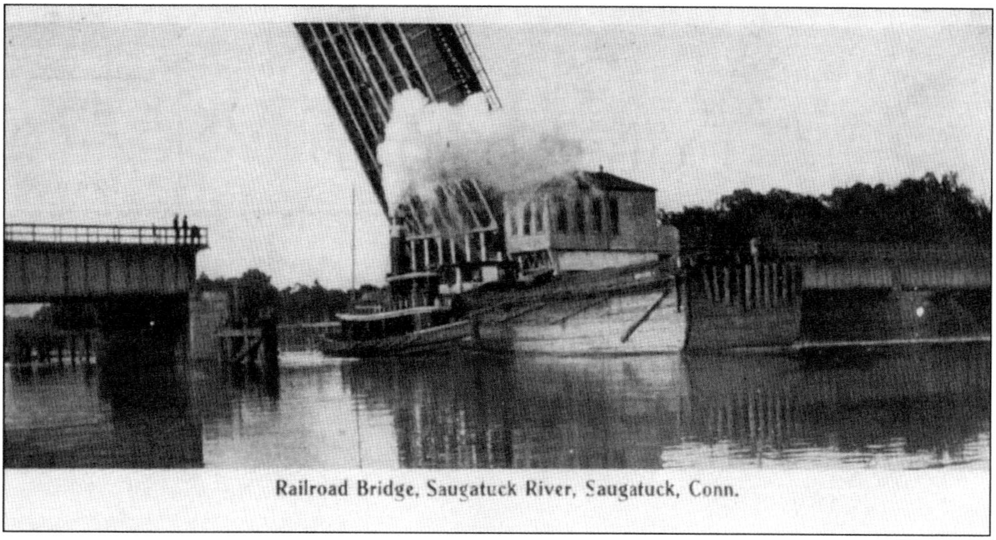

The Town sold the rights to the railroad right of way . . .

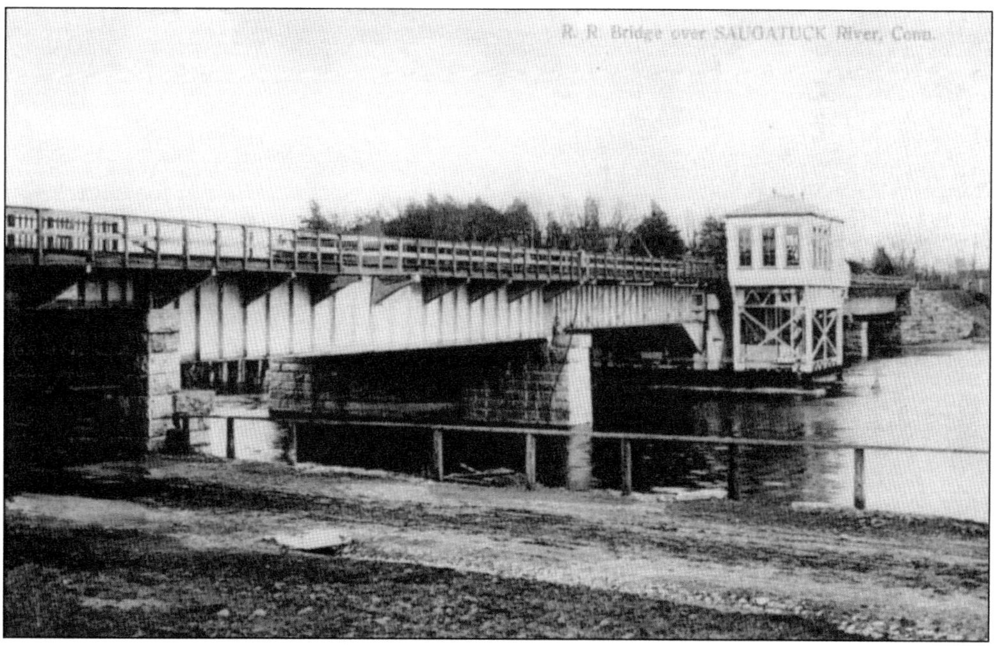

. . . in 1848 for $200. The first Saugatuck carriage bridge was paid for in 1873.

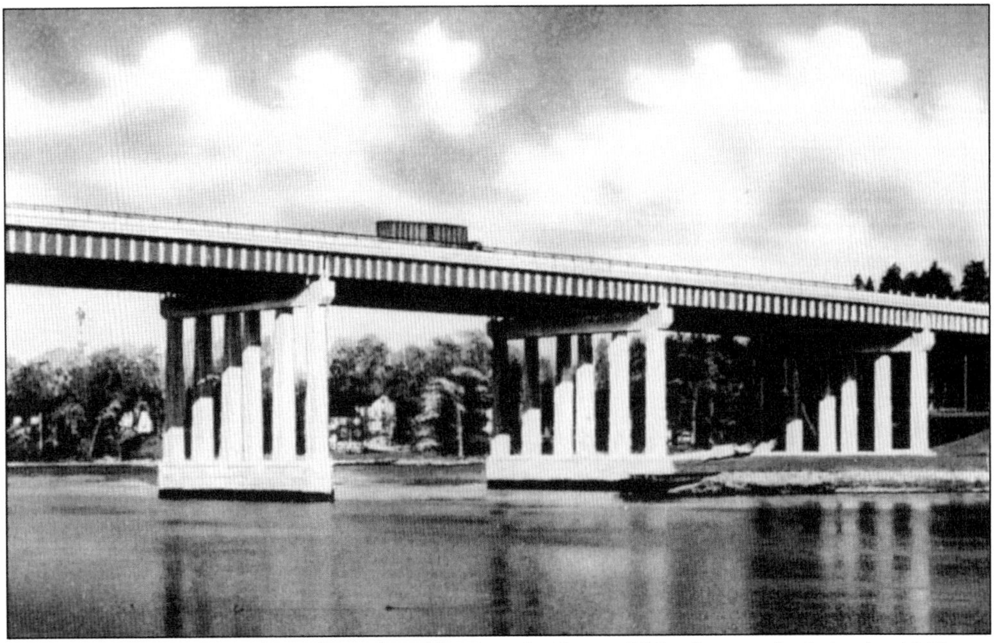

Located slightly upriver from the railroad bridge, the Route 95 bridge was built in the 1960s.

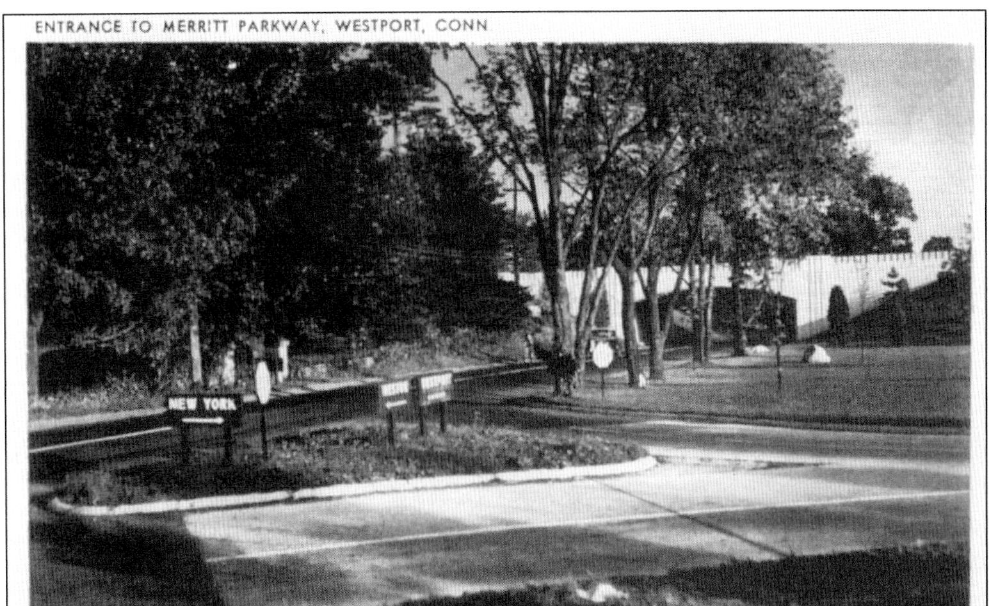

The Merritt Parkway, seen here when new in the 1930s, was called "America's First Parkway."

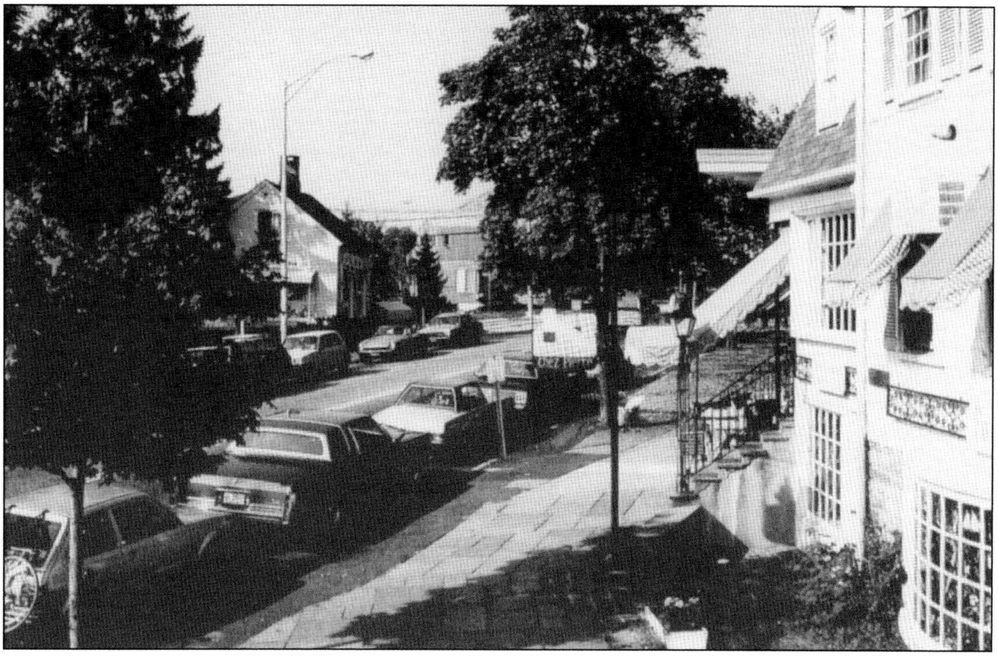

These contemporary postcards of downtown Westport . . .

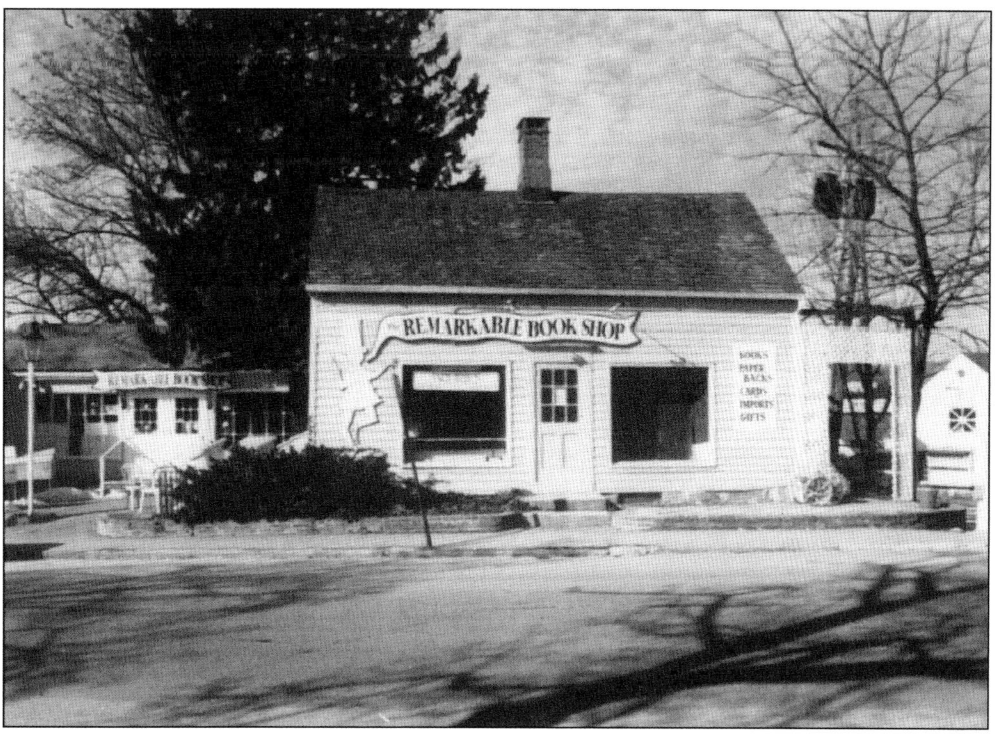

. . . are already out of date as the town continues to change. (Andrea Fine.)

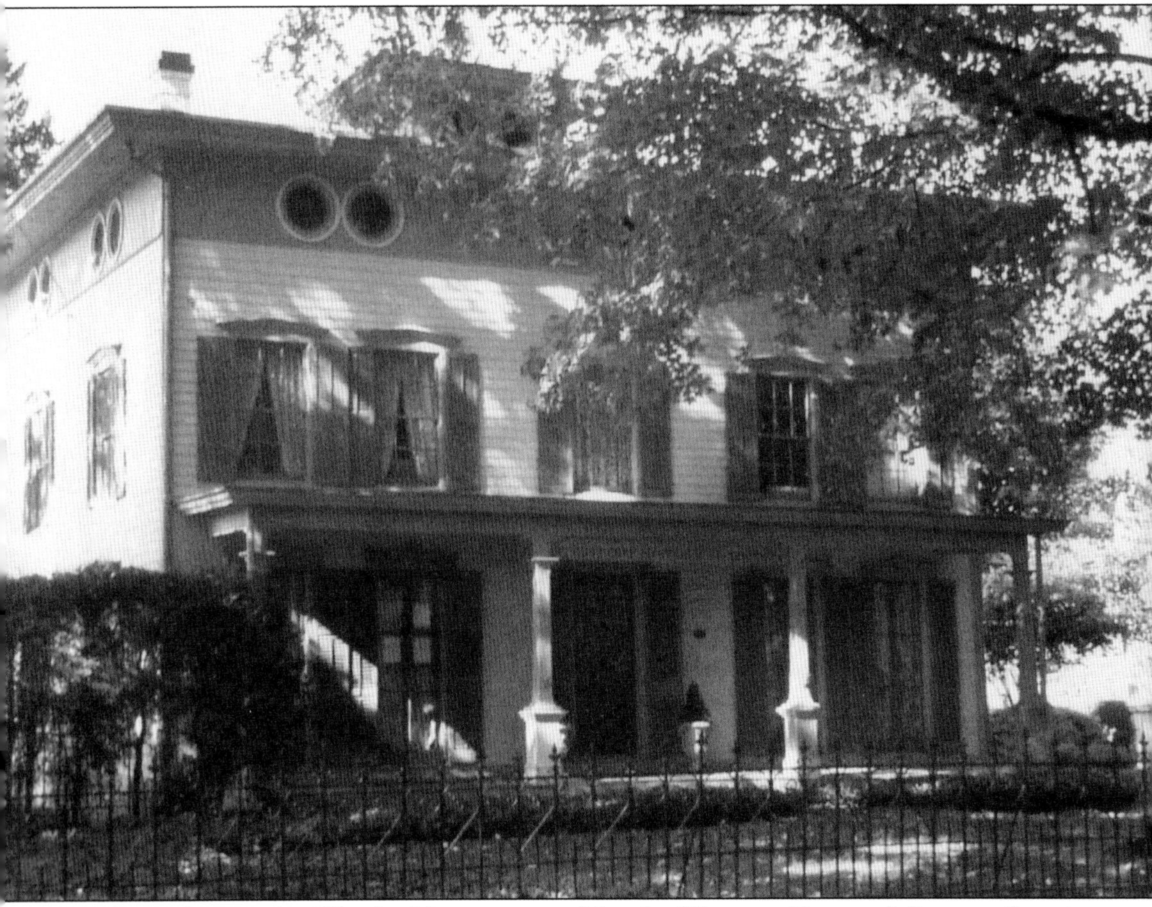

Shown here is the Wheeler House, operated by the Westport Historical Society. Captain Ebenezer Coley built a house, a salt box, for his son Michael in 1795. Throughout the 19th century the house had a succession of owners, including Morris Bradley, who enlarged and converted the house to the popular Victorian Italianate villa style in the 1860s. The style is characterized by the flat roof topped by a cupola, decorative brackets, "bull's eye" windows, and a gracious front veranda.

Bradley died in 1886 and the house was willed by his widow to their daughter Julia. Julia's son, Dr. Lewis Wheeler, lived and practiced medicine in the house until his death in 1958. He willed the house to his housekeeper, who left it to Christ and Holy Trinity Church with the wish that it be known as Wheeler House.

A fund-raising drive chaired by Joanne Woodward and Paul Newman enabled the Westport Historical Society to purchase the property in 1981. A parlor, kitchen, and bedroom have all been restored to their Victorian elegance. (Emily Reich.)

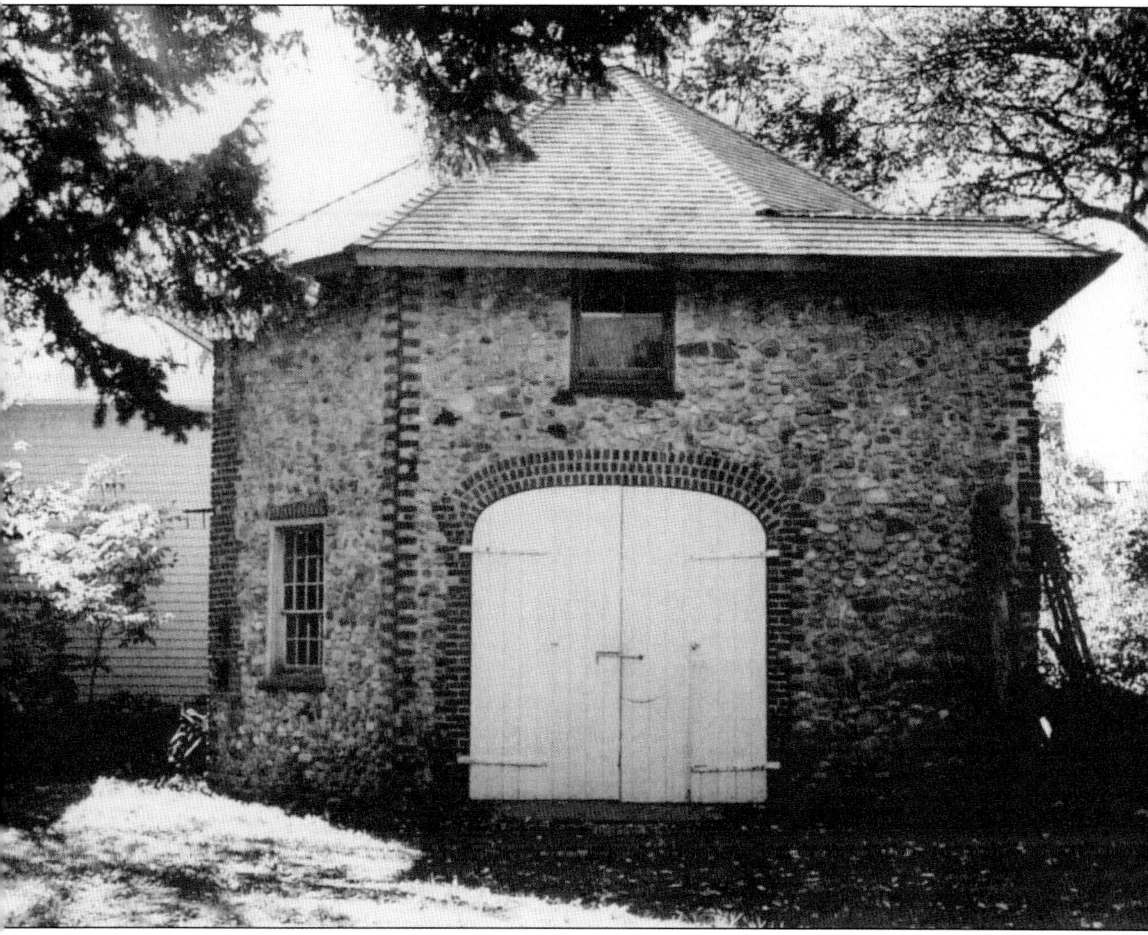

The Bradley-Wheeler cobblestone barn, located behind Wheeler House, is a seven-sided structure. It is the only barn with an octagonal roof in Connecticut. It houses the recently opened Museum of Westport History at the Bradley-Wheeler Cobblestone Barn, dating from the time of Native Americans to the present. Both Wheeler House and the Bradley-Wheeler Barn are listed on the national and state historic registers. (Emily Reich.)

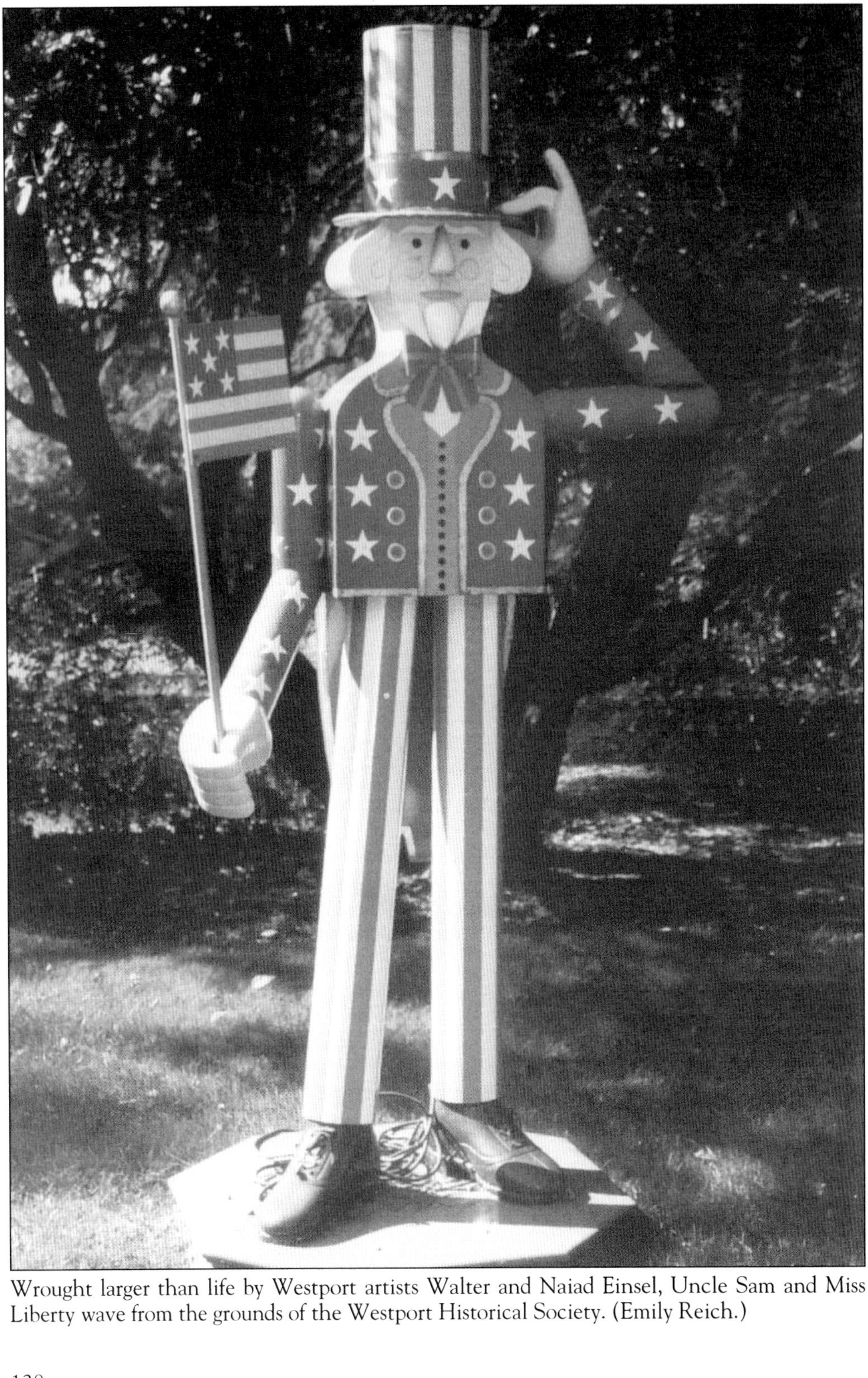

Wrought larger than life by Westport artists Walter and Naiad Einsel, Uncle Sam and Miss Liberty wave from the grounds of the Westport Historical Society. (Emily Reich.)